Best Wishes

D1395274

The Dawes Decades

The Dawes Decades

John Dawes
and the Third Golden Era
of Welsh Rugby

David Parry-Jones

seren

Seren is the book imprint of
Poetry Wales Press Ltd
Nolton Street, Bridgend, CF31 3BN
www.seren-books.com

First published in 2005

ISBN 1-85411-387-9

The publisher works with the support of the Welsh Books Council

Printed in Plantin by Cromwell Press, Wiltshire

The Dawes Decades

FOREWORD

T his year the Welsh Rugby Union celebrates its 125th anniversary. Since 1880 there have been many highs and lows for Welsh rugby, but three periods of its history can be said to stand out. They are the 'Golden Eras', identified by my biographer David Parry-Jones as those of Gwyn Nicholls at the outset of the twentieth century, John Gwilliam in mid-century, and finally the 1970s which this book is mainly about.

These periods were outstanding, and memorable for the heavy scoring by Wales which led to Triple Crowns and Grand Slams and also for the skills and penetration yielding victories to validate the 'Golden Era' epithet. I was fortunate enough to watch some of the Gwilliam games (though very young at the time) and later proud to play a leading part in my contemporaries' 'golden' era.

These periods differed in character, of course, but each manifested virtues which are very much the essence of Welsh life. Commitment, passion, skill, dedication and pride were all present plus a feeling of togetherness between supporters and players which is special. If there is ever to be a fourth Golden Era all these ingredients have to combine again.

Hence it is a huge pleasure, even as the covers of this book are being cut to size, to dwell for a moment on the achievement of the National XV throughout February and March 2005, and the pleasure the players, under their new coach, gave to the nation. Our supporters, somehow, have kept rooting for their heroes through thick and – mainly – thin, but it has been a long, long twenty-seven years since a Grand Slam was last achieved by Wales. Only two years ago, remember, the side which competed in the Six Nations tournament finished holding the wooden spoon. Now, against expectations, the Welsh can cheer again after dominating European rugby and achieving our ninth Grand Slam.

Much is made these days of the idea that 'winning is everything'. But the world-class players whom I had the good fortune to lead and coach in the Seventies wanted more than just victories. 'Winning in style' seemed a better motto to them, and their performances lived up to it. Games were played to win, but total satisfaction could only be achieved by the quality of performance – *Mwynhad Drwy Rinwedd*. This attitude was adopted by the 1971 British Lions whom I captained and who drew high praise from New Zealanders. It is undoubtedly to be found in the class of 2005. I am delighted to be able to congratulate squad members on a supreme campaign.

A single successful season does not qualify as a golden era, but might be the start of one. It is evident from the beginning of his reign as National Team Coach that Mike Ruddock had told his men to go out and express themselves, for which I salute him. Underpinning the preparation of his team has been intense fitness training, diet control and lifestyle changes shunning alcohol and late nights. And it is crystal clear that, along with the players, the coach has been determined to exploit skill, flair, space and blistering speed. Backs lead the way, forwards are allowed to join in. Sometimes brute force is necessary, but for the Wales of 2005 it would appear – happily – to be a last resort. Thrilling is the word I choose to describe the rugby they have played.

I would also congratulate Ruddock and Co for having won through by a difficult route. To win her last Grand Slam in 1978 Wales faced only four fixtures, two played at home and two away. Since then the odds have lengthened. Because there are now six participants in the European tournament, a side winning a Grand Slam may have had to play three of its five fixtures away from home. That is what Wales achieved in 2005. They did it the hard way.

Despite the despair felt by Wales in 2003 there were, I think, clues to a revival for those who were not afraid to recognise them. In autumn 2004 our team came within a whisker of defeating South Africa and the All Blacks. The two Tests were agonisingly closely fought, and the Welsh had almost re-discovered a capacity which had deserted them many moons before – how to win. Going back another year, however, at the 2003 World Cup in Australia, Wales showed tremendous spirit in defeats by New Zealand and then England, both of whom they led well into their cup ties. I think that is when the worm turned. David Parry-Jones takes up the story.

John Dawes

ONE

It went, as Shakespeare might have put it, "to the last syllable of recorded time". Once the Rugby World Cup competition of 2003 had shaken off minnows and also-rans at the Pool stages, it advanced with a blend of huge confrontations and dazzling pyrotechnics until the critical moment. That was when Jonny Wilkinson's accurate boot killed off Australia's challenge in the Final with a dropped goal some thirty seconds before the end of extra time. In England's grasp, the Webb Ellis Cup left the southern hemisphere for the first time.

Not that the six weeks of action had gone wholly as planned, or forecast. As the months went by before the kick-off in October, the New Zealand squad had appeared likely to peak at just the right time with impressive performances in July and August to signal their calibre. Alas, as they computed the odds, the bookies had failed to add in home advantage and passionate crowd support for the Wallabies in their semi-final, and an All Black side which had scored eight impressive tries against Wales could not raise its game on the day to reach the Final. The third great southern hemisphere nation, South Africa, also failed to leave her mark on the tournament and soon afterwards sacked her coach. France, who had come quietly through the early stages to face England in the other semi-final, were dismayed at the rain which fell for hours before the game and fatally blunted the cutting edge of tactics and skills better suited to sunshine and a dry playing surface.

And what of Wales? Despite a series of pre-tournament reverses in the southern hemisphere and then in their own Millennium Stadium, three victories over Canada, Tonga and Italy at the Pool stage guaranteed them a place in the quarter finals. Unexpectedly good form shown against New Zealand preceded a memorable clash with England in the last eight when Colin Charvis's men actually led the eventual winners at half time before exiting the tournament. Defeated Wales left the Suncorp Stadium bound for the airport; but the players' heads were held high.

The World Cup was not up for grabs during the decades evoked in these pages. But this does not mean that previous

9

clashes between the top nations were anything short of full-blooded. The title of Paul Dobson's history of Tests between New Zealand and South Africa is *Rugby's Greatest Rivalry* and has as its opening sentence Springbok 'Boy' Louw's advice to his fellow-countrymen before the 1949 series: "When South Africa plays New Zealand, consider your country at war". Even ahead of a World Cup tie it is hard to imagine a more uncompromising attitude being demanded.

In the northern hemisphere the summit of achievement during most of the twentieth century was a Five Nations title, preferably featuring a Grand Slam of four victories or a Triple Crown competed for among the original International Board member nations, the four Home Unions. Once or twice a decade the British Isles visited the southern hemisphere for long campaigns in the old Dominions – South Africa, New Zealand and Australia – where being a British Lion was, and remains, a special distinction. But tours by the Home Countries were rare; and furthermore, when one of them did venture south of the equator, the damage suffered could be heavy and demoralising.

But in the nineteen seventies – not necessarily so. Here was a decade which began with glory when a British touring party captained by the Welshman John Dawes flew off to make history in the Land of the Long White Cloud. On arrival at Auckland Airport the robust Scottish manager Doug Smith assured an astonished welcoming party of New Zealand media folk that his men would win the Test series by two games to one, with a fourth match drawn. By the final whistle at Eden Park on 14 August 1971, as the weary Lions began to look forward to their journey home, that was exactly how things had worked out.

Since the first British Isles side led by Bedell-Sivright went down to New Zealand 3-9 in the single Test of 1904, its successors had been regularly worsted with only two Test victories and a couple of drawn games to show for their endeavours down the decades. Meanwhile the All Blacks, as they were nick-named during their 1905 tour in the United Kingdom, were clocking up fourteen victories on their own patch, four of them registered in the whitewash of Campbell-Lamerton's 1966 tourists. When New Zealand visited Europe, moreover, they usually managed to play as if they had never left home, and defeat by British, Irish or

French opposition was always a rarity.

That is the measure of the achievement of 1971. To northern hemisphere nations, defeating the All Blacks in their den was the supreme achievement of the period, the equivalent of winning the World Cup. The welcome received by Dawes and the returning Lions at Heathrow Airport was hardly less frenzied than that accorded in 2003 to England's heroes. Was that Lions tour and the victory, then, the high point in the career of the captain? And, is there room for both Lions' tours and a World Cup tournament in the rugby calendar?

Dawes answers the first question guardedly. "It was undeniably a pinnacle. But I have to say that I look back more fondly on the Barbarians' display against the All Blacks at Cardiff eighteen months later. To me as captain, in the evening of my career, it gave total satisfaction. It was a victory in which we scored four tries including the Gareth Edwards score and a decisive one later which went through hands from all four Home Countries before J.P.R. Williams got the touch-down.

"Yes, we won. But what is uppermost in my memory is the fact that in eighty minutes of high-octane rugby no Barbarian gave a forward pass or knocked on. This was mistake-free football, not far from perfection: the Ultimate, you could say."

Certainly to any fan who saw the game it endures indelibly in the memory. Many of the 1971 Lions took part along with their captain, and endorsed the statement they had drummed out eighteen months earlier – that well-led teams focused on primary objectives would demonstrate how, from time to time, the southern hemisphere giants could be taken on and bested. Their aura of invincibility was no more.

In contrast, curiously but understandably, more than thirty years later John Dawes recalls a certain lack of jubilation after the tied final game in Auckland which gave his men their series victory. In those days of long-drawn-out tours, a longing for home kicked in during the final stages, which over-rode feelings of satisfaction. Karl Mullen's Lions of 1950 were away for seven months, which Dawes thinks must have felt like a life sentence. He can remember Carwyn James asking all and sundry in 1971 how it was that Ronnie Dawson's 1959 Lions managed to win the last Test having lost the first three – the coach simply had to know how they kept the *hiraeth* (longing – for home) under control. So Dawes's supreme highlight of 1971 was the crucial Third Test, which his team won by thirteen points to three to take a two-one lead which meant that they could not lose the series.

The British have always enjoyed tangling with New Zealand. New Zealand's ethnic origins and values are rooted in the United Kingdom; and her warmth and mutual understanding has always set them just above the South Africans, who were admired as opponents during the twentieth century though not always loved. But games on tour or in the British Isles against the two nations, plus Australia as her rugby union capability matured, have always been special: going head-to-head against one of them has unfailingly brought into play all the tensions, brute force and determination to win that are now the ingredients of Rugby World Cup.

For these reasons visits by the British Lions are prized by the rugby world; and there is no doubt that the long traditional tours they have made during the last hundred years were always eagerly anticipated by the host nations. In New Zealand now a lobby is making itself felt which is not altogether satisfied with the present flying visits paid by individual countries to the southern hemisphere; there is a yearning for the old days when, just like the bigger centres, Greymouth, Timaru, Oamaru, Marlborough, Pukekohe and the rest could be sure of hosting top rugby featuring major touring sides.

Dawes is with them, wanting expeditions by the British Isles to continue. Further, he would like to see a revival of inward tours to the Home Countries by the southern hemisphere giants. Does a reciprocal desire survive on the part of the latter? The Welshman quotes the great All Black lock forward and captain Colin Meads and the guaranteed enjoyment to which he looked forward from an evening under floodlights in the Welsh Valleys, a tough match with a Scottish Borders XV or a visit to the West Country. Fitting such all-embracing tours into an ever-more-crowded schedule of Test Rugby across the world will undoubtedly be a challenge, but it should be possible to achieve a four-yearly cycle alternating with the Rugby World Cup.

As for the latter, Dawes admits that he would have enjoyed meeting its massive challenge and leading a national XV aiming to be global champions. But as you would expect from a member of the dear, departed amateur sport he has reservations about the ethics and principles underpinning the new professional game. They centre on the ambition stated and re-stated by England coach Clive Woodward in the months leading up to his team's World Cup triumph: "We're not going to Australia to play well. We're going there to win". Dawes understands such a single-minded approach, but calls it "lowering the sights". To win is part of the objective; to win with style is better. And what is style? This book, and the man himself, will contribute to the understanding, and recognition of it.

A small sector of the one-time coal-mining village of Abercarn in the Ebbw Valley is known locally as 'Chapel of Ease'. Not all its inhabitants know the name's derivation; but almost certainly it referred to a small building demolished long ago (not to be confused with the English Baptist chapel which still stands in the vicinity). The parish's two Church in Wales buildings are located on the overlooking hillsides – at a height of several hundred feet in the case of Mynydd Islwyn, clearly a problematic venue to reach for attendance at divine service for the infirm, the lazy or those short of stamina. The theory is, therefore, that the building which conferred its name upon the location was a chapel of 'ease' in the sense of 'convenience'; that is, for those villagers who felt unable or disinclined to climb to evensong at the top of the hill, here was a 'convenient' alternative place of worship.

At any rate, it was in this part of the Western Valley (so called to distinguish it from the eastern one containing towns like Blaenafon and Pontypool) that Sydney John Dawes was born in June 1940. The Abercarn in which he began growing up was wholly typical of South Wales Valleys, having expanded and prospered for over a century thanks to busy collieries and metal foundries. Bisecting the village was a canal (now all but obliterated by the A467 dual carriageway) navigated by barges which took coal to Newport Docks for export. The Prince of Wales Colliery was among its early users, a pit which suffered one of the most horrendous accidents experienced down the years in the Welsh coalfield. The explosion of 1878 killed two hundred and sixty four men and boys; sadly the history of the Welsh mining communities is all too often scarred by such statistics. Other nearby pits founded in due course included the Abercarn Colliery, while there were more shafts to the south at Cwmcarn and immediately up the valley at Newbridge. Today, where the great winding gear wheels used to turn constantly like lazy black windmills on the Valley floor, neat, clean industrial estates have been laid out with ample space for car-parking. No-one now marches to work in hob-nailed boots.

The other great change to the Valleys in the last three or four decades has been their greening. As late as the 1960s mining concerns including the National Coal Board still habitually dumped their black waste on the bleak and ugly tips which disfigured the hilltops. In 1966, perhaps inevitably, came the Aberfan disaster resulting from a monstrous landslip which slithered and careered its way down upon the village, causing grievous loss of children's and adults' lives. Soon public opinion and pressure prompted a two-pronged drive to expunge the threat posed by such spoil-heaps to communities housed below them and at the same time restore lost verdure to the Valleys. Nowhere in South Wales has green replaced black more comprehensively than on the hills beneath which Abercarn nestles – half way between Newport on the coast and Ebbw Vale at the edge of the Brecon Beacons. Even the Ebbw river looks fresh and pleasant at the start of the twenty-first century.

This was John Dawes's domain as a child. It communicated with the outside world via the canal and its locks, an industrious railway line whose cargoes were coal and steel, and some main roads whose chief users were buses which were always full in days before mass ownership of motor cars. Small boys could roam the valley floor without fear of being run over, just as they could puff and pant their way to exhilarating release on the boundless heights that lay above Cwmcarn or over towards Mynydd Islwyn: the kind of hill-top kingdom that dreams are made of.

In John Dawes's recall, the family he knew reached back a couple of generations to his paternal grandfather William, who followed the practice of the day by begetting a large brood which included two daughters and three sons (one of them John's father-to-be, Reg) in addition to an adopted daughter. They lived at Crumlin, close to a viaduct built to carry the Newport Abergavenny and Hereford railway above the Western Valley on its journey from Pontypool to Neath. Since demolished, this was a graceful structure, whose light and airy appearance prompted a writer in *Railway Times* to observe that people almost expected a gentle breeze to bring it toppling into the meadowland below. The young Dawes does not seem to have crossed it by train, but he and his small pals often ran a little way along it for a dare.

Before the start of World War II grandfather Dawes up-rooted his family, all of whom emigrated with him to the Bristol suburb of Fishponds with the exception of John's father. Although moving house to Chapel of Ease the latter stayed put in his job as a blacksmith at North Celynen, one of the two collieries located at Newbridge, just down the valley from Crumlin. Few signs survive of their one-time dominance in the landscape, since in recent times the spoil heaps were eradicated by the process of 'washing'. This made available small coal that had been rejected as useless in the long-gone boom days but by the middle of the twentieth century was a substance worth recovering and selling. Apparently a Yorkshireman called William Pepper became a millionaire as a result – one of the long list of mainly English entrepreneurs who have made money under the noses of the resident Celts. In his school holidays the young Dawes took a paid job in the washing routine which involved making sure the 'hopper' did not clog up. If he took his eye off it for twenty seconds, it did just that and coatings of black slurry had to be scraped laboriously off the machinery. He remembers dirty fingernails.

John's mother Gladys, whose maiden name was Harris, had lived in Chapel of Ease for a number of years. Like her husband she was part of a lively family who were regular, committed chapel-goers. Her father was an organist who played at morning and evening service on Sundays, and accompanied mid-week rehearsal with the choir. Evidently the Harris tribe was big in the locality, with cousins, nephews, nieces and other relations based nearby. After a century of pit village life, with its constant closeness of contact, Mrs Dawes would well know that a degree of inter-marriage had been inevitable. As for herself, she ran a scrupulous and orthodox Welsh household, along lines dominated by 'respectability': a simple lady of the Valleys, a housewife who was completely focused on her job and who, her son recalls, did not particularly want to know about the world beyond Abercarn.

However, John Dawes is in no doubt about the family genes which contributed to his own athletic ability and prowess, and speaks warmly of his father's gifts and abilities. In his prime, Reg was a lean, sinewy man weighing around twelve stone, who possessed a natural gift of speed which he cultivated until his retirement from active rugby (by which time he probably turned the scales at fifteen stone). The early years saw him making appearances for Abercarn and Crumlin RFCs, and it appears that he played now and then for Abertillery. In those days such teams were at the forefront of Welsh rugby, and Dawes senior won recognition and acclaim up and down the Western Valley from the members of many rival clubs. Later, as a spectator, he would take John to matches involving the so-called 'first class' sides of the day. His attitude to big, competitive rugby was that of a fanatic, which he remained until the end of his days.

In the World War II years, life here did not greatly differ from that in peacetime. Most menfolk in employment were miners or tin-workers, who escaped call-up to the armed forces because the continuance of their output was held to be vital to Britain's War Effort. Their wives bought rationed goods at Abercarn's bright little shops. Couples sent their children to Gwyddon School. Congregations would worship and sing the great Welsh hymns at the Presbyterian Church of which Lady Llanover and her husband Sir Benjamin Hall (creator of Westminster's 'Big Ben') were patrons.

And for relaxation, combined with a measure of self-education, the Abercarn Miners' Institute boasted a snooker table as well as a select library and reading room which stocked weekly magazines and daily newspapers. In local pubs many a pint helped to quench the thirst of men who had been toiling underground or in the tinworks' heat and now, off duty, were simply dedicated to hitting double-top on a dart board. Such a scenario was standard for much of the twentieth century in a South Wales valley at a time before heavy industry toppled over and gave up the ghost.

So much is certainly not to say that Abercarn's adults were unaware that there was a War on. The bombing of nearby Cardiff and Newport, and the terrible damage done to Swansea, could not escape them. For the children it was different: at only four or five years of age, young Dawes and his small pals were unconcerned at what was happening in the wider world of grown ups. Rarely, he recalls, did aircraft, friendly or hostile, fly over the Valleys of Wales – let alone drop bombs on them. Thus his most vivid wartime memory is of the street parties held in Chapel of Ease to celebrate the end of hostilities in Europe and later the Far East. He remembers the fun that he enjoyed without quite comprehending why there was this cause for great rejoicing.

Other, more routine, events looked forward to by mining families and their children were Sunday School 'treats' or day-trips, the usual destination being Barry Island. Dawes went to Sunday School regularly until his late teens, relishing the debates and discussions about tricky moral and ethical dilemmas. Also, once he had begun his secondary education at Lewis School, Pengam, which was a couple of bus rides distant from Abercarn, attendance at Sunday afternoon classes in the chapel vestry made sure that he did not lose touch with friends from junior school days.

Today a busy and productive Ysgol Gymraeg at the centre of Abercarn ensures that a goodly amount of the Welsh language can be heard in the village streets and in a sizeable number of homes. Likewise, a hundred and fifty years ago the language and culture of the homeland was championed by Lady Llanover, with her zest for all things Welsh from tall beaver hats for womenfolk to regular regional eisteddfodau. In between these eras, as in many other parts of Wales, the acquiring and use of the language would seem to have been a low priority. Members of Dawes's generation will remember beginning their third year at secondary school by having to choose between French and Welsh. Many pupils covered themselves by opting for the former since it was recognised by all British universities as an acceptable 'second language' when would-be students applied for places. The same did not hold good for Welsh outside the University of Wales.

As it happened, Dawes would go from Pengam to Aberystwyth, so its validity or non-validity was not an issue. It was at Aber that 'Welshness' first began to be meaningful to him, while London Welsh RFC in the mid 'sixties was a kind of cultural finishing school where every Saturday Old Deer Park was transformed into a Welsh-speaking, Welsh-cheering islet in anglophone west London. Dawes says that a season there had more of an effect on his essential 'Welshness' than a whole up-bringing in Newbridge and attendance at a school in the homeland. Anyway, he seems untroubled by his inability to speak the old language of Wales and puts up with the leg-pulling of contemporaries like Mervyn Davies: "Does John speak Welsh? Well, he just about knows what 'Dim Parcio' means."

The next staging post in the youngster's educational advance was his move to Lewis School, one of the mid-century examples of 'Direct Grant' schools which took fee-paying boys and also successful scholarship applicants. Among the latter category were Dawes and fellow Old Boy Neil Kinnock. The school's location was within Glamorgan, but its pupil catchment area spilled over the border here and there, permitting admission to a small number of Monmouthshire children whose eleven-plus examina-tion performance had been impressive. Thus Dawes was offered one of the places reserved for primary school pupils from Abercarn and district. He says that the school's academic achievements, dating back to its Foundation in 1729, seemed excellent and a regular half-dozen State Scholarships came its way each year in the mid-twentieth century. In other words it was an opportunity not to be missed, even though acceptance would necessitate bus journeys of up to an hour at the beginning and end of a school day which perforce lasted nine hours.

It is fair to observe, and Dawes does not disagree, that the profile of Lewis School (named after a Founder) was less than high in the overall pattern of south Wales's secondary schools. This was the heyday of the grammar schools, whose reputations were underpinned by prowess on the rugby field. At this time Neath Grammar School, Cowbridge and Pontypool-based West Mon ruled their respective roosts; their boys won Secondary School caps against the other Home Countries. If not quite comprising a closed shop, the top-performing rugby schools were choosy about who should appear on their fixture-lists, and for long Lewis School played sides like Caerphilly Grammar School and the several suburban Cardiff 'High' Schools.

At their primary schools most sporty little boys had been accustomed to playing football in the yard at playtime, kicking the life out of well-used, dirty grey tennis balls. Occasionally, at eleven years or thereabouts, they might represent their school against rivals not far away and suddenly find how hard it was to control or even to kick the ton-weight soccer balls of the day with their wrap-around panels. But despite outings with their fathers, few of them had had a chance to handle that different article with a point at each end, the rugby football. Certainly in John Dawes's memory is the distinct idea that he had never handled or even seen one at close quarters until he moved to Lewis School. But soccer – 'footy' – was out; here rugby was king.

Not that the future British Isles captain had much influence on the position in which he should play. For reasons best known to the Lewis School masters of the day his early role was that of hooker: "Er, I didn't care for that very much". He prevailed upon one of the rugby masters to move him to scrum-half, where he stayed until the fifth form, moving to open-side wing forward in the sixth. It seems as if his only experience of the back division came when he turned out for one of the Newbridge XVs in the school holidays. However, when he looks back it is clear that the detail at this career stage is less important: Dawes's main aim was just to be involved in rugby teams; that is, he was moved and excited by the 15-man synergy which he perceived that the game – uniquely – held out.

In the School's teams were some gifted contemporaries who would go on to bring distinction to the rugby game and some-times influence its development. Maes y Cymmer-born Derek Morgan is a prime example of this, a native of Monmouthshire capped nine times by England for whom he qualified fortuitously through time spent at Durham University (he became President of the RFU just in time to celebrate England's World Cup victory). Dennis Hughes of Newbridge was winning caps at the same time as John Dawes while, having joined Newport, Peter Rees claimed several on the wing at the beginning of the sixties.

These advances, with the shaping of some top-notch players, were not being achieved accidentally. To improve its competitive game, Lewis School had really needed to include a few of the bigger and more fashionable schools in its fixture list. Thanks to expert and tireless coaching by school staff, plus some skilful networking, considerable progress was made in Dawes's two or three seasons with the first XV. The masters whose positive input he salutes today were Caerphilly-born Bryn Jones and a West Walian called Roy James. These were numbered among the self-less amateurs of the pre-coaching era in the schools, men who ran rugby but at the same time might be a junior master teaching mathematics or a Latin scholar. Such men did not need to be highly-trained PE experts: next to the subjects they taught they adored being in charge of the School Rugby XV and motivating it. In John Dawes's final years he can remember that, thanks to Roy James's westerly connections, Llanelli and Neath grammar schools were written into Lewis School's fixture lists – and, what is more, began to be defeated occasionally.

During their school holidays Dawes and some of his contemporaries at Pengam benefited from a move made by Bryn Jones onto the committee of Newbridge RFC. This led to a small, select group of Lewis School sixth formers being invited to train with the club. They went through their warm-up routine at a short remove from the heavyweights of Newbridge's teams, something that could have been regarded as stand-offish and divisive by the veterans with whom the boys were sharing the practice area. Instead, a number of the Newbridge players paid Dawes and Co the compliment of coming to see their exercises from closer quarters, before moving off to go through the paces themselves. Imitation is, of course, the sincerest form of flattery. As for the precocious sixth formers – well, their desire to play the fifteen-a-side game in grown-up company was whetted, and one or two of them found that a pint of bitter or shandy tasted great after a hard bout of training.

A bonus at this particular club and its evening practice periods was the presence of David Harries, a nippy scrum-half in his playing days who along with Cadfan Davies at Bridgend can probably claim to have been a pioneer of intensive coaching in South Wales – certainly their work commitment antedated the WRU dictum of 1964 stating that all clubs should appoint coaches. Harries is remembered by all who have known him as a rugby dictator, achieving reforms and getting things done at Newbridge through sheer will-power. Although an un-paid coach the energy and drive he injected into practice sessions was considerable and he was also a taskmaster who goaded his men towards giving their all. His methods paid off, and in 1965 Newbridge – "relative minnows in those days", recalls John Dawes – took the unofficial Welsh Championship title with some great displays.

By the end of his schooldays Dawes's commitment to playing the rugby game and exploiting the limitless possibilities it held out was well founded. At school the rudiments of the game had been brought home to him and he had begun to think hard about how best to exploit them. Regular visits to Newbridge RFC had opened up aspects of the club system into which he would soon fit. And, importantly, there was icing on the cake in the shape of regular world-class fixtures played at Cardiff Arms Park which could be reached by bus or train from Abercarn in under an hour. Thus as a teenager Dawes can claim to have watched every match played by Wales in the old stadium during the fifties (when Swansea ceased to stage International fixtures).

And what games they were. The Welsh teams of the day secured two Grand Slams in the Five Nations Championships of 1950 and 1952. South Africa were opponents in 1951, a dropped goal by Hansie Brewis denying Wales a share of the honours in a thunderous clash of giants. Dawes also remembers being at the Arms Park in December 1953 to see what, at the time of writing, remains the last victory by Wales over New Zealand. In his mind's eye he can see Clem Thomas's speculative cross kick being gathered by wing Ken Jones who sprints twenty-five yards for the winning try. And he admits that this period and those games turned him from an interested onlooker into a passionate supporter of rugby football at the highest level and of his country's players.

And well might that be. In the inter-War years from 1919 to 1939 the backs produced by Wales had been outstanding, from Bowcott and Vivian Jenkins through to Wooller, Tanner and Cliff Jones. Alas: it is clear from the scribes of the day that no administrator, selector, teacher, or even media analyst had been able to lay down a regimen which might advance forward play. It was always vigorous and competitive, but evidently ingenuous. The greatest Welsh feat in the thirties was the defeat (for a second time) of New Zealand; but it was the backs, living off no more than forty per cent of possession, who got the 13-12 result.

Now, suddenly, as the new-age fans and would-be acolytes like

John Dawes came to watch post-war international rugby, there was a man called John Gwilliam leading Welsh XVs to the heights. This inspirational leader knew that skilful forward play, with delivery of quality possession from set piece and the loose, was the priority – with backs like Lewis Jones, W.B. Cleaver, Jack Matthews, Bleddyn Williams and Malcolm Thomas delivering the killer blows that inevitably followed.

It is probably fair to suggest that like other teenagers Dawes enjoyed and exulted in the action of the day in carefree fashion. Maybe it was on his way home by bus that he strove to recapture images and action in his mental recall of what he had seen. But in a youthful way he was becoming a thinker on the game and its inner workings: Why did we win? Why did we nearly lose? Why was that try scored? Did a punishing penalty goal have to be conceded?

The aim was to understand and exploit possibilities for their own sake. Such an idealistic view occupied one end of a spectrum, perhaps a more intellectual one than the other end of it which included the zestful pragmatism of Ireland's Ronnie Dawson: "What does the result matter? – as long as ye win!"

TWO

The steps taken by young people to advance from school to tertiary education are hazardous ones which can make or break future progress. They have to choose the right college or university, and hope that it will admit them. Their selected course of studies must be one that will stretch without baffling or demoralizing them. In all likelihood they must immediately start coping with being self-sufficient, learning about washing and ironing and maybe cooking food. For the first time in their lives they will have serious money to look after and expend. Most significantly, they have fled the nest; there are no parents on hand to comfort them or re-build morale in times of crisis.

For a few would-be scholars it is all too much and they opt out at an early stage. There are others who battle through while admitting to waves of home-sickness. John Dawes appears to have fallen into a third, select category which takes the new challenge in its stride. But he is quick to explain that with a demanding schedule studying chemistry, and the rest of his days full of rugby football activity, he had little or no time to pine for the comfortable up-bringing that he had left behind.

Wales is proud of the college which admitted the Abercarn youngster for the pursuit of his studies. Founded in 1872 Aberystwyth, or simply Aber as the alumni call it, was the first college of what would eventually become the University of Wales. The great railway builder David Davies of Llandinam directed some of his huge fortune towards the new foundation, and by the turn of the century *Y Coleg ger y Lli*, the College by the Sea, was making a prestigious name for itself and laying down a template for the succeeding generation of such institutions in Wales.

But its perceived academic excellence lies in disciplines like the law, politics and the culture of Wales. Most people would be less aware of the respectable Chemistry faculty boasted by the College. In all likelihood John Dawes's knowledge of Aber was equally rudimentary; and he is frank enough to admit that he cannot recall why he chose to apply to it. Presumably there would have been a master at Lewis School able to point him in the right direction; while if you look at it from the College's point of view an applicant who was not only at home in chemistry labs but had also been playing some first-class rugby as a schoolboy clearly had a strong case for admission. At all events Aberystwyth accepted young Dawes, who duly reported to the Dean of Admissions in September 1959.

His journeys there would always be long and tortuous. In the fifties the young men who owned cars were rarities among whose number he did not feature. In those days the country was criss-crossed by the railways, which made it possible to travel around Wales by train or up and down it. Ultimately you would reach your destination but the progress took time – too much for many people's liking. Buses were an option, though not much quicker than trains, and Newbridge RFC were sometimes able to offer their young centre a lift. But the method which solved most students' problems was hitch-hiking. The Dawes technique was to stand at a likely point beside the main road to the west and wag a thumb vigorously. It was also important to wear your university scarf, the passport to a lift.

His arrival at the College, and the ranks of its sportsmen was hardly felicitous, since he was nursing a muscle pulled on the traditional West Country tour undertaken by Newbridge in early autumn just before the College term began. Consequently, all he could do in his first few days was register on the quadrangle notice board his interest in playing rugby, plus apologies for being unable to take part in trials. In such situations people feel pretty marginalised; and by the time the final trial arrived he had still been unable to show off his ability.

This is where a new pal stepped in to give some help. Cardiffian Denis Horgan, a product of St Illtyd's College, was by now Aber's Rugby Club secretary and speedily recognized that a class act like Dawes could not be left on the sidelines. He fitted the freshman into one of the teams as open-side flanker, moving him to centre for the second half. Those were the forty minutes which defined the position in which John Dawes would play for the rest of his career, for after the game Horgan suggested that the newcomer should feature permanently at number twelve (where he quickly secured a place in the College's team which he

24

never lost). Dawes grins: "Only later did I realise that Denis himself was an open-side flanker!"

The man of Gwent had been quick to make an impression on Aberystwyth rugby. However, his first reaction to the town where he would live and study for the next three years was not favourable; he found the place tired, unappealing and right off the beaten track. Only gradually did it begin to win him over; but once that had happened he was in its thrall for ever. Always, the moods and movements of the sea could fascinate people brought up in land-locked environments. Students never tired of walking the promenade, at the northern end of which they 'kicked the bar'. There was spectacular scenery to admire throughout the year, especially brilliant when the winter snows decorated Pen Dinas or Constitution Hill. However, given a benevolent coastal climate, the sports pitches lying beside Llanbadarn Road were usually playable and even in the depths of winter it was rare for rugby and soccer fixtures to be called off.

In 1959 Aberystwyth's hub and administrative headquarters was Hen Coleg – the Old College. This was a gracious building erected close to the town centre on spec about a century earlier as a grandiose terminal hotel to serve rail travellers – a development which to the relief of generations of students and their tutors never took place. Then, up on Penglais hill, sparkling new buildings for Botany, Zoology and Geography were the first examples of the new and the modern on what is today a well-populated campus. It was a short walk from either of these starting points to the Chemistry School, which was presided over by a a senior lecturer, Orville Thomas. Although also President of the rugby club he sternly, and regularly, made it plain to fresh in-takes that they were there to work and that adherence to their time-table was obligatory. From the outset John Dawes accepted the need for such discipline, and although he created time in his schedule for extra fitness training he was determined that his studies should not suffer.

His day began with a lecture at nine a.m. after which students moved to the laboratories for practical work. There were two 'recreation afternoons', on Wednesdays and Saturdays, the latter of which might find Dawes committed to an away game with the rugby XV. "Orville proved very tolerant," he recalls. "But if I missed half a day's study and maybe a lecture, I took care to borrow a friend's notes for copying up on Sunday morning."

As he reflects on his up-bringing John Dawes acknowledges that, from the viewpoint of a South Wales valley community, the horizon is close at hand and limited. The occasional outings with Newbridge RFC had introduced him to new places, new life-styles and new people; but always there awaited the return to a small town existence. At the outset he had thought that Aberystwyth might be in the same league; but gradual realization told him that a university town contained new types of people with a wealth of different experiences from his own, who were well worth knowing and hearing from. His mind was experiencing exactly what universities are supposed to confer: a profound broadening through the consistent experience of other disciplines and expo-sure to his peers' knowledge and points of view.

In the rugby sector alone there was a number of such people. A large lock forward called Jack Davies captained the College team in Dawes's second year and brought to bear his experience with Cardiff RFC. He gave his side huge commitment and momentum, and preferred leading by example to bullying or tub-thumping. "And," recalls Dawes, "although he enjoyed a pint or two he knew that I was not yet a drinker, and yet never tried to tempt me to imbibe alcoholic drinks." Good team-mates included another lock called Wyn Thomas, Gwyn Thomas, who had propped for Cardiff, Jeff Roberts from Abertillery, who would eventually succeed to the captaincy, plus a man whose all-round sporting ability was greatly admired by Dawes – John Hitchins who was elusive on a rugby field besides being something of a sprinter and a fearsome fast bowler.

Then there were experiences of the outside world. For two important reasons Dawes vividly remembers trips to play west Wales town or village clubs. The first is that, the roads of the time being what they were, two hours or so were always available for chat somewhere near the back of the coach. Sessions like these, with pep-talk style conversation on the outward journey and post-mortems on the homeward run, perpetuated the question-ing and analysis beloved by the fast-improving centre and reminded him of unpalatable truths such as the disgust a pack feels when backs kick away hard-won possession.

The other reason has to do with force of circumstances. At set pieces, a slender student pack taking on teams stuffed with farmers and foresters could scarcely hold its own with the sheer brute strength of such opponents. This led Dawes to ponder how to win matches in defiance of such a disadvantage. He and the brains trust on the bus concluded that the answer was to move scraps of possession consistently towards the wide open spaces on the pitch where it could be successfully re-cycled by back row forwards who might be slighter than their opponents but could reach the break-down first. This almost certainly accounts for the extravagant miss-moves and long, long passes to wings which would become the hallmark of the Dawes style. The supporting attribute it needs is vision, which does not come straightaway, but can be worked towards.

At Aber there was, of course, an agreeable social side to the sport as well. Just as most rugby teams prefer playing at home to travelling so, in mid-century, many sides which did not boast club-houses would make for a friendly local tavern after the final whistle and their shower. UCW RFC and their opponents regularly homed in on The Ship in the centre of Aberystwyth for post-match hospitality, though no-one can tell why their choice was a pub whose lounge could comfortably accommodate no more than a dozen heavyweight drinkers let alone thirty thirsty players and quite possibly a referee. The post-match schedule comprised a brisk trot from the sports ground for the 5.30 opening time – and within half an hour there would be standing room only. Soon after the first round of drinks reached the tables the singing began under the baton of Porth-bred Glyn Rowlands; forty years on the non-stop Negro spiritual medley which was their signature offering can still be heard in pubs and clubs on the morning of an International match at Cardiff when the Former Students get together. What is more, the same conductor is in charge and, as was ever the case, the medley contains nothing smutty.

Alcohol had featured no more than modestly in John Dawes's career hitherto, but by his second year he was downing the occasional half of cider which, because it is made from apples one supposes, those new to drink can mistakenly imagine to be harmless. A year later, on the evening after his Finals had been completed, he and a couple of pals decided to celebrate with a

27

grand pub-crawl to take in thirty-six hostelries including other favourites of theirs like the Angel and the Farmers. Alas, the outcome was one of the very few recorded failures in the Dawes career: after visits to just six pubs the three discovered that even rising from their seats to leave was beyond them, at which early stage the grand tour was aborted.

To be completely at ease a student living a long way from home ideally needs a good base, and in his second year Dawes was fortunate to discover excellent digs with a family called Savage at Sandmarsh Cottage near Pont Trefechan, the bridge over the Rheidol at the entrance to the town. rugby players were evidently popular with the Savages, who were pleased to take in another future Welsh international in the shape of Dennis Hughes twelve months later. In due course Mary, a daughter of the house, was to become his wife.

In his final year Dawes became captain of the College rugby club. The process was somewhat arcane, and even he himself is at a loss to know how it happened. But not for the first time Denis Horgan, who was still at Aberystwyth doing post-graduate work, seems to have been the fixer, and with his encouragement Dawes "sort of eased a way" into the captaincy. Perhaps he is being over-modest; it was known that the Wales selectors had become interested in his ability, and it is a fact that there was no-one at Aber remotely able to compete with him at this time.

His period in the ranks had been a successful one for the College team, and now Dawes enjoyed being at the helm as UCW met new and stiffer challenges. The Welsh Championship, in which the half dozen colleges of Wales competed, provided a thorough test at what amounted to a pool stage before its title-winners moved on to the UAU – Universities Athletic Union – championships.

As well as being fiercely fought the Welsh ties were great levellers. Sometimes these might bring you up against a man who was still intent on choosing the right position for his gifts. Such a player was D.K. (Ken) Jones, a brilliant product of Gwendraeth Grammar School (also attended by Carwyn James) whom the UCW side had to deal with in a crucial fixture with Cardiff University. Jones was at stand-off half, where it is remembered that initially the Aberystwyth XV closed him down comfortably. In the second half D.K. was switched to centre, where suddenly he began revealing the quality that would later make him a British Lion.

As things turned out, Aberystwyth overcame domestic opposition to be involved in two UAU Finals, both played at Moseley RFC's headquarters, The Reddings. To John Dawes's chagrin both games were lost, by small margins. He compares the UAU Final to the Varsity match, with every combative ambition present plus a do-or-die state of mind – in addition to the sheer desperation that followed if you lost. As captain, in his last year at Aber, he declares that UCW should have won their Final against Leeds, but paid the penalty for a negative approach, with too much kicking from stand-off half (by the unofficial choir conductor Glyn Rowlands). Certain members of the back division, too, lost concentration and made defensive mistakes. Tough: but defeat is part of the rugby scenario and players must be able to suffer it with grace and dignity.

During this period in his career John Dawes could be forgiven for thinking that his star was in the ascendant. What forbade him was an innate modesty; he truly did not credit the idea that he was International material. But now, team-mates of his were scorching away to round off gorgeous tries and the ultimate arbiters of the day – the 'Big Five' selectors who picked Welsh teams – had recognized cause and effect: the way passes laid on by him found speedy team-mates un-marked and in open country. Certainly the Newbridge wings had begun to enjoy the licence the youngster's vision was providing for them. That is why during his last year at the College by the Sea he had started to be selected for International Trials, and indeed sat on the Welsh bench during a game against Ireland (in those days it was no more than token recognition, since the Laws did not yet allow the replacement of injured players).

But now the halcyon days were over. John Dawes duly left Aberystwyth with his BSc degree, which meant that he would be able to embark on the career in teaching that had become his ambition. Maybe, he thought, a second string to his bow would be a good idea and that it would pay him to get qualifications in physical education, or PE. Loughborough College admitted him to bid for a post-graduate diploma which would occupy one further year and send him confidently into the jobs market.

Dawes was evidently a trifle undecided at this stage about where his rugby loyalty now lay. He actually played a college trial game under an assumed name, giving a smart display as a running full-back. However, his identity could not be kept a secret for long, and the Colleges' rugby club looked forward to fielding their new recruit from the top ranks of Welsh rugby. It was at this point that he showed some of the independence and certainty of action that would stand him in good stead in life and rugby. In effect, he advised Loughborough that, having spent three years at Aberystwyth, he felt he owed a debt to the club that had nurtured him, Newbridge RFC, and wished to travel at weekends to play for it.

Dawes is very fond of owning up to 'good luck' (though he is also aware of golfer Gary Player's observation that "the harder I practise the luckier I get"). And probably he was fortunate that a senior member of staff was none other than John Robins, a Cardiffian who propped for Birkenhead Park in the immediate post-War years, who was a member of John Gwilliam's 1950 Grand Slam side, and that same summer toured Australia and New Zealand with the British Lions under Karl Mullen's captaincy. Robins understood the young man's position and made sure that no bureaucracy stood in his way or tried to change his mind. Newbridge were suitably appreciative and provided petrol which allowed Derek Morgan to undertake the long car journey to the Midlands and ferry Dawes to wherever the club were playing each weekend. On one of these trips the passenger asked point-blank why his old school-mate had opted to represent England. The reply was candid and blunt: the Welsh selectors' preferred number eight forward was the athletic Alun Pask, whom Morgan felt he would find it difficult to displace from the National XV.

Besides good company, another advantage John Dawes gained from outings with Newbridge was that, at least once a fortnight, the Welsh selectors could readily monitor his progress – he was never out of sight or out of mind. Now grooved into the centre position, he was gaining in confidence and willing to take risks which mainly paid off. His displays occasionally drew media criticism, notably from the Thomases, father and son. The influential 'J.B.G.', and subsequently Wayne, wrote that he had "dodgy" hands and "lacked a fine edge of pace"; but breadth of vision more than compensated for such perceived shortcomings. The running by most backs of the day was opportunist, whereas the young Newbridge centre gave himself chances, and enough time, to survey the broader state of play.

Although not part of the Loughborough rugby set-up, he enjoyed a constructive friendship with John Robins. Oddly enough at Pengam, as at a number of sites in South Wales, there was a fives court on which he had enjoyed plenty of exercise. Now he was introduced by Robins to squash – in effect, fives with a raquet – a game that had yet to take off in the Wales of the day. He recalls with amusement his early efforts, beginning with the need to warm up the ball, before which it obstinately refused to bounce. Although short of stature, Robins was an immensely powerful athlete able to pass on basic skills and tactics plus the importance of anticipation and reaction to an eager novice who was able before too long to deliver an action-packed forty five minutes. After a shower, the talk would usually be about rugby with Robins's input revealing many of the secrets of front five play. Such sessions amounted to regular, invaluable, master classes.

For people in Dawes's age group there was also a cadre of post-graduate students at Loughborough with a certain maturity which gave their company instant appeal, and who had valid opinions to pass about different sports and the diverse training regimes they demanded. As at Aberystwyth there was plenty to learn from a peer group in other disciplines, and Loughborough fulfilled the promise it had held out from the start. The time passed quickly, and by the summer of 1964 John Dawes had added a Diploma in PE to his degree, and the job-hunt could start.

There was now a new factor which would influence the search. At the end of term that same summer John married the woman to whom he had become engaged, Janette Morris, whose home was Penygraig and who had attended Pentre Grammar School. Bent on a career as a singer (her soloist brother had a good enough voice to win a prize at the National Eisteddfod) she had attended Nottingham Training College and now wished to develop her progress in London. Although working in the metropolis was not exactly what he had looked forward to, John her husband decided to go along with her ambitions and obtain a post there.

This he did. But not, as might have been expected, at a school where rugby was the dominant winter game. Instead, he accepted an offer from Spring Grove Grammar School, which played Association Football. Its Headmaster was Gordon Lister who, though a north countryman, happened to be a follower of rugby union and knew of the applicant's progress in the game. Things now fell into place, for a job in the chemistry department was vacant and the Welshman got it. Soon, his pupils were won over by the knowledge that their teacher was a man of some distinction in the sporting world, and always gave him attention and good discipline.

For his part, Dawes had done some scheming. He wished to keep his Saturdays free to continue his rugby career, and the best way to do this was to join a soccer school. What is more, he had already decided after sporting contact with London Welsh RFC in Wales, that this was a club whose Corinthian approach to the game was one that he could live with and take satisfaction from. He would, therefore, join it. At this point in time, he knew nothing about the hand-to-mouth amateurism which infected the Old Deer Park approach.

But in one respect the Exiles were, and remain, professional – and that is the traditional warmth of their welcome. The totally focused and tireless committeeman of the time, Dick Ellis – a kind of unofficial accommodation officer – recognized that here was a potential first-team man who should be helped to fit in. He it was who travelled widely in south west London to secure a flat which was ideal for the newly-weds. It was owned by a bachelor called Morris, who lived alone, and comprised a lounge, kitchen, bedroom and bathroom, all for £3.15s (£3.75p) a week. The landlord called upon his tenants only rarely – usually to beg a hot bath. All told, therefore, Mr and Mrs Dawes had a soft landing in west London, where life seemed to be arranged to their advantage. They appeared to be well-equipped to exploit it.

And at Old Deer Park, John Dawes was poised to give a dear, highly respected rugby club the shaking-up of a lifetime. But at first his input was that of an apprentice.

THREE

A strong Welsh presence in London has endured at least since the Middle Ages when, for a while, a couple of Kings called Henry and the wonderful Elizabeth I ran much of the British Isles from their Court. It was a magnet to which their fellow-countrymen flocked for preferential treatment in the establishing of successful businesses. The nineteenth century saw the heyday of the emigrant Cardiganshire dairymen, who exported a cow or two to the East End to satisfy the cockney demand for fresh milk. During the twentieth century Wales produced more than its necessary share of schoolmasters and was able to release those surplus to requirement. Many chose to settle in London thus maintaining an old-established tradition which was paralleled by the presence of Wales's future doctors on courses at the city's teaching hospitals.

And when a need for exercise and sport was identified, what could be more natural than these young men's desire to play rugby football? The game had taken Wales, certainly the south, by storm in the later decades of the nineteenth century when landowners and farmers allowed energetic youths the freedom of their meadowlands to compete with neighbouring communities who had formed 'clubs'. Now, in their adopted territory, London's rugby playing immigrants were keen to meet top opponents: Wasps, Rosslyn Park, the Harlequins and Richmond were all well-established – and the Exiles wanted a slice of the action.

Though the early performances of Welsh enthusiasts in the metropolis are not well chronicled, there is general agreement that scratch games involving them were taking place as early as 1882. However, it seems that London Welsh RFC was formally created in 1885 in a meeting at Anderton's Hotel in Fleet Street. The main impetus came from a certain Dr T.J. Pryce-Jenkins, who practised at rooms in Hills Place – where, from the start, players injured in action for the club got free attention.

As well as being 'Exiles' (the term has stuck despite the faint stigma of banishment which it carries) London Welsh were also nomads in the early years, playing at Raynes Park, the National

33

Athletic Ground, Cricklewood, Tufnell Park and a host of other venues including the oddly-named Tee To Tum fields at Stamford Hill. After 1919, however, nearly all home games took place at Herne Hill before the 1957 move to Old Deer Park. Rosslyn Park RFC had been its previous tenants for sixty-three years – a span which their successors of today are satisfied to have eclipsed.

Besides being in a more accessible quarter of London the new headquarters were an improvement on what had gone before in a very important detail: the first team pitch. Veterans speak with a slight curl of the lip of the playing surface at Herne Hill, which was vulnerable to the slightest shower of rain and turned into a mud-heap under anything heavier. Nor were its basic facilities much to boast of and, all in all, players preferred not to go there unless they had been selected to appear in a match. This probably helps to explain members' resistance to organized training, and even punctuality, aspects of a London Welsh sporting ethic that dismayed the products of finishing schools like Oxbridge, Loughborough and St Luke's in the West Country, who drifted in the direction of Old Deer Park after graduation.

But, from 1957, there was no question of criticizing the new ground's pitches. The responsibility of a Mr Ken Sales, they always looked good, even in midwinter, and only heavy frosts could cause cancellations. It is true that, after eighty minutes' combative exercise on a greensward that is absolutely perfect, men feel that they could have continued for another twenty minutes. This was the case at London Welsh RFC's new headquarters, and made for deep satisfaction. For players it was always like running 'on top of the ground'.

Despite the meanderings around London in the search for a sporting sanctuary, plus perennial cash crises, the attraction of comradeship was powerful and there were always newcomers knocking on the door. Though cherry-picking throughout the twentieth century was not guaranteed or infallible, some of the greatest players ever to represent Wales had graced the club's ranks in its first five or six decades. The *crème de la crème*, so to speak, would include Willie Llewellyn, Teddy Morgan and 'Boxer' Harding who played in Wales's 1905 victory over New Zealand. Wick Powell, Harry Bowcott, Vivian Jenkins, Claude Davey, W.T.H. Davies and Haydn Tanner all played a few games for the club while stationed at Aldershot during the War. In their heyday, these men were world-class players whom big crowds came to watch and be thrilled by, while later stars included Trevor Brewer, Arthur Edwards, Bryan Richards and Robin Davies. Up until 1959 seven club members had toured New Zealand, Australia and South Africa with the British Isles. A strong supporting cast assisted such front-runners to achieve notable, if erratic playing success.

During the pre-Dawes years there were no official league titles or Cups to compete for but, in terms of raw publicity, successes in the end-of-season Middlesex Sevens drew headlines in plenty. Between 1930 and 1960 the Exiles went to eight Finals, their three wins outstripping those of close rivals. In 15-a-side fixtures they had achieved twelve consecutive wins in 1929-30 and enjoyed long consecutive runs without defeat at home in 1925-27 and 1936-38. Though, on their day, they were evidently good enough to beat English club sides statistics show that until the nineteen-sixties victories over Welsh opposition were few and far between. A comment in *The Sportsman* tersely summed things up after the reigning Champions Cross Keys had scored five tries in a 23-point win at Herne Hill: "the Valley side was composed mainly of young, strongly-built miners who are very fit – which is half the battle"

But, all in all, it was a well-balanced club that an ambitious John Dawes joined in the autumn of 1963, whose priorities were to have serious fun in order to raise a thirst and, if possible, to win a match. Should the second aim remain unfulfilled then - too bad boys, there's always next Saturday. Fifteen more pints please, barman.

It was not a place where Dawes had expected to settle down. Had it not been for Janette's career ambition the young couple would certainly have stayed put in South Wales – with John committing himself to Newbridge RFC. There would have been nothing surprising about this, for in mid-century and even into the nineteen-seventies top players nurtured by Valleys clubs stayed loyal to them – Alun Pask, Haydn Morgan and the Pontypool front row of Graham Price, Bobby Windsor and Tony Faulkner were good examples.

Had that happened, the centre might have suffered a certain hardening of his rugby arteries. He recalls a certain same-ness about Newbridge's seasons, which were combative and highly sociable without ever presenting new challenges. That said, he cannot recall anything basically wrong with the rugby the club played under David Harries's guidance as coach – and, remarkably, he is on record as stating that it "compared well with London Welsh's carefree approach". Its efficacy is borne out by the 'unofficial' Championship title taken by Newbridge in 1964-65 – which delighted its former club member, by then in his second season in London. The move had been made and, says he, "If I was going to play my club rugby in London, Old Deer Park was the place to be. I was now so certain of my Welsh roots and basic Welsh-ness that playing for Richmond or Wasps or even Harlequins held no attraction at all. And, with hindsight, had I not opted for London Welsh, all the things that happened to me would simply not have happened."

If you drive up the Western Valley in search of rugby clubs you have only to follow the A467 to pass them one after another – Risca, Cross Keys, Abercarn, Newbridge and so on all the way to Ebbw Vale. In other words, you cannot miss them. It was rather different when the new Exile, fresh off honeymoon, set out on his first outing to Old Deer Park to report for training one August Tuesday evening, only to lose his way. A number of pedestrians whom he asked for advice after getting off the number 73 bus in Richmond were unable to tell him where the rugby ground was located and only, finally, at London Scottish's clubhouse was he sent in the right direction.

Having found his bearings, he speedily recognized the splendid acreage where London Welsh had been headquartered for half a dozen seasons. The young John Dawes had enjoyed occasional games there with invitation school sides, and now on hand to welcome him were some of the backroom figures whom he had met when the club paid its regular visits to the homeland (touring in Wales at Christmas-tide and Easter featured in its Founders' mission statement).

He was impressed by the turn-out on this summer evening. A best-guess suggested that perhaps a hundred vigorous and athletic bodies were engaged in physical jerks, sprinting, passing, dribbling and kicking. But after donning a track suit and standing at the touchline ready to involve himself, Dawes realized that he could not recognize a single participant on the pitch. The fact was, no member of the First XV squad was to be seen. 'Hm. Strange,' thought the newcomer. He was soon to realise that the club's top players found routine training highly resistable and usually stayed at home.

Experience of London Welsh logistics soon followed. A West Country tour was to occupy the first weekend of the 1963-64 season, and the card informing the new recruit that he had been chosen to play also stated that he was to be picked up by club skipper Bryan Richards, an elusive little stand-off half, in Hounslow early on the Friday evening. No information was included about the means of travel – coach or car – and Dawes had only the faintest recollection of what the once-capped Richards looked like. The wait until a Morris Mini (which also contained the large Robin Davies) finally picked him up seemed interminable – not to say miraculous, given the identity problem of the passenger to be taken on board.

These were first tastes of the club's happy-go-lucky attitudes to organizing rugby matches, getting fit for them and developing a style of play. How to sum up the last-named at the time? "Typically English" is John Dawes's terse comment. What did that mean? "Well, simply that Old Deer Park was the beating heart of Wales in London – but the rugby being played there was, in a word, foreign. Big forwards were the norm, not mobile but just about able to win set-piece ball. This was then released to a back division that was supposed to make things happen."

In this context Dawes recalls members of the then tight five – the captain of the 1962-3 season Gwyn Lewis, the very popular Islwyn Jones, Colin Mallows (a giant of a man) and the like. Their presence was down to Vernon Davies, a former captain of the club whose slogan now was, 'We must have bulk!' Dawes thinks that it took two whole seasons to make him change his mind.

Nonetheless, the big fellows could ultimately claim to have made their contribution to a memorable 1963-4 season which brought just ten defeats from thirty-six games. Roger Michaelson, a highly successful erstwhile captain of Cambridge, had come on strength, to torture his forwards at training and goad their big match performances, while after Christmas a significant arrival was Ken Jones, fresh from gaining his Blue in a losing Oxford side at Twickenham. "From that time," recalls Dawes, whose partner in the midfield Jones would become, "everything took off, and we went unbeaten to the close of a season that had included a win at Cardiff for the first time since 1931, plus a more than creditable performance in defeat against the Newport side which had recently toppled the touring All Blacks." In fact, for the most part the big Welsh clubs still carried too many guns for opponents who were physically lightweight by comparison; but there were a number of convincing wins over English opposition, both in London and out in the shires.

"All things considered, we did well," was the Dawes summation of his first term.

Roger Michaelson might have succeeded Richards as club captain had he not decided to return to Port Talbot for a twelve-month. In the event the choice fell upon another Cambridge man in Haydn Davies. This product of Idwal Rees's rugby academy, aka Cowbridge Grammar School, was a gifted all-round sportsman good enough to play for Welsh Secondary Schools at cricket and the winner of a Blue for rugby in 1958. His two caps were gained in 1959 – after which admirers at Old Deer Park divined that being a family man took precedence over setting aside time and effort to bid for further International honours.

He brought a rather laid-back attitude to leadership, with an example set for his team that might perhaps be called minimalist. He is remembered for last-minute arrivals in changing rooms which left small time for team talks or planning – not to mention a distinct absent-mindedness exemplified by the occasion when he turned up for the bus trip to a fixture in the Midlands without any kit. "What did he think about on the journey from Mill Hill to Richmond?" John Dawes still wonders. "Haydn was really talented, but by the time we were team-mates he seemed to have few rugby ambitions to spur him. When the time came to hang up his boots people had the impression that he had no regrets at calling it a day."

During Davies's captaincy the foot had been taken off the accelerator. After a first year with the club which was, on reflection, more successful than people were expecting Dawes was to experience a very ordinary second eight months in 1964-65. This was doubly frustrating, since he had become Davies's vice captain and was given the post of coach, in accordance with the Welsh Rugby Union's coaching advisory panel dictum of the day. The new responsibilities also carried clout: he could now exert influence and introduce radical reforms. A quiet revolution was underway.

Dawes remembers occasions and events that played a part in it, in accord with his inner determination to transform the club's approach. The first target was training, which he admits he set out to make obligatory. By mid-autumn Old Deer Park, without floodlights, was dark in the early evening, so that no fast-moving manoeuvres or combined operations could be practised in safety or with any definition. The club had been fortunate to reach an agreement with the Welsh Guards based at Chelsea Barracks which allowed them to use the gym on Wednesday nights where at least press-ups and other body-building exercises could be carried out. But though numerous members took advantage of the facility, Wednesday evenings were still conspicuous for the absence of first team players whose bonding, at the very least, might have been strengthened. If not exactly angry, the hon coach was very frustrated: "I quickly reached the conclusion that, for all their dash and bravado, London Welsh were a team who turned up five minutes before kick-off, ran around hopefully, sank a few beers afterwards and went home. Those few who did stay behind often sang more energetically than they had played."

At this time John Dawes regretted that the club was unable to train on turf at its headquarters, to which, he speculated, players might more easily be attracted than to an Army barracks. Suddenly, that became a possibility. Along the pavements of Kew Road, which runs past Old Deer Park, there sprang up a number of the new-fangled sodium lights which were beginning to illuminate large tracts of suburbia. They shed just enough light over the railings onto the Exiles' rugby training area for running and speed-work, usually without a ball – and, sure enough, there really did begin to be a rise in the number of people who turned out.

Four people, including the coach, now set an example which slowly shamed team-mates into the regular training that he was bent on introducing. He names John Ryan, later a Wales national XV coach, Glan Richards, a remarkable young wing who remains a senior member of the club, and Rowley Richards, a scrum-half from the Maesteg area: "We four trained every week, twice a week, at Old Deer Park, and tried to persuade others that this could and should be done. Next year, when I became captain, I appealed to the Committee for backing to run compulsory training at HQ, receiving a reaction that was not much more than lukewarm. Once more there were heroes who helped me to win the moral high ground by being the rod with which their teammates could be coerced into following suit. Tony Gray, Colin Gibbons, Gwilym Treharne and Trevor Davies all lived in Essex; twice every week all of them left work (at school or in the office) at half past three; travelled all the way across London; and trained like demons before leaving for home – which they reached by midnight if they were lucky. At training they were ever-present."

The sodium lights were a tremendous advance, but of course even their use had limitations – sprinting and jogging, jogging and sprinting, over distances and in ten-metre bursts, was all they permitted. But the habit of attendance at training was undeniably catching on, and when the lighter evenings arrived turn-out remained high. At this juncture a kind of touch-and-pass routine was introduced in which personnel of all London Welsh's seven teams took part, with maybe seventy five trainees on each side. This would take place on the Druids', or second team, pitch which became a morass by season's end. Such was its quality and resilience that by the end of June it would always be grassed again.

The really important break-through, however, one which delighted Dawes, was that the First XV had fully accepted the new discipline. Ultra-high fitness was the long-term aim and, indeed, a requirement if London Welsh were to be equipped to play the kind of rugby desired by their coach. Further progress came, incidentally, three seasons later when the club 'scrounged' what a committeeman describes as some 'ancient but serviceable' floodlights which lit up most of the main pitch. Sometimes they blew a fuse, but they did make it possible to introduce basic handling moves along with scrum and line-out practice.

Happily, it seems that this new, 'focussed' approach was not altering the clubhouse character of London Welsh RFC. If anything, the new player attitudes amplified the post-match *hwyl* and spontaneous entertainment which enlivened the evenings after matches and training. Celebrities would often put in an appearance, and the impromptu arias that Gwyneth Jones (Islwyn's wife and later a Dame) would sing – unaccompanied – were heard in silence and capped by tumultuous applause. Stanley Baker was in the company from time to time, not to mention the Burtons, Richard and Elizabeth (Taylor). It was special – despite the shortcomings of the pavilion, which deserved its description as 'an old shed'. Always a gregarious man who mixed easily with players and fans, John Dawes enjoyed these evenings, but equally important to him were Sunday morning meetings of his 'inner cabinet'. They were a feature of the rugby seasons once he and Janette had moved to Sunbury, and took place at a congenial riverside pub. By now Roger Michaelson had returned to London, and he and the coach were usually joined by such as Colin Gibbons and Neath-bred David Richards. After the initial banter these think-tanks embarked on in-depth post-mortems concerning the previous day's performance.

Such developing friendships helped to dispel any lingering home-sickness nursed by Dawes. He admits to uneasy feelings in his first English winter mainly stemming from London Welsh's attitude to the game, which had been a rude shock to his beliefs and aspirations. He found himself questioning what he had let himself in for. Was he going to stick this out? Could this club's amateurism really be turned around? Did he really want to be playing for it? Such mental turmoil, it seems likely, affected his form which, in his opinion, took a dive. There were weeks when he fully expected to be dropped, and not until he received his match invitation in the post did he breathe easily. As we shall see, the WRU's 'Big Five' had been keeping an eye on his progress, and would begin to award him caps. But not until early 1964, when his club's record and performances improved, did he fully come to terms with the new situation.

The one aspect of London Welsh's week-to-week existence which did not need tweaking was away trips. Cars driven by indi-viduals had given way to coaches, on which the players reverted to Welsh Rugby Type, consuming large quotas of beer and other post-match alcoholic treats. Those from west London began the excursion by travelling to Russell Square to board a coach belonging to Evan Evans Travel, which was readily accessible to team-mates based in Essex or inner London. Only then did the journey to Wales or the Midlands or the West Country begin. At the end of the trip, everyone travelled back to Russell Square before the final flog all the way back to western suburbia. Dawes's numerous Aber contemporaries revived the old Spirituals routine, on the bus and at home in the clubhouse.

The coach's thinking on leadership and captaincy, conceived at Aberystwyth, was now beginning to be profound, and he was pondering constantly about how you got the best out of an assortment of disparate talents which needed to blend into a team. He had listened attentively to Bryan Richards in the early days, before discovering that, as a traditional Welsh-style stand-off half, his main preoccupation was with his own game – whose intent and directions had to be best-guessed by support players. Therefore, the coach had to develop his own methods of controlling and inspiring his men. The journalist John Hopkins recalls witnessing a typical training session taken by Dawes in New Zealand, as coach to the 1977 Lions: "A definitive training pattern began to emerge... The man with the ball has to sprint when I blow the whistle," the coach would shout. "One blast means sprint forward, two blasts means run ten yards backwards. Three blasts mean jump in the air. Off you go!" The seeds of such a non-stop, whistle-controlled routine were planted at Old Deer Park?

There were, of course, the senior citizens such as Gwyn Lewis and Islwyn Jones who, John Dawes readily admits, were steeped in their very effective ways. They could contribute hugely, but by quarter to five they were not necessarily thinking about the game's progress so deeply as the pints waiting on the bar. Yet their knowledge of the game as played up-front (where their coach had not appeared since his sixth form days) was profound: in the bar, especially after a beating on the pitch, you just sat and listened, allowing your morale to be lifted again by the voices of experience.

Those two men typified the 'bulk' priority of Vernon Davies which John Dawes, when he became club captain at the start of 1965-66, was determined to dispel: "I wanted to change things, and to bring in 'footballers' who could run with the ball and tackle in the open spaces – in every position." Such virtues could be most clearly seen in Sevens rugby, where players without these skills would very quickly be exposed. As training for Sevens tournaments took over after Easter, the coach was enabled to identify the kind of men he wanted. Good examples were Brian Evans at 13st 10lbs and George Patterson at perhaps 13st 4lbs. It was not realistic to expect consistent possession from set pieces, but at least such raw-boned locks were mobile enough to reach the breakdown first and initiate attacks. Such a selection and match strategy was more than enough to see off top English opposition, though not necessarily to overcome streetwise Welsh sides who would kick for touch in the knowledge that possession could be recovered.

London Welsh kept up the search for men able to deliver height, weight and sufficient speed to play within their newly evolving style. In due course Mervyn Davies would come on strength along with Geoff Evans and Mike Roberts – neither, perhaps, remembered for scorching pace but, if given the ball in open play, able to do something creative with it. Probably the example-setter in this number, whom Dawes remembers with respect, was the South African-bred lock forward of Welsh descent Ian Jones, who had packed down for Oxford at Twickenham. He won a single cap (under Dawes's leadership) against Ireland, only to be subsequently dropped. His captain of the day grins, "He was included to win line-out ball, but the trouble was – as he was unknown in Wales nobody threw in to him, so he was totally unable to make his mark! ...by the way, we lost and I was dropped too."

Ian Jones's cost-effective and masterly ingenuity at bending London's public transport system to his own convenience is remembered with affection and admiration. In order to reach Old Deer Park from Hammersmith he would board a bus for Hounslow and in due course ask the conductor for a single to Shepherd's Bush. "You're going the wrong way," he would be told. "Oh, sorry. I'll catch another one," would be the reply as Jones got off. This procedure was repeated for as long as it took him, on board possibly half a dozen buses, to reach Richmond - and drew applause from team-mates when he arrived. Dawes pays the large lock a glowing compliment: "As a front five forward he brought to London Welsh more of what was missing at that time than any other man; the first of our succession of iron-hard players up-front. Back row forwards like Tony Gray and John Taylor came along soon – but Ian Jones was always in the engine room."

Weighing up the plus points that were accruing at Old Deer

Park, it is worth dwelling for a moment on the return to London rugby of Roger Michaelson after his spell back in the homeland. It is clear that from the outset John Dawes had valued the brand of perpetual motion introduced to training sessions by the former Cambridge number eight. His leadership of the Light Blues in their Varsity match triumph of 1962 was full of sound and fury, and inspirational – virtues which he now brought to bear for the Exiles. Immediately on his return to the ranks in 1965 he hit it off anew with the captain who, for his part, knew that the 'donkeys' would be whipped up to top speed. Michaelson was to play a magnificent support role during the Dawes seasons in west London. He had won his solitary cap against England in 1963, and it is one of the great mysteries of twentieth-century Welsh rugby that his dynamic presence and leadership qualities could not secure him a permanent place in the back row of the National XV.

As for his own game at this time, John Dawes looks back dispassionately. Maybe the Press critics who said he lacked the speed to make breaks had a point. But the role he was cultivating at that stage of his career was as an exploiter of width. He was playing constantly with immensely speedy and elusive wings, such as the Oxford Blue Andy Morgan, while Gerald Davies would be with the Exiles soon. There was also the Blaina-born Gareth James, a natural sportsman who represented Wales at tennis and, as a rugby full-back, was never slow to shout at his captain under a high ball, "Yours!" His main virtue in John Dawes's estimation was a determination to run everything, from any position, and he was pretty quick.

Aware that his side boasted wings and a full-back who travelled like express trains, it came as no surprise that the captain simply transferred the ball to their hands. Simply? Much more: a skill which was activated correctly, accurately and with perfect timing. Maybe he himself seldom set a stadium on fire; but his wings did. The media did not see him as a centre who cut out extravagant openings; but support players had only to run the tries in.

By the close of a highly successful 1965-66 season John Dawes and London Welsh had a quorum of men able to play the Exiles' New Rugby. That is, the playing side was looking after itself. But all clubs need an *eminence grise,* and at Old Deer Park the head guru lurking in the background puffing away at his pipe and sipping gin and tonics was Harry Bowcott (Cardiff High School, Cambridge University, Wales and British Lions). By 1965 a well-established member of the 'Big Five', Bowcott was a clever debater able to time his entry into selection arguments exquisitely. He assured the club captain, on one of the frequent journeys to Cardiff which they made together, "When the claims of London Welsh players are under scrutiny I simply keep my mouth shut – confident that the others will pick them for me!" Doubtless his civil service background under-pinned this 'Yes, Minister' kind of detachment which meant that he knew how and when to push his case and when to keep his mouth shut. A lot of caps began to be awarded to the Exiles.

But though very influential, Bowcott never let club allegiance over-ride his commitment to the cause of the National XV. In any case, at Old Deer Park he was simply first among equals. Other strong administrators sat on the committees such as Vernon Davies, Johnny Price, Stuart Davies, Ronnie Boon, Dick Ellis and Len Davies (a chairman of selectors who was supportive to captains). Dawes also remembers warmly the input of Colin Bosley, among the most unlucky of men during his playing career but now a busy networker who kept London Welsh in touch and in tune with developments affecting Home Counties rugby. These were the people who now took a bold decision to build a bigger, more modern HQ and launched the very successful Appeal which made the scheme feasible. The burgeoning club spirit of the time is exemplified by the £40 each contributed by the players themselves – a considerable chunk of money in those days. Their willingness to stump up was a hammer blow which bludgeoned older and retired members into following suit.

Evidently John Dawes was satisfied with his developing power-base at Old Deer Park. It is clear that he now knew exactly what he wanted: what sort of rugby London Welsh should play and how to persuade the club of it. For a relative newcomer that may sound over-confident, even arrogant. But such certainty, allied to specific targets, is among the qualities which separate great leaders from their followers. Another one, of which Dawes had a large amount, is stubbornness and a capacity to win arguments. A forceful and persuasive personality was maturing.

At this time, he says firmly, it was hard to credit that his rugby career would move up to international level (despite being assured by Vernon Davies that winning a cap was simply a question of time). Sitting on the bench for Wales was a mere distinction rather than any guarantee of active service. Since then, he had been playing many miles away from the South Wales rugby hot-bed and the scrutiny of the Welsh selectors.

Thus the call to the colours of 6 March 1964 to play against Ireland in Dublin the following day had come like a bolt from the blue. Since he had not been in the team named a week or so before, Dawes imagined that he was summoned to Ireland for another afternoon on the bench. But to his initial mystification, on his arrival at Dublin Airport next morning the WRU committeemen detailed to meet him began congratulating him and pumping his hand. Only then did it emerge that one of the selected centres, Ken Jones, had withdrawn with a leg injury which failed to mend, and he, S.J. Dawes, was to take the field against Mike Gibson and Co.

It may have been a shock entry into international rugby, but at least he did not have eight or ten days to spend wondering if he was up to the job. Instead, thrown in at the deep end, he experienced the full force of an Irish XV which found itself 6-5 in front with ten minutes left. Then it was that the wing, Stuart Watkins (scorer of the earlier Welsh try) found some space on the Irish left in which to exchange passes with John Dawes, and the new cap went smoothly in for a try that gave his side the lead. David Watkins added another and Keith Bradshaw sealed the win with a third conversion.

France frustrated Wales's title ambitions by snatching a draw in the final Championship encounter of 1964. Dawes's part in the Dublin victory meant his retention for the game in Cardiff, where he had spent so many magical hours as a teenager on the terraces watching marvellous Welsh performances. Played on a sticky pitch, this game was by no means a classic and Wales were lucky to avoid defeat.

It had been four years since Wales had played the Springboks and held them to 0-3 on a waterlogged Cardiff Arms Park. That May, John Dawes found himself chosen for a five-match visit to South Africa when revenge would be a priority. As it happened, the tourists went into the Test with three wins under their belts plus a 22-9 defeat by Northern Transvaal at Pretoria. Alas for their hopes, the outcome in Durban was a 24-3 defeat, the worst suffered by any Welsh side since 1924 when Scotland's victory margin at Inverleith reached 35-10. Half time was reached at King's Park with a 3-3 score-line, after which tries by Marais, Hopwood and Smith supported by Oxlee's excellent place kicking obliterated Welsh hopes.

"We were certainly in the game for forty minutes," John Dawes recalls wistfully. "But after the interval they caught us off balance straightaway, and from then on it was catch-up rugby. After half time we were never in it."

The young London Welshman had had his first experience of the ruthless, relentless approach which characterized South African rugby through the twentieth century. Not until 1999 would Wales gain a first victory against the 'Boks'.

FOUR

B etween the Wars the Welsh backs who won caps, especially in the thirties, were among the best rugby players this pocket-sized country has produced. Some of them, as noted in Chapter Three, were tempted to Herne Hill and played a few games there before deciding to stay and seek their fortune in the Metropolis. These men included stars like Vivian Jenkins, Ronnie Boon, Harry Bowcott and others. Then there was the procession of talented performers who took a look at what London offered before deciding to remain in the homeland. This group included such as Maurice Turnbull, Cliff Jones, Wooller, W.T.H. Davies and Tanner. Whatever their allegiance dictated, however, the quality of such players brooks no argument.

There can be little doubt that if those men had been serviced by powerful, well-drilled packs they could have tucked Titles and Triple Crowns under their jerseys for a whole decade before World War II. Sadly, although their raw strength was not in question, the Welsh packs of this era had no-one like England's W.W. Wakefield able to conduct master classes on forward play. The critic E.R.K. Glover lamented in his *Western Mail* 'Notebook' after one International match in 1938:

> As usual there was never a heel from the loose... we are no nearer an appreciation of the principles of the loose heel than we were before... Mauls are still conducted with the players standing nearly upright; and, worse, forwards join them from the side rather than the back.

The immediate post-War packs were hardly any better. But suddenly, fortuitously and in the absence (injured) of players senior to himself, a formidable captain in the shape of John Gwilliam arrived to grip Welsh forward play by the short and curlies and lift it to a calibre where it could hold its own not just with Englishmen and the Irish but with South Africans and All Blacks too. For career reasons he did not tour New Zealand with the 1950 Lions but, when men like John Robins and Rees Stephens brought back insight into the way that All Black forwards worked, Gwilliam was all ears and willing to learn. His captaincy lasted just three seasons, after which the top Welsh forwards had become street-wise enough to live with any packs in the world.

This sea-change lasted through much of the fifties, and was appreciated by backs like Cliff Morgan who played on until 1958 when he exchanged his rugby boots for a BBC Wales microphone. He was in the first Welsh side to be defeated by France at Cardiff, but was gone a year later when the French followed that win up with a first Five Nations title. South Africa came on tour to the UK and won the Cardiff Test 3-0 in December 1960, after which Wales was involved in some wretched and forgettable games, mainly through indecision about whom to select at number six (worn in those days by stand-off halves). The death in a car crash of the gifted Ken Richards meant that the Welsh selectors put all their confidence in David Watkins of Newport, who began his Wales career at stand-off half on an icy afternoon in January 1963. Almost more important than a cap that day was the underclothing issued to the Welsh team.

As we have seen, John Dawes missed the first two Internationals of 1964, making his debut at Dublin a few days short of his twenty-fourth birthday. By the end of that year he had appeared in the drawn game against France and been gunned down by the Springboks at Durban. So: what impact was Test Rugby making on the newcomer?

For a start, Dawes agrees with all the other players of international rugby football that their first Test match went like lightning. "Start! Pfft! All over," he recalls. "It's very hard to remember detail from my debut. I think I handled the ball twice, the first time putting in a diagonal chip towards a corner flag which the Irish defence just reached before the Welsh attackers. Later there was the inter-action between Stuart Watkins, winning a second cap, and myself which resulted in a try. That's not something you can ever forget! But if you check with the various Press accounts of the game it will become clear that from a Welsh standpoint it was run by Clive Rowlands at scrum-half and David Watkins at stand-off. Not a handling game."

So the story that Dawes likes to tell with a grin is not about the match so much as its aftermath and the receipt of his cap. It

arrived by post the following week at his London address in a
tattered old box which had once held a pair of shoes. That was all,
with no word of thanks and congratulations from the selectors
and not even a compliments slip to say where it had come from.
But evidently there was nothing unusual about what happened,
and in Dawes's memory this sloppy, off-hand system endured at
least until the nineteen-seventies.

A variety of factors may have contributed to the curious sense
of unease experienced by him during the thirty-six hours in
Dublin. One was the kind of game the Welsh were bent on playing; it scarcely mirrored the direction in which things were now
moving at Old Deer Park. Secondly, geographically Dawes was
playing his rugby out on a limb and hence a stranger to at least
half of his new team-mates. It has to be remembered that his
arrival on the International scene took place in Welsh rugby's
Middle Ages, when match preparation amounted to little more
than a slap on the back after a Friday practice session followed by
a trip to the cinema; and men being capped for the first time
faced a magic circle of acceptability into which they had to break.

The newcomer recalls not knowing, for a start, why he was
suddenly deemed good enough for the International XV, and what
was to be his role on that particular afternoon. This was partly
since skipper and scrum-half Clive Rowlands was not an analytic
leader but an out-and-out motivator who believed simply that
matches could be won by men prepared to die for their country,
or at least for their auntie Gwladys. He knew that his enthusiasm
would be wasted on men who wanted to concentrate and think
before games started, amongst whom Dawes was numbered: "I
didn't need that approach". There were some, too, in the pack like
Brian Thomas and Brian Price who could also do without being
harangued. So 'Top Cat', as Rowlands was affectionately nick-
named, targeted the more emotional members of his teams, such
as Dai Morris and Denzil Williams. Dawes even suspects that in
his playing days as Wales captain (as distinct from his later coaching role) the scrum-half actually needed to release such torrents of
emotion to pump up his own self for the fray. As for tactics, if his
men learned anything of them beforehand it could be summarized
in one word: 'Kick!'

Pretty soon, his players realized that he had a way of, as it were, challenging them with his gaze and a determined jaw-line to be at their best from the kick-off. A player with whom he managed to lock eyes became the object of the next five minutes' noisy soliloquy. Hence some of his more thoughtful squaddies avoided eye-contact for all they were worth and cultivated the art of gazing studiously at the floor.

Interestingly, in the debate about which position on the rugby field is most suitable for captaincy Dawes comes down emphatically against scrum-half: "No, it is quite the wrong position". He agrees that New Zealand does leave decision-making and control to the 'half-back', as he is known, but this is made possible because of the supremacy habitually secured by All Black packs, giving number nine extra inches and seconds in which to work. Captaincy and inspirational play are usually the tasks of their back row men. Although the greatest scrum halves, gifted men like Gareth Edwards, usually made correct decisions, survival is a priority in the position and there is much to say for control being given by European sides to stand-off halves. But Dawes concludes that his own position, centre, is the perfect one for captaincy: in the midfield he was in touch with all sectors of his team, and had space and time in which to judge quality of possession and reflect on the state of the game.

What all of this adds up to is that, in his own carefully-chosen words, Dawes "did not feel he belonged" to the Welsh team of his early years, whose approach was alien to the way he felt about the game: "We were not adventurous. Our style was limited. The traditional excitement of the national game was absent. Don't get me wrong – representing my country was magical, but the way we played in the mid-sixties was sometimes mundane. I felt little elation.

"Nor was there feed-back from the 'Big Five' which we players could absorb and learn from. The selectors kept their distance. We knew their identities – without actually knowing *them*, so that after a year winning Welsh caps I had still to hold a meaningful conversation with any one of them. The most encouraging statement made about my game in that time came from Stuart Watkins. I heard that he was on record as saying, 'If I were allowed to choose a centre to play inside me, it would be John Dawes every time'. This Newport wing had only one cap more than myself, but that statement by him in the Press made me feel, for the very first time, that I was actually making a contribution."

In the unimpressive 11-11 draw with France of 1964 in Cardiff Keith Bradshaw missed six out of eight kicks at goal, any one of which could have brought an outright Five Nations title instead of the eventual tie with the Scots. Now, anticipation was sharpened by the first-ever tour to South Africa by a Welsh side but, as noted earlier, the tourists were put to ignominious flight in the second half of the Test at Durban.

Though he had seen Springbok number eight Doug Hopwood almost single-handedly thwarting Wales on a Cardiff quagmire in 1960, Durban had clearly been the first real eye-opener of John Dawes's early International career. The Springboks, he recalls respectfully, were blessed with superb physiques not to mention fitness which had reached the high peaks thought necessary to tame the Welsh (all this, of course, in the romantic mid-century era when they could indeed present a vivid threat to any rugby nation in the world). Significantly, beatings that Wales had managed to give New Zealand and Australia by this time had all happened on home soil, and now they were learning how hard it can be to play International games when the crowd at the stadium is noisily hostile and home is thousands of miles away. Dawes vividly recalls the few minutes after half time when Lionel Wilson dropped a goal for South Africa, a signal to his side that they should engage a higher gear. This happened; exit Wales from contention.

What also made an impact on the Welsh tourists was the good, normally dry, weather in South Africa. An average Welsh season is full of rain, which in turn makes for quagmire conditions on midwinter rugby pitches (England's too). That is why groundsmen prefer to leave grass long, so that it stands a better chance of surviving the cold weather. Dawes remembers that London Welsh often played Harlequins in the last fixture before the annual Varsity match at Twickenham: "The grass there was left to flourish from late summer right through the autumn; and by their early December clash any member of Harlequins or London Welsh ordered to place-kick at goal would find that he could see only that half of the ball which was not covered by grass."

So he has some sympathy with a view expressed thoughtfully

by the World Cup winning skipper of Australia in 1991, Nick Farr-Jones, as he perceived the onset of Wales's decline in the late nineteen-eighties and the beginning of the nineties: "They should give their pitches a long rest at the turn of the year, after which groundsmen will be willing to cut the grass much shorter – and that in turn will assist much faster running by backs and forwards alike. The Welsh have been handicapped by coping with five-inch high grass, and they won't be nimble again until they do something about it. In addition, they are a slighter, lighter race than many of their opponents; on heavy grounds it is harder for such players to get into the game than it is for heavyweight opponents."

One exception to that rule was a Welshman who made his International debut in January 1965 and contributed to a Cardiff victory over England. John Dawes's judgements are normally cautious and considered, and he is not in the business of rave reviews. But he singles out the late Terry Price (Hendy, Llanelli, and Leicester University) for special praise: "a giant of a youth who had scored two tries from full-back in a 1964 Trial, he pumped a hundred per cent into the eight appearances he was to make for his country. His early death in a road accident was a huge tragedy."

This nineteen-year-old full-back is certainly remembered for his physical attributes. His broad shoulders had put New Zealand's cruiser-weight flanker Waka Nathan out of action in a crash tackle when Llanelli met the All Blacks in 1963, and he was an immense defender. He also carried a kick like a horse which was both valuable up and down the touchlines and delivered dropped goals and conversions from anywhere inside opponents' territory and beyond. Finally, although in his time full-backs were not yet regular attackers, his thrust on the move could break tackles and leave markers spreadeagled on the floor. Perhaps the ultimate tribute paid to him by Dawes, who played just in front of Price, is this: "Ahead of his time, he always wanted to run and, all in all, I have the feeling that if the boy had not chosen to go North he would have had a big, extended career in Union – and even the great J.P.R. Williams might have had to wait three or four years before claiming the Wales full-back position."

Price contributed eight points in the February victory at Murrayfield which was a very close call in the visitors' favour.

Then Ireland were seen off in Cardiff by fourteen points to eight, a victory which brought Wales a tenth Triple Crown. Price was again a match-winner with a conversion, a penalty and a dropped goal from forty-five yards, but John Dawes had to leave the field with concussion after five minutes and missed a lengthy period of the first half being treated by Dr Jack Matthews. In the changing room the team physician gave his patient the required treatment, finally asking, "Can you see anything out of the window?" "Er, just a bit," came the reply. "OK, back you go," said the good doctor happily. How things have changed since those days.

The Triple Crown of 1965 was a great morale booster to both the happy fans and the Wales team in which Alun Pask gave great displays not only as one of the pack but also as an emergency member of the back division when Dawes was off the field – replacements had yet to be allowed. Afterwards Clive Rowlands caused a brief stir by telling the media Press conference, "Losing John was the best thing that could have happened to us". Then, realising that his phraseology was unfortunate, he hastily explained, "Er, that really made us fight all the harder. If Ireland couldn't crack us then, they never would."

Triple Crown or not, it was the final Welsh game of the winter which first gave John Dawes the satisfaction, and the kick, which he had confidently expected to experience in international rugby. Rowlands and his men set off for Paris in the spring with high hopes of adding a Grand Slam to their conquests of the Home Countries. They knew that their opponents were not to be taken lightly; by now the one-time apprentice Frenchmen had kept Wales on the back foot for the best part of a decade.

Among a brilliant group of backs were the admirable Boniface brothers paired at centre, while the pack featured two of France's all-time greats in Benoit Dauga and the immense Walter Spanghero. André Herrero was no mean flanker, and the whole machine was driven by one of the most dynamic captains of French rugby history, Michel Crauste. A native of Lourdes, he boasted a nickname calculated to deter any faint-hearted opponent – Attila. Now, following a draw in Dublin and defeat by England, his team were not in a position to take the title or a share of it; but they were determined to frustrate the Welsh at Colombes.

And they let loose a hurricane in the first half, playing dazzling rugby to run in four tries and establish a 19-0 lead by the interval. The visitors looked dead in the water; as John Dawes puts it, "We hadn't turned up". Clive Rowlands, however, was at his most histrionic during the interval, smacking fist into palm and telling one and all that their Auntie Gwladys would not be amused. Dawes, Stuart Watkins and Dewi Bebb were stirred to positive action and claimed a try each to eat into the French lead. Terry Price struck two conversions for 13-19.

"At this point I really thought that this game was so challenging, and our second half mood so exhilarating, that we could win it," recalls Dawes. "Alas, Paul Dedieu kicked a vital penalty which put our opponents two scores out of reach and we faded. But it had been stirring stuff, out of rugby's top drawer. We still finished as Champions."

That match moulded the Welshman's respect for the game as played by France. In his pantheon, England qualify by reason of efficiency, New Zealand for continuity and France for her capacity to produce sudden inspired and devastating passages of play. Many readers will remember the 1999 World Cup semi-final in which the French, trailing the All Blacks 17-10 at half time, came out for a second forty minutes of bravura which gave them a tremendous 43-31 victory.

"That blitzkrieg is exactly what we encountered in 1965," says Dawes. "Every time we took our eye off the ball in the first half France swept past us to score their four tries. The ingredient we could not cope with was novelty. Successful rugby at the highest level demands intense concentration and we were disconcerted every time the French dipped into their bag of tricks. At the time their teams possessed far higher skill levels than we did. And all their players knew, should one of them make a mistake, how to put things right instantly. To combat this kind of brilliance and assurance you really have to live in their shorts. We hadn't. We took the Championship, but fell at the Grand Slam hurdle."

Although he had performed more than adequately through the 1965 Championship season, Dawes drew a blank the following year when D. Ken Jones, Keith Bradshaw and his Bridgend co-centre Lyn Davies were the preferred midfielders. Again just one result denied Wales a Grand Slam, when Irish flair undid the hopes of Alun Pask's side in Dublin.

In a sense Dawes could afford not to lose any sleep over his continued omissions from Five Nations games by the Welsh selectors. His Herculean labours at Old Deer Park took the lion's share of his energies and were now paying off. However, in December 1966 he did find favour, paired at centre with Gerald Davies for the Test against the touring Australians. Once more, in defeat, his rugby education would be enhanced.

Although always popular visitors, the Wallabies had never beaten Wales, home or away, through fifty eight years of trying. They were perceived beforehand as rank outsiders, for Wales were the current champions of the northern hemisphere and had not lost in Cardiff for three years. Their chosen team was experienced, contained some very powerful men, and above all was thought to be street-wise in a manner that Australians could not yet claim – rugby in their country was still a minority sport.

The mighty, however, would fall. At twenty minutes the scores were level at 6-6, Wales having scored a try through Haydn Morgan plus Terry Price's penalty, against a dropped goal by Phil Hawthorne and a penalty by Jim Lenehan. The latter then came into the line from full-back to score at the corner, hitting a goal-post with his conversion attempt.

The crowd waited expectantly for the home team to strike back. To raise their hopes, it appeared at one stage that the tourists would lose Hawthorne with a depressed fracture of his cheekbone, but the stand-off bravely decided to remain on the field, soon converting a smart try by Alan Cardy. Their fourteen points would be enough for victory even when a late rally by Wales brought Dawes a try converted by Price. At the final whistle tears of happiness poured down the cheeks of manager Bill McLaughlin at this first-ever successful incursion into Wales by the Wallabies.

Dawes confesses to astonishment at the pace with which Australia launched attacks from all quarters of the pitch. The sheer speed of their inter-passing took his breath away as the Welsh three-quarters tried to close down spring-heeled opponents. At scrum-half, skipper Keith Catchpole whisked the ball off one stride like lightning to Hawthorne from whom it flew on its way to wings Boyce and Cardy. At other times full-back Lenehan would arrive at top speed between or beside the centres, a devastating move given that his opposite number, Terry Price, was not enjoying the greatest of games. It all added up to nourishing food for thought – which the future captain of the British Lions digested greedily.

There was more grief for the Welsh in 1967 when, again without Dawes, their heroes plummeted to the bottom of the Five Nations table as a result of defeats in succession by Scotland, Ireland (in Cardiff) and France. This was despite the emergence in the midfield of W.H. 'Billy' Raybould alongside Gerald Davies. Though puzzled at his treatment by the 'Big Five' selectors Dawes was pleased at the pairing for his club's sake. Gerald Davies, he knew, was rapidly becoming a world-class three-quarter while Raybould, a recent arrival from Cardiff, may not have been the easiest of centres to track but could make wonderful breaks when on song. Those around him just needed to keep up.

There was finally the surprising, even incredible, result against England at Cardiff when a team of Welsh no-hopers – among whom Dawes would love to have featured – turned the tables on the visitors and galloped to a 34-21 victory which will always be remembered as Keith Jarrett's match. On his debut he ran up 19 points with a try, five conversions and a penalty to equal the Welsh individual scoring record held by Jack Bancroft. Gareth Edwards won a second cap while David Watkins played his last game for Wales before going North, leaving the field clear for Barry John.

The next incoming tourists to Wales were New Zealand on a seventeen-match autumn visit hastily arranged after the calling-off of an intended trip to South Africa because of apartheid difficulties over the Maori contingent in the squad. The All Blacks saw off England, Wales (13-6), France and Scotland but were denied the chance of a Grand Slam because of Irish fears that the foot and mouth epidemic of 1967 might be brought across the Celtic Sea into the Republic's farming regions.

John Dawes, again side-lined by the Welsh selectors, made an appearance for East Wales (incorporating London Welsh) against the tourists because of Raybould's last-minute withdrawal with shingles. It turned out to be a great game in which to feature. The tourists came to a bleak Cardiff Arms Park in December fresh from a convincing 23-12 win over Monmouthshire when their line was not crossed. They fielded what was, on paper, a second XV which nonetheless included McCormick, Gray, Strahan and the tour skipper Brian Lochore. A midweek crowd of 30,000 packed the Park to see whether a home team built around Cardiffians could dent the visitors' hundred per cent record.

Although the pre-match words to the scratch Welsh team might have been spoken by John Dawes they actually came from the lips of another Newbridge-bred man – the coach, Dai Hayward: "We must keep the ball away from their forwards. And we must run in attack from everywhere – from near our own line or even behind it. We have the backs to shake them, and we will do so." It proved to be the right strategy, All Black coach Fred Allen saying afterwards, "We were glad to escape with a draw."

East Wales went into the lead twenty minutes into the game. Slick line-out possession secured on the Welsh right by Cardiff's Lyn Baxter encouraged Barry John to drop for goal. Fatally the New Zealand backs spent one moment too many looking upwards as the ball sped over their heads towards the target. As it faded to the left Frank Wilson chased and fell on it close to the New Zealand corner flag for a try that full-back David Griffiths just failed to convert.

The combined Welsh side stayed in the lead for fifty minutes, twice denied scores that might have given them the result. The truly controversial incident came when wing Keri Jones kicked over New Zealand's line and went after the ball at full tilt, only to be taken out by a very late shoulder-charge from McCormick. Far from incurring a penalty try, the full-back was not punished at all. Another questionable judgement by referee Frank Lovis was his refusal to award a second score to Wilson after he had pursued a chip ahead by Gareth Edwards which bobbed awkwardly over the All Blacks' line. No glory for East Wales in the end, then, only an honourable draw as Bill Davis set up an unconverted All Black try ten minutes from time for Tony Steel. Barry John continued to pepper the vistors' posts with drop kicks which were just off target – and the All Blacks had saved their unbeaten record by a whisker.

This had been John Dawes's first experience of All Black

power, and once again clues to the way leading opponents played were not lost on him. He would have been in sympathy with the pre-match opinion expressed by Hayward: "New Zealand have shown on this tour that they have few weaknesses; but they can be made to look harassed." That, of course, is what happens to any machine into which a spanner is thrown – it stutters and grinds to a halt. But to do that kind of damage to a New Zealand side on a rugby pitch their opponents must be prepared to play out of their skins – as a pack wonderfully led by John O'Shea had indeed done.

Half way through the 1968 Five Nations John Dawes was restored to the National XV for matches against Ireland in Dublin and France at Cardiff, for the first of which he was given the captaincy that had been taken away from Gareth Edwards (only to be returned to him two weeks later). It turned out to be a faintly farcical afternoon on which I reported in *The Times*, for which I had just started writing about Welsh rugby as a freelance. That is the reason why, from the Lansdowne Road Press box, I had the best possible view of the incident which nearly caused a riot, with the crowd calling for the head of referee Mike Titcomb – a likeable man who made a mistake in the afternoon to which he owned up in the evening. It came after Ireland had laboriously created a 6-3 lead through a Mike Gibson try and a Tom Kiernan drop goal to a Doug Rees penalty. It was not a game to please the crowd and the action they were now to witness pleased them even less.

There was about a quarter of the game left when Delme Thomas won good line-out possession some 35 yards from Ireland's line, and Edwards dropped for goal. The ball curved away at the last moment and passed at least a yard outside the left-hand goalpost. So certain was I of the miss that I took my eyes off the touch-down by an Irish catcher of the ball to write in my notes, 'Just off target'.

When I looked up again it was to see Mr Titcomb haring for the half way line, whistle still in mouth and arm in the air. The Welsh players were trotting in the same direction, though I noted a degree of hesitation before Edwards followed suit. Meanwhile the Irish, lining up behind Mike Gibson for a re-start on the 22, were clearly mortified when they realized that the goal had been given and their lead was wiped out. They trooped reluctantly to the half way line.

The kick-off was now delayed for four minutes while the unhappy Irish fans hurled fruit, cauliflowers, coins, bottles and even themselves over the barriers and onto the pitch. The players of the two sides clustered protectively around the referee until gradually the crowd's wrath expended itself.

Titcomb now drew heavily on his instinct for survival. Some two minutes before the end of proper time the home team forced their way to the Welsh line and camped on it, delivering thrust after thrust at a weary defence. Finally, a full nine minutes into time-added-on (only five of which were strictly legitimate), the flanker Mick Doyle forced his way over for a winning try. Tom Kiernan's conversion attempt was just wide, but its fate did not matter to the ref, for either way Ireland had won and he now preferred the safety of the tunnel. That evening he gallantly admitted, "I really thought the ball had gone between the posts. Evidently I was wrong. That kind of mistake can happen to anyone."

Magnanimously John Dawes agrees. He takes cover behind the tongue-in-cheek comment that he had a poor view of the kick (unless he had slipped onto his back in the mud or an Irishman was twenty yards offside he must have had an even better view than I had). However, there was more than referee errors for him to think about after the match. He had lost it, and had a feeling in his blood that he might now lose the captaincy too. He was right. Edwards was put back in control for the final game of the 1968 Five Nations tournament, against France.

Diminutive Doug Rees was enjoying a short period as Wales full-back after the departure to League of Terry Price – though a greater contrast with his predecessor can scarcely be imagined. Against the French he placed two penalties but could not convert a Keri Jones try that made up a promising Welsh lead of nine points to three. It turned out to be not enough, for on this visit to Cardiff nothing was going to stop France completing their first-ever Grand Slam. Skipper Christian Carrere scored one try and Lilian Camberabero another, while the latter's brother added eight points with the boot to clinch a vital win which was their seventh in a row. France were now a world power.

In the summer of 1968 Ireland's captain Tom Kiernan led the British Isles on a major tour of South Africa, the twentieth such overseas visit to take place. Ten out of a thirty-one strong party were Welsh, a surprisingly high proportion in the light of a below-average Five Nations campaign which saw them finish fourth. However, when the Lions came home in August 1968 what they would need was a month or two without heavy commitments. This meant that they were not to be considered for the September tour of Argentina to which Wales were committed and whose personnel would include only a minority of seasoned Internationals. Soon it was revealed that John Dawes was to skipper the party, and would be the only capped back to travel.

At that stage in twentieth-century rugby Argentina were no more than a remote outpost. Combined Oxford and Cambridge teams had been there on tour, bringing back good reports of the Pumas' progress but not hinting at any grave threat which they might present to a senior member-nation of the International Board. Beyond that, John Dawes states, the WRU had done next to no research and, with hindsight, had grossly underestimated the nature of their young team's task.

Not untypically, preparations were muddied by controversy over management personnel. The era of coaching had arrived in Wales, with a supremo appointed in the shape of Ray Williams as National Coaching Organiser. He had an outstanding track record and had persuaded the 'Big Five' to install the former Ebbw Vale forward David Nash as National Team Coach a year previously. But early on it was announced that the assistant to the Manager, Glyn Morgan, was to be the elderly Harry Bowcott who, having just passed the age of sixty, was emphatically not someone who was going to don a track suit to rehearse a team. There was consternation: how could Wales accept the concept of coaching only to abandon the idea at its first major overseas challenge? Nash, who had taken Wales through the Five Nations campaign, resigned in disbelief and disgust commenting, "It made me wonder if my input had been at all worthwhile." The General Committee were the guilty men, and also received the resignation of Alun Thomas, chairman of selectors.

Bowcott stuck to his guns, and got his glamorous trip. However, there was a compromise which saw Clive Rowlands appointed as team coach. Thus when John Dawes accepted the captaincy he knew what style of control to expect. But what lay in store for Wales?

"The answer is that no-one had a clue," is his blunt response. "That was one concern; the next one was that an early-autumn tour was not a wise undertaking since, in those days at any rate, Welsh players were unlikely to be match fit and battle-hardened in September. There was a general feeling that a Welsh team, even without its top players, would be able to overcome the Argentinians in the two Tests that lay in wait, but this was not founded on good research."

Inevitably, things went belly-up. As a matter of routine today's tour managers go on reconnaissance to check accommodation, venues and the like. The young Welsh tourists of 1968 were billeted at a country club which, in the Argentine winter, was short of visitors and anything that could be called exciting. Accessing the night-time fleshpots, or even simply shopping, was half a day's journey, there and back.

The visitors were very distressed after the first game against Belgrano. A prop called Miguel Cole, who had probably had a bang on the head, walked from the field and sat for a while on a touch-line bench saying that he felt unwell. Later came the news that he had been moved for treatment in hospital where he had died. It was no consolation when the Press revealed that he had suffered a blow to the cranium in his previous game and should not have played so soon afterwards. His Argentinian team-mates wept openly, the tourists were distressed, and the after-match function became a damp squib. The Welsh were without *hwyl* and zest four days before the next game.

That brought a win over a Provincial XV, but from then on the results went downhill. Defeat in the First Test was followed by a draw with Argentine Juniors, a defeat of another Combined XV and the final 9-9 draw in the Second Test. The young side was simply not good enough, and by sending out a below-strength party the WRU had shot itself in the foot. Back in the UK Harry Bowcott commented, "Youngsters like Phil Bennett and certainly our new discovery at full-back, J.P.R. Williams, came of age on a tour when the odds were stacked against us. The Pumas were allowed by referees to put in late tackles, obstruction and a series of crimes [sic] at the line-outs. As soon our men infringed we were penalized." However, John Dawes recognized a basic mis-match, and once again he had been unable to win undisputed command status for himself at International level.

The Five Nations challenge early in 1969 saw the London Welshman invited by Clive Rowlands to join the regular squad sessions at Aberavon aimed at mounting a more mature and coherent challenge in Europe – not to mention the visit to New Zealand due that summer. Dawes grins at the recall of squad week-ends at the local Lido, a kind of early sports centre where Rowlands' men went under the cosh. The younger players behaved themselves and were tucked up in the team dormitory by eleven p.m. – which was when the old hands would go out for a curry. Thus the atmosphere at breakfast-time could be recalled as somewhat foetid.

However, Dawes was in sympathy with the National Coach's aims and gamely endured the weekly trips to Wales in the company of medical student J.P.R. Williams plus teachers John Taylor and Mervyn Davies, even though the two soccer pitches at the players' disposal were often under water and not strictly suitable for rugby training. It was at this time that Gareth Edwards suffered badly from what came to be called 'Cardiff hamstring' which obliged him to spend time on the physios' tables rather than getting wet in the Welsh winter.

However, when the tide was out the squad moved happily onto the beach, whose sands tested hamstrings and other leg muscles. One particular exercise run by the coach, Dawes recalls, began outside the Lido and finished up on Swansea Bay. Another feature he remembers from these occasions concerns the crowds who turned up to watch the Welsh team going through its prepa-ration. They were happiest leaning against the railings of the promenade, which gave them a grandstand-type view. Previously, Welsh squad training had either been non-existent or held behind closed doors – so being able to feast eyes on their heroes was an agreeable novelty for the fans.

But: was S.J. Dawes really playing a useful role there?

FIVE

Dawes felt vaguely troubled as the 1968-9 domestic season went past the half way stage and he celebrated a twenty-ninth birthday. Despite being part of the squad which trained at the Afan Lido, he recalled being advised by tour manager (and Wales selector) Glyn Rowlands in Buenos Aires that "your best days are behind you". Notwithstanding, he clung to the hope that he was still good enough to play International rugby for Wales. But as the Five Nations tournament progressed he found himself sitting regularly with Dennis Hughes on the Welsh bench. Thus he was putting in the training and enduring the travelling weekends without having anything to show for it. The chance to visit New Zealand with Wales later in the year was all that prevented him and Hughes from packing their bags and departing the scene.

It may be the lingering memory of being distanced in this way from the action which prompts strong criticism by John Dawes of the replacement laws as they work at present. Theoretically they allow a coach pressing the panic button to send on from the bench all the spare members of his squad, who turn a fixture, literally, into a different ball game. The International Board in Dublin periodically reviews the situation, and is thought to think at present that it is just about satisfactory. But there are radicals like Australia's Eddie Jones who, extraordinarily, favour unlimited rolling subs who come on and off as required. At the other extreme are conservatives who argue that replacements in the final twenty minutes should only be for injured men. This camp, in which Dawes belongs, also thinks that the wholesale injection of new players in the final minutes cheapens the winning of caps.

Interestingly, he also speculates about the damage done to the morale of men who are taken off by the coaches, something which can be appreciated most vividly in soccer's Premier League. A player who is taken off after a poor hour on the pitch trudges down the tunnel with a feeling of demoralization and failure while his replacement is fairly jumping for joy. Finally, what about the fans? People who have paid good money to enjoy the play of, say, Shane Williams can be excused for feeling short-changed if he is taken off with a quarter of the game still to go. Dawes hopes that the IB will keep deliberating, and will act.

As the 1969 Five Nations tournament neared its close the London Welsh captain began telling himself that, maybe after all, he was not up to it. The competition for places in the centre did not seem to be inordinately strong. Ken Jones had gone into retirement, to be followed by Keith Bradshaw. The young Gerald Davies was brilliant but slight of frame. Keith Jarrett was enigmatic. As a player, as opposed to a leader, Dawes could not be said to have let Wales down – and yet he was not being selected. Would not Harry Bowcott and his fellow selectors give another chance to someone who, if apparently not earth-shattering, got the basics right and made very few mistakes? Well: not straight-away, if ever, it began to seem.

It did not help his mind-set either that his professional and private lives were under some strain at this time. The major surgery which secondary education was undergoing meant that Spring Grove Grammar School had become a Senior Comprehensive School for 14-plus pupils, fed by a junior school close at hand. It was ill-equipped for his subject, chemistry, which Dawes claims is a hard one to teach in any circumstances.

Crucially, while the grammar school had possessed two laboratories each for physics, biology and chemistry, in which pupils from entry upwards could carry out fruitful experiments, the former secondary modern school attended by younger children had no such facilities in which to introduce them to the sciences. Thus the Head of Chemistry envisaged pupils coming into the upper school without the necessary grounding in chemistry laboratories or classrooms. He could therefore see that the flow of talent into his Department would dry up. The A-level and O-level candidates in whom he was interested would be in short supply, and he might well find himself obliged to teach a bland General Science course which, most emphatically, he had no wish to do. So slowly, despite the friendship which had grown with head-master Gordon Lister (and which survived), a resolve built up in him that sooner, rather than later, he must make a career move.

Domestically, things were different, too. Although master-minding the progress of London Welsh RFC was exhilarating, the price Dawes had to pay was five, sometimes six, evenings of spare time spent in the Club's interest: selection of its seven teams (this took place at the Cock Tavern near Oxford Circus), training nights, plus a Saturday match from which he might not return until late evening. Finally there were the Sunday morning think-tanks at Sunbury or frequent journeys down to squad training sessions at Port Talbot for which the Exiles' representatives departed at four am, and were never late. Today's new breed of professional players might consider this a punishing schedule – and Dawes was an amateur.

The result was that time spent at home was at a premium, especially when the children, Michael and Catherine, arrived in the space of twenty-two months. As good Welsh parents John and his wife debated adding Rhodri and Llunos to their offsprings' birth certificates, only to demur; living in London they had become aware of the English capacity for tortured pronunciation of most 'foreign' names, and there was no way they wanted 'Llunos' to become 'Clinnos' in the Anglo-Saxon way.

Although financial considerations had obliged Janette to abandon hopes of a professional singing career, her membership of amateur choral groups demanded a rehearsal discipline that matched her husband's devotion to his rugby activities. She evidently shouldered the chief responsibility for the children's up-bringing but often, when both parents' presence was required elsewhere, baby-sitters had to be brought in. Such a scenario was difficult for the couple, putting strain on their marriage.

On arrival at Old Deer Park, however, Dawes's spirits never failed to be lifted by the atmosphere of a rugby club which was going places. Now, he delights to look back on the kudos which membership of London Welsh held out to some of Britain's finest players of the day. Men queued up to get on London Welsh's books. And their captain loves to look back on the valuable input many managed to deliver.

A product of Neath Grammar School, hooker Brian Rees had captained Cambridge before joining London Welsh. The official club history describes him as offering "a rugged dependability in the front row". Dawes puts it more bluntly: "On a rugby field the charming Brian was a ruffian, exactly the type of hooker needed by us. The trouble is, referees knew of his 'hard man' reputation.

"Once, after a forward fracas in a game against Harlequins one of the opposition's front row men broke away to show the referee what were apparently bite-marks on his cheek. The official called Brian over, saying, 'number two, I'm sending you off for biting'. Brian threw his head back, laughing. So did we all when his gums were revealed to be toothless. Needless to say, he stayed on the field!"

Rees was in fact a key component of the Dawes Plan, phase two, which demanded a front five who could hold their own with any team in the land. The next important recruit, therefore, was Geoff Evans, a product of Llandovery College who now checked in at 6ft 4ins and 16 stones. He could throw that weight around effectively, handle in the open, and run around a bit. Most importantly he would develop into an expert ball-winner at the line-out.

Though she bore him in England John Taylor's mother was Welsh, and after his spell at Loughborough Colleges (where he moved from centre to the back row) her son was warmly welcomed at Old Deer Park. He had starred in the magnificent Colleges VII which took the Middlesex Sevens title of 1966 and was destined to win the first of twenty-six caps in 1967 (when, to his annoyance, he would start being described by Bill McLaren as 'Wee John Taylor'; he was 5 feet 11). Back in Wales there were some puzzled frowns at his entry into the Five Nations fray, but the fans were soon to acknowledge his speed and hitting power at number seven.

Taylor became the perfect partner for Tony Gray at the tail of the London Welsh line-out. The latter could win ball, whereas Taylor was fast enough to stay in touch with attacks or defence by the back division. The pair were thinkers, too, who once experimented with throwing the ball into line outs. This expedient, however, kept the thrower stranded on the touchline and out of the action for valuable seconds. After a while it was abandoned.

But the greatest coups for London Welsh as they climbed into British rugby's aristocracy had yet to arrive. Bridgend-bred, Millfield-educated John Peter Rhys Williams (henceforth J.P.R.) competed at the Junior Wimbledon tournament in 1965 and won it. Next came a few cameo appearances for Bridgend RFC in 1968 before, early that autumn, the youngster found himself on an Argentina-bound plane with the 'Wales B' touring party. For once, the selectors of the day deserve credit for identifying, at the age of nineteen, so prodigious a talent.

During the tour John Dawes learned that, on his return, JPR would be pursuing his medical studies as a freshman at St Mary's Hospital, and lost no time persuading him to join London Welsh. But 'Mary's' competed, very successfully, for the Hospital Cup, whose Final was regarded by the medical community as an occasion second only to the Varsity match. Thus Registrar Tommy Kemp, a former England International, had assumed that the future doctor would play for the Hospital. It was only after a series of fractious telephone conversations that Dawes could convince him that the young man in question was, in all probability, the next Welsh full-back and simply had to be allowed regular games at top club level to continue making progress. Eventually a compromise was struck: since London Welsh played only at week ends, it felt able to release its star newcomer to Wednesday appearances for St Mary's, with his assurance that he was perfectly happy to turn out twice a week.

"He was a hot property," recalls John Dawes. "Nobody who saw him play, or has watched the video-tapes, can be in any doubt of his huge sporting skills augmented by great composure. I recognized his calibre when watching him under the high balls which the Pumas loved to pump up. 'Mine', he would roar – and besides opponents, he was happy to knock team-mates sprawling if they interfered.

"From those early days I found myself impressed by his self-discipline. Dating from his first appearance for London Welsh at nearby Richmond he was always first into the changing room and into his match strip. Naturally, at the beginning he had a youngster's reserve; but this was something that masked tremendous confidence – which, in turn, he may have brought from his tennis. On the field, other players might match his speed, or his handling – but not the undiluted aggression with which he bristled. On seeing him for the first time in our team room John Taylor frowned, saying *sotto voce*, 'Who is that child?' Soon, he knew well enough." As for the Old Deer Park regulars, they were saddened at the demotion of Gareth James to the status of utility back. However, James himself took the setback well and cheerfully played where he was selected, while JPR swiftly developed into a good all-round clubman who was evidently liked by members – whom he liked too.

On his return to Old Deer Park from Latin America John Dawes was quick to realise that the Exiles lacked a certain component that would enable their pack to compete – on all fronts, with any opponents. This was, simply, another really tall and burly forward to win consistent ball at the line-out. The packs which played International Rugby in Britain immediately after World War II were fortunate if they contained two players over six feet tall. Soon, six feet two inches became the norm for top line-out forwards who had grown up on better, healthier diets in the post-War years, while by 1968 there were plenty of men around who measured six feet four. Dawes had Geoff Evans, but needed other jumpers. His prayers were about to be answered.

The son of a Welsh International lock forward, Mervyn Davies was born and brought up in Swansea where he learned his rugby at Penlan C.S. and Swansea College of Education. A move quickly followed to his first teaching job at Mitchett Junior School in Surrey, with a brief spell playing rugby for Old Guildfordians which was too tame for his liking. So, up the A3 as it then was drove the twenty-one year old to knock at the gates of London Welsh. Having played a game or two for Swansea, he was able to present the Exiles' committee with a recommendation which the club had given him, and soon found himself chosen at number eight for the Third XV. That was when his promise was noted by a junior selector – but no-one at Old Deer Park, or indeed in British rugby, could have foreseen his sensational rise.

In a Foreword contributed to Davies's autobiography *Number Eight* (Pelham 1977) John Dawes wrote: "We decided to try him out in the First XV, in the knowledge that flankers Tony Gray and John Taylor could help to break him in safely. Looking back to that gamble, I can still scarcely credit what now happened. After six club games Mervyn was called into the Probables side for a Final Trial at Cardiff Arms Park (which the unfortunate Dennis Hughes missed through injury). Two weeks later he was winning a first cap at Murrayfield in a Welsh team which beat Scotland 17-3, the start of an International career which would bring Mervyn thirty-eight consecutive Welsh caps and two highly successful tours with the British Isles."

The unique input of 'Merv the Swerve' will always be remembered at Old Deer Park – always bearing in mind his one-time captain's assurance that 'swerving' along with side-stepping were skills that the number eight never actually possessed! No matter: for John Dawes the key attribute of Davies was his height. At six feet, four and a half inches he could virtually guarantee line-out possession from a long throw, either held and driven or the 'off the top' variety which so delights scrum halves. Moreover he was equipped to compete for opposition throw-ins, often stealing them and always interfering with their intentions. Suddenly, therefore, his presence at Old Deer Park dramatically amplified the kind of game London Welsh could play.

Another new arrival of the period was Mike Roberts, who stood 6 feet 4 tall, a third forward of that height. He was a much-travelled player who attended Colwyn Bay C.S. and Ruthin before moving into and out of teams such as Liverpool, Colwyn Bay RFC, Trinity College Dublin, Birkenhead Park, Irish Wolfhounds, Oxford University, Surrey, London Counties, Barbarians – and, to their satisfaction, London Welsh who, some speculated, paid the most generous expenses. His presence meant that at any point in a line-out the Exiles now had a ball-winner, and as Dawes remarked, "That was when the running game that I had been coaching ceased to be a necessity and became an option. Our game-plan now had variety."

One other newcomer was greeted at Old Deer Park with enthusiasm that out-did even the welcome which had greeted JPR and Merv the Swerve – mainly because Gerald Davies was not so much a young hopeful with great promise but, rather, the finished article. John Dawes recalls, "We were dumbfounded when, having turned out a few times with us the previous winter, he took a teaching job at Christ's Hospital near Horsham in the autumn of 1970 and applied to join London Welsh full time. I can tell you, it was like Pele or George Best asking to be taken on."

The club broke a recently-adopted rule in accepting him. His school time-table often kept Davies in the classroom until early evening, making it impossible for him to train with team-mates on week-nights – a chore which had been made compulsory and which, some members thought, should apply to Gerald Davies. Three considerations enabled the wing's application to be pushed through: firstly he was known to be a fitness fanatic who could be trusted to train hard at Horsham. Secondly, his detached position on the field was not wholly integral to the effectiveness of the team; and thirdly, he was a world-class player whose availability no club on earth could ignore.

At this point, since henceforth T.G.R.'s manifold skills will be dwelt on from time to time, it is interesting to quote briefly from his autobiography of 1979 the reasons why he chose to play at Old Deer Park. They all boil down to the presence of John Dawes:

> He had a perceptive eye on the essentials of coaching, he knew how to conduct training sessions, he knew what he wanted of a team, he had the sensitivity of a player, he knew ultimately his men's strengths and weaknesses, and he knew the on-field pressures... John Dawes also had, and this was one of his strongest points, a broad vision of how the game should be played. It may be argued that in those days he had the players at London Welsh to play an expansive game; it is to his credit that he allowed this to happen.

Its potency was now be demonstrated to the rugby public in the homeland. The London Welsh tours at Christmas and Easter were welcomed by Wales in the way travelling circuses are received: as boisterous, colourful visitors who entertained wonderfully but presented no serious threat to opponents. Match reports in the Press would comment kindly, "though pretty to watch, London Welsh could get nowhere against the blunt cohesion of the home pack". Or, "Despite their colours being lowered London Welsh received a tremendous ovation as they left the field." Coverage in the Welsh Press by writers like J.B.G. Thomas inclined a little towards the patronizing.

The statistics, as the Dawes revolution kicked in, show how the Exiles could win both home and away against a sprinkling of second-rank sides. But always, from 1965-6 to 1969-70, the major clubs in Wales continued to be hurdles which could rarely be surmounted. The win percentage rose steadily from the beginning of the Dawes era from 67.6% to 75% in 1968-69, yet at Cardiff, Newport, Llanelli and, usually, Neath, they went down to defeat. A thrilling exception was the 1969-70 double over Newport who had started the season by defeating South Africa.

So the success rate of 81.9% is just one of many, many reasons why 1970-71 stands out in the memory of John Dawes and in his club's centenary publication *Dragon in Exile* written by Stephen Jones as an *annus mirabilis* and the climax of a revolution in attitudes and achievement. As will be seen in due course its personnel played key roles in the advance of Welsh and British rugby football; but their progress came off a marvellous platform of club efficiency and flair. Certain victories are recalled by Dawes as particularly gratifying.

One was the tour fixture on a bitterly cold Boxing Day at Stradey Park. Llanelli had won eight of the last nine games between the two clubs and now, to add insult to injury, kept the visitors shivering in a bitterly cold December gale before taking the field. The tannoy apologized to all and sundry, explaining that queues of late-arriving spectators were the reason for a delayed kick-off. London Welsh had received no such information – and later learned from a mole in the Scarlets' changing room that high level, time-consuming talks on remuneration were the true reason for the hold-up.

In my match report for *The Times* I wrote that, "Llanelli's much-vaunted front row... were made to look like camels by Freddie Williams, Tony Baker and Trevor Davies" – not at all the sort of thing it had been possible to write about London Welsh packs in the preceding years. However, with five minutes of proper time left the visitors still trailed 0-3 to an early Llanelli penalty placed by Andy Hill. This was when JPR threw caution to the wind and joined every attack in an effort to snatch victory, and it was his pass which sent sprinter-wing Terry Davies scorching to the corner flag for a try to tie the scores. Afterwards, Phil Bennett admitted to feeling relief at that point, telling his team-mates behind the posts, "Don't worry, we'll get the draw. JPR will never put this conversion over." Alas for the Scarlets, young John placed a fantastic kick into the wind which fairly zoomed over the crossbar without travelling more than twenty feet from the ground.

Time was up and the full-back prostrated himself in front of the chagrined but sporting Scarlet fans in the grandstand. His team-mates leaped in the air like New Zealanders doing the Haka. In the main bar afterwards I remember John Taylor enthusing, "That is the result I've looked forward to ever since I joined this club."

Another game which Dawes remembers well, for personal reasons, was the away win of February 1971 over the club that had helped nurture him. At this time Newbridge were not performing well, and their 19-6 defeat by London Welsh was the seventh in a row. The visitors' four tries included one by Mervyn Davies, by now the holder of nine caps, and kept them on course for end-of-season titles which had hitherto eluded them. I covered the game, and chose to pass comment on John Dawes:

> At 30 he remains a remarkably elusive runner, while the timing and direction of his passing is a model for the younger generation. During his seven seasons in London his club have risen to become one of the most formidable and entertaining units in Britain. It would set an impressive seal on their reputation if they can sustain their challenge for the Welsh clubs' unofficial Championship.

The Exiles failed narrowly in that aim, finishing second to Bridgend. But other honours in plenty came their way including three *Sunday Telegraph* Pennants as Champions of England, Champions of Wales, Champions of England & Wales, plus a third successive Middlesex Sevens title. However, what certainly gave the captain deepest pleasure was his men's record against the big Welsh clubs, featuring home and away doubles against Neath, Pontypool, Newport, Aberavon and Swansea plus the victory at Stradey Park. Only Cardiff and Bridgend lowered their colours and, in England, London Irish and Coventry.

Those occasional blemishes on an otherwise outstanding record prompt comment from Paul Beken, co-author and statistician of *Dragon in Exile*, "The eight seasons from 1965-66 to 1972-73 are generally regarded as the best in the Club's history, with hugely impressive results. But these do not reflect the fact that the demands on London Welsh's playing strength were colossal, and the results were often achieved with teams half of which were drawn from the Druids. Over a period of four or five years, the Club never lost a game when it was at full strength. That really puts things into perspective."

Such sentiments did not emanate only from Welsh admirers and supporters. The great Coventry and England centre David Duckham would write a few years later in his autobiography,

"John Dawes steered London Welsh to an almost impregnable position. His influence had brought about an amazing transformation in the club's style."

And, some time before Duckham retired, other writers – professional ones – were taking an interest in the Exiles and turning up in strength to watch a side that won with style. Keeping tabs on his old club, Vivian Jenkins brought a *Sunday Times* presence to the Press box which Stephen Jones from Cross Keys was subsequently happy to perpetuate. David Frost of *The Guardian* often crossed Kew Road with his wife Pandora to watch the action. The *Evening Standard's* J.L. Manning wrote a lovely colour piece on the visit of Llanelli. Clem Thomas, Tudor James, J.B.G. Thomas and John Billot would drop in, and John Dawes appreciated the technical insight of the *Sunday Express's* John Reed. From time to time the BBC's outside broadcast units, often from Cardiff, invaded the Park to record some of the red and white magic being weaved down on the pitch.

And perhaps the most intriguing conversion to the London Welsh way of rugby was that experienced by John Reason of the *Daily Telegraph*. This acerbic writer was rugby union's high priest for a couple of decades, and it was his bad luck as an Englishman to be at a peak professionally when the national rugby team that he would so love to have praised was no more than ordinary. Certainly he began to be a regular visitor to Old Deer Park, and John Dawes goes so far as to suggest enigmatically, "We sensed that John Reason wanted 'to be on our side'. His rugby values were basically our own, and it was no surprise either that in due course he developed a firm friendship with Carwyn James."

Later, when the victorious Lions of 1971 returned from New Zealand Dawes set up a 'talk-in' involving half a dozen of his top players who would jointly record for posterity, orally and in print, the lessons that were learned on tour. No sponsor-style assistance was given by the RFU or the WRU. It was left to the North London Polytechnic (whose staff Dawes had by then joined) to stage the event and record it, while John Reason pitched in to acquire the copyright and publish the exchanges on cassette and in print with the title *The Lions Speak*. Today, the transcribed narrative of three decades ago is still vital and valid.

It seems appropriate to end this chapter with recall of the Exiles' triumphs at the Middlesex Sevens, since in a sense the sevens game is the bare bones of the kind of rugby that John Dawes had taught his men to play. There had been an isolated success in 1956, when Colin Bosley, Robin Davies, John Leleu and Carwyn James were in action for the club. Then came a period of London Scottish dominance lasting until 1968, after which London Welsh embarked on a four-year winning streak. By early May Old Deer Park was commandeered by the cricketers, and though still training there the Sevens squads kept themselves fine-tuned for Twickenham by competing in local tournaments, which they often won.

"Our run of successes at 'HQ' drew boos from the Twickenham crowd each time we took the field," recalls John Dawes, smiling at the memory. "But far from being upset we took this as a compliment, or challenge, which put us on our mettle. Also, in fairness, we noted that as we left the pitch, having chalked up yet another victory, there was only applause."

The captain played in three of the successful Sevens, the exception being 1971 before the British Lions toured Australasia. The touring party came to Twickenham, but had to leave for Eastbourne where routine preparations were to take place. As the players got up, the loudspeaker announcer wished them luck Down Under, and the crowd responded with a standing ovation.

In successive Finals London Welsh defeated Richmond, Harlequins and, twice, Public School Wanderers. The Exiles' teams contained searing speed in the shape of Terry Davies, Colin Gibbons, Alan Richards and, just once, a reluctant Gerald Davies who admitted to finding the long waits between the early ties somewhat tedious. Bill Hullin was in four of the successful Sevens, sniping away at scrum-half, while JPR played at prop a couple of times. Dawes was usually at stand-off half, from which position he could control the play, which in Sevens demands periods of ball-retention, even on the retreat, interspersed with sudden, dynamic surges into any suggestion of a gap. A welcome recruit to the squads as their coach was the former Wales full-back Gerwyn Williams, by now a teacher at Whitgift School. He is remembered for his emphasis on the discipline demanded by the seven-a-side game.

So: Dawes had brought London Welsh to the boil as a side which could batter opponents into submission or out-smart them by brilliance in the open field. Now, he could confidently leave it on a kind of supercharged auto-pilot while he paid obligatory visits to South Wales and the Welsh squad. And then, suddenly, his international career was re-born, with selection for the XV to meet England at Cardiff in April 1969. This was a golden opportunity to play again at the game's highest level. It had to be grasped.

SIX

John Dawes had been very patient through the early exchanges in the 1969 Five Nations campaign. For the third match running he found himself on the Welsh bench, at Colombes, against a French side captained by Walter Spanghero in which Pierre Villepreux, Jo Maso, Eli Cester and Jean Iracabal were the menacing new stars. An extraordinary try by Gareth Edwards plus one from Maurice Richards converted by Keith Jarrett gave the visitors an 8-0 lead at half time which appeared to point the way to a first victory in Paris since 1957. But the second forty minutes saw Wales squander a series of excellent scoring chances; allowing France to get a draw thanks to a Campaes try and Villepreux's accurate goal-kicking.

So although the possibility of a Grand Slam was ruled out Wales could still take the Championship title with a good result against England a month later in Cardiff. But Gerald Davies would not be available for that decisive encounter, having dislocated an elbow in the final minutes at Colombes, when twenty-year-old Phil Bennett became the first man to win a Welsh cap as a replacement. At the time, only two players could be nominated for that role and perhaps Bennett's all-round ability saw him as the preferred sub. Dawes stayed on the bench reflecting on a missed chance to make history.

Then, suddenly came consolation: his selection to partner Keith Jarrett in the centre against England. Dawes was overjoyed. But equally, he knew only too well that this might be his last chance of becoming a fixture in the Welsh team.

In recent years Welsh rugby (and soccer) squads preparing for big games have habitually secreted themselves in the luxurious and tranquil hotels which have sprung up in the Vale of Glamorgan. Practice facilities are readily to hand, and there is minimum contact with fans. New Zealanders as a race, and that includes those who have coached the Wales XV in recent years, are instinctively countrymen rather than city slickers and their preferred venues in which to tune up for big occasions are located as far from noisy fans and boozy pubs as possible. The

Welsh protégés of Graham Henry and Steve Hansen accepted the discipline, though what they really thought about such places was reflected in references to one hotel as the 'Jail of Glamorgan'.

John Dawes thinks that something precious has been lost by these moves out of town. In particular he cites the team head-quarters used in his playing days: "Everyone's adrenalin started to flow when we checked into the Angel at the junction of Castle Street and Westgate Street around tea-time on the eve of a big match. Some today might call it an ancient pile; an older genera-tion prefers the description 'traditional'. Lying between Cardiff Arms Park and the Castle, this down-town position makes it unique, something which no other nation can claim. During an International Rugby weekend the Angel is at the hub of the city."

By 1969, as a holder of ten caps, Dawes knew exactly the routine to expect before taking on England, beginning with greet-ings and handshakes as players and officials checked in. A main meal brought everyone together, at which the most expensive dishes could be ordered since the WRU was picking up the bill. Nor, in those days, were there any regulation diets. For the play-ers it could be chips with everything. The meal finished early so that the squad could stroll down Queen Street to catch a feature film at one of the city's big cinemas of the day like the Capitol or the Olympia.

The players would have held a vote for the film they wanted to see, and there was seldom disagreement – westerns and good comedies were popular. The best seats in the house would have been booked and, before the big film started, team masseur Gerry Lewis was despatched to buy ice lollies and tubs of vanilla for the team to lick, for all the world like a gang of small boys. As the end-titles rolled it was back to the Angel, with perhaps one or two of the forwards stopping on the way for a pint. The players were paired in double bedrooms and most would conscientiously have got their heads down at a sensible time. Gerry Lewis was always available if one of them wanted late night attention to relax him, and was often busy until one o'clock in the morning. Gareth Edwards certainly enjoyed a small hours rub-down, which Dawes thinks may have given him some psychological comfort as well as a physical glow.

Hotels, especially rugby hotels, are often the scene of high-jinks and rowdy behaviour into the early hours. Dawes avers that teams he played for never, ever experienced any bad behaviour with night-time noises-off that might have kept them awake: "The supporters were guests in the hotel as we were, and all around us. We could sense their hopes for the morrow – that was something else that got the blood coursing through your veins. But they invariably respected our wish to get a good night's rest. Downstairs in the lobby they might politely wish a player good luck."

On Saturday mornings the Welsh XV would re-surface in dribs and drabs. Some men preferred a lie-in and took no breakfast. Others had breakfast in bed. A majority reached the dining room, where once again there were contrasting choices. Dawes remembers the toast-and-honey preference shared by his fellow London Welshmen John Taylor and JPR And ready on the table there would be a large bunch of grapes awaiting consumption by Brian Thomas in the manner of Roman emperors of old. Later on in the morning some players ate a light luncheon. The Dawes verdict is that when a man took the field he would not wish to feel over-full of food. On the other hand, an empty stomach was not the thing to play rugby on either.

Next he recalls a vital and compulsory part of the count-down: the team gathering at eleven o'clock: "This was quite a short-lived affair, used by the coach of the day, Clive Rowlands, for his wake-up call to the troops. Top Cat would go through his whole routine, of flashing eyes, challenging juts of the jaw, reminders about Aunty Gwladys plus a few impassioned sentences in the Language of Heaven – which, even if some of us could understand it only imperfectly, made for a tremendous peroration. Then he would take his exit, stage right, glaring". The coach would re-appear before his men again shortly before the game was due to begin.

The players would have been instructed to report to the changing rooms ninety minutes before the kick off. A further release of adrenalin would pump up the team as they left the hotel and walked the Westgate Street pavement, either solo or in pairs or threesomes. "It was not quite like the parting of the Red Sea," recalls Dawes, "but the fact is, the supporters made space for us. There were claps on the back. There were expressions of good luck and hoorays, and shouts of 'Stuff 'em' and the like. Again it sort of blew your mind; and reminded you that you were going into battle for these lovely people. They evidently thought we could see off the invaders. Well, not a bad idea! Why not?"

The Westgate Street Experience left the players in no doubt that the fans were behind them. The nation was united to beat off the imminent threat. Maybe, as visitors to Cardiff in the weeks just past, individuals in the team had become used to cries like, 'Go back to London, you city slickers' (aimed at London Welshmen) or 'Get back to Llanelli' or 'the Valleys are where you belong'. But now the tribes had come together, their total support steeling the players – their champions.

Suitably supercharged the players moved on into the great half-finished palace of rugby, where on this day in 1969 the crowd would be limited to around 29,000 by reconstruction work being carried out on Cardiff Arms Park. In their new, ample changing rooms the Welsh XV could dimly hear the rumble out on the terraces and sense the growing passion. Some showed their delight as Gerry Lewis conducted his traditional ritual and presented to each man his match jersey (no 'shirts' in those days). Others, including John Dawes, were quiet, preferring to concentrate on the task ahead and the opposition which would have to be subdued in order to be defeated. It was a time to focus. And the visitors on this day were the old – the oldest – enemy. The English were not just at the gates – they were camped next door down the corridor.

There was a quick formality still to be seen off before taking the field, and that was posing for team photographs. Most people respond eagerly to the command, 'Say Cheese!' and International Rugby players are no exception. Interestingly, after a number of years' pressure exerted on the WRU the Former Internationals have been given a generous sector of the Millennium Stadium's ground-level space in which to create a hospitality lounge where, on big match days, they can meet old team-mates and re-live old memories. On the walls, team photographs of bygone XVs are the ice-breakers which, decades on, can still start tongues wagging.

A quarter of an hour before kick-off, with Rowlands back in attendance, the captain called for order to deliver his last pep-talk. As skipper on this day (in the absence, injured, of Brian Price) Gareth Edwards could already demonstrate the fluency in

English and Welsh of later years speaking to other audiences; but now, at twenty-one years old, he contented himself by listing the simple orthodoxies he wanted everyone to put into practice. Then came the call from Irish referee Paddy D'Arcy, the move to the pitch, the ear-bursting welcome, and standing at attention for the anthems.

As it happened, England were by now a little way into a decade of zero success and small distinction which would last until their magnificent Grand Slam under Bill Beaumont. The writing on the wall could be said to have started two seasons earlier with the astonishing 34-21 defeat at Cardiff. But this was now history, and the men in white were still the side to be feared by their four European rivals. In 1969 they fielded a team which looked mighty strong on paper, featuring powerful, experienced forwards like Pullin, Rollitt and Rogers and a back division built around the centres John Spencer and David Duckham. Today the man John Dawes would keep under observation was not one of that burly pair but the gifted Moseley outside half, John Finlan. It was his angles of running, and the kind of ball he handed to the midfield, which had to be watched – in order to work out how the attacks would be carried on. Such anticipation would allow the English centres to be up-ended by 'aggressive defence'. Attacking play could come later.

This softening-up process by the Welsh now occupied the whole of a first half which finished at 3-3 after a Bob Hiller penalty cancelled out by Maurice Richards's unconverted try – the first of four that the wing would finish with. After their forty minutes of hard labour the second half brought the home team rich rewards triggered by Jarrett's pair of penalty goals. Then Barry John scored a masterly try out on the left, bobbing and weaving his way past England's corner-flagging defenders with dummy after dummy. Dawes recalls: "I was fooled three times into thinking he was passing to me! But he went all the way to the line to emphasise the latest step he had taken in his progress towards full maturity. This was Barry's best game to date for his country. He was also learning to take advice without taking offence. If you quietly suggested at some stage that he might have made an error of judgement, there would be a quick nod of the head – and the same mistake would not be made again."

However, the day belonged to Richards. Adding three second-half tries meant that he was bracketed with Willie Llewellyn (1899 v England) and Reggie Gibbs (1908 v France) as one of Wales's record individual try scorers in a single match. His total of six tries in a Championship season was also a shared record. Richards usually got the ball with men to beat, though the Welsh midfield could take some of the credit for creating the opportunities he seized. Dawes's comparison between Richards and Gerald Davies is interesting: the latter, the slighter of the two, could side-step defenders without losing speed, whereas the six foot two inches Richards was willing to slow down almost to a standstill before stepping away with devastating speed off the mark and, when needed, the power to brush off the remains of a tackle. His display on this day was a match-winning one (and, as will emerge, he was to make Kiwi jaws drop at some of his running in New Zealand during the summer tour).

As he reflects on the thirty points to nine victory John Dawes observes: "The under-dogs, which we always were against England, had done it. If Wales beats England it doesn't really matter if we win the rest of the season's Championship games or not." The sentiment is tinged with hyperbole, but most of his fellow countrymen will know what he means. Of the losers, he thinks that our large neighbours were entering an era of rugby when there was talent available but no vision about how it should be forged into a team. For example, there was selectorial indecision about the respective merits of the strong-running, orthodox stand-off half Richard Sharpe and those of Bev Risman whose different styles could dictate whole game-plans. Again, it took Wales's Carwyn James, in 1971, to select David Duckham on the wing where his speed and footwork could thrive in space.

By their World Cup triumph England had eliminated most shortcomings, thanks to the calm but ruthless control exercised by Clive Woodward and his management team. Their European rivals had always feared the potential which has now been realized. The English, as a race, are certainly burlier than the Welsh. They have more first-class clubs and therefore more players to choose from. There is big money to employ the best available specialist coaches. The reactionaries whom Will Carling was once heard to call 'old farts' have departed, and 'team England' is a mean machine.

Three and a half decades ago, however, coaching, as pioneered by Ray Williams, was yielding dividends for the Welsh. The Coaching Organiser's method included getting club coaches to communicate with each other in pursuit of a joint, authentic Welsh 'style' which had been absent from the game for over a decade. Llanelli, under Carwyn James, subscribed to his philosophy; Dai Hayward was taking Cardiff in the same direction. And the London Welsh contingent felt at home, since this was how their club was now playing. Dawes states looking back, "for almost the first time I felt a hundred per cent comfortable in a Wales jersey – a round peg in a round hole." He was delighted, though not surprised, to be named a few days later in the Welsh party for the short summer tour to the southern hemisphere.

For a seven-match tour there is little doubt that modern selectors would choose a thirty-strong squad, even perhaps adding in a third scrum-half. In 1969 the visitors' strength at the outset was a mere twenty-three players (it became twenty-four when Vic Perrins flew out after Jeff Young was injured). Newport, as the newly-crowned club champions, supplied five men including the captain, Brian Price. Four Cardiffians were on strength, while the Llanelli contingent included manager Handel Rogers plus the then President of the Welsh Rugby Union, Ivor Jones.

If the tourists were overwhelmed by it, the frenzied welcome accorded them by New Zealand's fans was only to be expected. Although the British Lions had been Down Under several times during the century, this was the first time that the Welsh toured there as a rugby entity. The recently-crowned European champions had defeated New Zealand three times in eight Tests down the years – beginning in 1905 when Gwyn Nicholls and Co had the effrontery to deny the First All Blacks a hundred per cent record by beating them in Cardiff. Ever since, New Zealand had wanted revenge.

Of course, the British Lions had fielded Welshmen in plenty. In 1950 Bleddyn Williams and Jack Matthews were heroes to admire. Malcolm Thomas and Rhys Williams were the giants of 1959, while David Watkins and Alun Pask shone in an otherwise lack-lustre party of 1966. In 1969, however, nobody attracted quite the hero-worship reserved for the WRU President of the day. Veteran players and supporters queued to shake the hand of Ivor Jones, especially in Dunedin where his two tries of 21 June 1930 had helped to crush Otago 33-9. This match was well described in a book called *With the British Lions in New Zealand 1930* written by a former All Black from Canterbury, Geoffrey Alley. The next chapter was headlined 'The First Test; One Up to Britain. Ivor Jones Did It' above the score-line Britain 6 New Zealand 3. This is how Alley chronicles the winning try:

> Suddenly the goddess of Fortune turned her face away from the hotly attacking New Zealanders and smiled quite openly on Britain, which had never managed yet to defeat an All Black team. Ivor Jones, the unmanageable Welshman, broke away from the fuss-and-bother going on near the British line and simply set sail for the New Zealand goal, over eighty yards away. Confronted by George Nepia in the opposition's 25 Jones released a pass to fellow Welshman Jack Morley who went in for an unconverted winning try.

So, the President's autograph promised to be in great demand. But first there was a late-night internal flight to catch onwards from Auckland to New Plymouth, where the Welsh were to kick off with a game against Taranaki in the lee of picturesque Mount Egmont. Here the warmth of New Zealand's welcome was immediately experienced, though a one a.m. performance on their hotel balcony to serenade a main street packed with fans demanding some Welsh singing was a mixed blessing for the travel-weary players. Valuable sleep was lost: the selected side to meet the north islanders had a mere thirty-six hours in which to acclimatize and get its act together. What is more, the first of two Tests against the All Blacks would take place only three days later.

The schedule which the WRU had agreed before its men's departure would be the subject of bitter criticism when the time came for a tour post-mortem. In those early days of long-haul travel on big, wide-bodied aircraft little was known about the effect of jet-lag on travellers. It can interfere with all manner of bodily functions, and the working of the mind is slowed. With hindsight, it is worth speculating whether the Welsh might sensibly have played Australia and Fiji at the outset of their tour instead of embarking first on the New Zealand leg. In the latter country, too, perhaps the Tests might have been played consecutively at the end of the tour. Anything, surely, would have been preferable to playing two big games during the first week. Since those days, and maybe partly as a result of the Welsh experience of 1969, itineraries are now scrutinized with far greater thoroughness than of yore.

Such speculation pre-supposes that the tour, with its two Test defeats of 0-19 and 12-33, was unsuccessful. Even confronted by such numbers, John Dawes is unwilling to accept that view. He points first to the results against three of New Zealand's leading Provinces, beginning with a draw against Taranaki that could have been a win had not the Welsh been sleep-walking for much of the time. A week later Otago were overwhelmed 27-9, their first defeat by a British side for forty years. If 1930 had featured a match-winning display by Ivor Jones, the year 1969 witnessed sheer magic by Maurice Richards who scorched his way to a brilliant hat-trick of tries. Keith Jarrett indicated that he was now acclimatized by contributing fifteen points with the boot and Barry John dropped a goal.

The final provincial match took place in New Zealand's capital city. Captained by the All Black prop Ken Gray, Wellington had enjoyed a successful decade during which they defeated the 1965 Springboks and the 1966 Lions. But they failed to live with the visitors on this occasion. Maesteg's Ray 'Chico' Hopkins, a bundle of energy at scrum-half, deputized for Gareth Edwards for the third time and, John Dawes recalls, celebrated a neat try by jumping twice his height in the air.

Maurice Richards, almost inevitably it seemed, went in for another memorable score. Decades later, thoughtful reflection highlights the fact that the wing's heavy scoring in a series of representative matches had been achieved while playing outside none other than – John Dawes. The other interesting feature of the Athletic Park game was that the London Welshman was appointed captain of his country again, a pointer to the future, given that Brian Price was expected to retire on the tourists' return home. The victory rounded off three decent displays against Provinces who Dawes insists were "at the top of their game" and playing not far below Test level.

However, in the first of the two fixtures that really mattered the sky fell in on the Welsh. It had been made clear that, having missed Wales's last International match through injury, Gerald Davies would be an automatic choice for the First Test, so John Dawes sat out the game, heavy-hearted as his team-mates were swept aside by a New Zealand XV under Brian Lochore. "It was eighty minutes of sheer misery on a playing surface like a bog," he recalls. "One vivid memory: when Jeff Young had to leave the field, his replacement Norman Gale was a single bright red object rushing around the field like a firework in the company of twenty nine muddied oafs."

That playing surface plus the Christchurch weather told against the Welsh, since their gifted back division could never get into the game. The All Black pack, with toughies like Muller, McLeod and Lister prominent, proved unstoppable, securing a monopoly of gilt-edged possession to be deftly used by scrum-half Sid Going. Dick, McLeod, Lochore and Gray were scorers of tries, two of which were converted by full-back Fergie McCormick, who also kicked a penalty. Wales could not score.

The reason for Young's departure was a broken jaw inflicted on him by the All Black lock Colin Meads. The hooker was the third Welsh player in a decade to be damaged by the big fellow's recklessness. At Cardiff in 1963 Wales skipper Clive Rowlands was taken out ruthlessly by Meads with help from Briscoe after calling a mark on his 22-metre line and had to be stretchered from the field in pain from a displaced disc in his spine, while a mere penalty for offside went against the All Blacks.

Next, in the final Test played by the 1966 Lions, Meads had flouted the Laws by illegally charging David Watkins as he took a penalty kick to touch. The little man remonstrated angrily with the immense farmer from King Country, only to be knocked out cold. The referee told Lions captain Campbell-Lamerton that he could do nothing about the incident since he had been unsighted, an excuse that would be laughable if it were not so pathetic.

And now, in 1969, Meads got away with mayhem once more. According to Dawes, Young had indeed tugged the jersey of an All Black opponent, probably Kirkpatrick, to prevent him from harassing Gareth Edwards. Again the big lock decided to take the law into his own hands, landing a punitive haymaker on Young's jaw which obliged the hooker to leave the field, his tour over. To add insult to injury a penalty for interference was awarded against him, while the All Black escaped with a warning.

What all this means is that Meads, lauded the world over for outstanding ability and unparalleled power play, must have been in more than fifty Tests without ever quite understanding what discipline was all about. Sure, punches were swung far more frequently in rugby's Middle Ages than they are today; though very often, rather than doing huge damage, they were ill-aimed expressions of frustration. Meads, however, was a big hitter; and the blows which felled Watkins and Young were precisely aimed and deadly. Few Welsh fans shed tears for the All Black when Jeff Kelleher sent him off in a Test at Murrayfield. Rogue elephants ought not to be allowed to roam paddocks; if they are not to be shot they should be shackled.

The second, more far-reaching aspect of this Welsh tour was the slanted displays of certain referees – 'homers' as some of them were branded – notably Pat Murphy who controlled both Tests. In Europe's annual Championship series it had been the case since 1884 that neutral referees were appointed to matches between the Nations, a lead which the southern hemisphere countries would take nearly a century to follow. Early discontent about their slowness to fall into line had surfaced in 1959 when Don Clarke kicked six penalties to win a Test for New Zealand by one point despite the four tries scored by the British Isles tourists of the day. Now, a decade later, an unsigned account in the new Welsh Brewers' *Rugby Annual for Wales 1969-70* carried further highly critical comment:

> Inevitably there was dissatisfaction with New Zealand referee-ing, and until there is a system of neutral referees New Zealand will have to accept that criticism, even suspicion, will continue. Referee Pat Murphy, who controlled both the Tests... allowed a couple of New Zealand tries that would have been rejected in British Rugby... refereeing problems have become accepted hazards for touring teams in New Zealand and South Africa, and the Welsh players were often seriously perturbed.

An outstanding referee of the later twentieth century, Clive Norling, thinks that Welsh protests, along with those of the 1959

Lions, did contribute to the change of policy in the three major southern hemisphere nations. Though not in time for the 1971 Lions in New Zealand (whose four Tests were, in fact, well refereed by John Pring) action had been taken by 1976, when Scotland's Norman Sanson was flown to South Africa for the Republic's Tests against France. New Zealanders were still in charge of their own country's Tests against the 1977 Lions but five years later Roger Quittenton was a first neutral official for the All Blacks' game against Australia. For their 1983 Tests against Ciaran Fitzgerald's Lions France's Michel Palmade was flown out to take control – from which point New Zealand's administrators toed the neutral line.

John Dawes is totally in sympathy with the way things worked out. He underlines, too, how any kind of bad refereeing, whether malign or simply incompetent, can undermine the confidence of highly-strung players in big games and cause them to react in regrettable ways. An outburst recalled by him from Wales's last game in New Zealand came from the normally even-tempered Barry John who, after Wales had conceded the third of Fergie McCormick's penalties, hurled the ball away and shouted at Mr Murphy, "What's the next New Zealand penalty going to be for, ref?" Dawes had to silence him, snapping "For God's sake – that'll only cost us more points."

The Welsh build-up to that Second Test at Auckland was far from the most confident and eager that Dawes had experienced. Despite the wins in Dunedin and Wellington a fatalistic mood seemed to dominate preparations, with the feeling that Wales were out of their depth and defeating New Zealand was not a possibility. Neither coach Clive Rowlands nor skipper Brian Price could raise morale, though John Dawes assured everyone who would listen that, "If the forwards can get us forty per cent of the ball I reckon we can give New Zealand a run for their money."

With that aim uppermost and mindful of the ordeal in the Christchurch swampland Wales selected the biggest pack that they could field. Brian Thomas was put into the front row next to Gale and Denzil Williams. Price and Delme Thomas were in the second row, with Dennis Hughes joining Mervyn Davies and Dai Morris at the back. All to no avail; the Auckland weather was dry and calm, and Welsh donkeys trundled around a pitch that was better suited to race-horses. In their eagerness at least to draw the two-Test series Wales's planning had immediately come unstuck.

Further, the Welsh share of possession was well under that demanded by Dawes. Reckless indiscipline played into the hands, or the boot, of Fergie McCormick who set a world individual scorer record for International Board countries with a 24-point haul comprising five penalty goals, three conversions and a dropped goal. The All Blacks' tries were run in by George Skudder, Ian MacRae and Ian Kirkpatrick. A Jarrett penalty gave the tourists the briefest of leads; he later kicked a second and scored a try. But the highlight of the game for John Dawes (in a re-shuffled three-quarter line with Gerald Davies moved to wing at the expense of Stuart Watkins) was a marvellous try by Maurice Richards.

Give or take a couple of thousand Welsh *émigrés* and a small number of travelling fans, the 58,000-strong crowd was getting noisily behind the All Blacks when Richards totally shut them up for a few minutes. Given excellent possession some thirty-five yards out he found that only McCormick barred his way to the line. Says Dawes: "I remember that Maurice went right up to the full-back at top speed. There he came to a complete halt before feinting to go right, where McCormick prepared to dump him. Instead he left the tackler for dead with an extravagant side-step, accelerated immediately – and roared away on the outside to reach the corner flag.

"The try itself was sensational. But so was the effect on the crowd. An eerie silence prevailed over Eden Park. It was born of complete puzzlement about what had actually happened – in the video age we have instant hindsight at our fingertips, but rugby supporters in those days did not have the advantage of action replay. In their bafflement that afternoon the Kiwi fans even forgot to applaud Wales politely. They were wondering, What has this Welshman done to our Fergie, the best full-back in the world? Only turned him inside out. The fans could hardly credit what they had seen.

"Puzzlement? The fact is, you see, New Zealand doesn't do side-steps, or even footwork. At New Plymouth I remember a few of us visiting a school rugby practice session where some twelve-year-olds were being put through their paces. The rugby master had divided them into two groups: ball carriers, and tacklers whose job it was to put them on the grass. This happened mechanically for the first ten minutes, at which point one small boy sold an outrageous dummy, jinked, and sped past his opponent. We began to clap, before realizing suddenly that the master was hauling the youngster over the coals: 'You will take the tackle,' he howled, wagging a finger under his nose. 'You must take the tackle and make the ball available'."

There you have it. The Welsh like their rugby to be full of the unexpected, including side-steps, dummies and spur-of-the-moment decision-making. The New Zealand model is a machine which functions efficiently and always obeys orders. Should a part malfunction, an identical replacement will restore perfection. The main virtue for their young backs is straight, strong running, not the caperings of would-be Barry Johns or David Duckhams. Such school visits were carried out with a good grace, but though Handel Rogers told his men that they had a duty to pay calls on Welsh societies these had to be limited eventually since training time was being eaten into. The Welsh *émigrés* were delighted that Wales had come to New Zealand but, Dawes thinks, found the calibre of Europe's champion nation a disappointment.

What Brian Price's team learned in New Zealand was all about the gap which needed closing between All Black rugby and that played in the northern hemisphere. Says Dawes, "We found out how much better we had to get. The truth is that, since Wales had last beaten New Zealand in 1953 the gap in skills and vigour had perceptibly widened each time we met, in 1963, 1967 and now 1969. Mainly, this divide between our nations was about possession of the ball. And the lack of it."

The Welsh party knew they had escaped from New Zealand's pressure-cooker rugby climate the first time they went training in Australia. Whereas, in the country they had just left, two or three thousand rugby-mad Kiwis would invade a stadium where the Welsh were at practice to watch from the terraces, in Sydney rugby union was small beer. Dawes relates how room for the tourists to train had to be commandeered on any convenient public park with piles of track-suit tops doing duty as goalposts. Nobody came to watch.

Once again, with Skirving and now Stuart Watkins unavailable through injury, Gerald Davies was selected on a wing, the right one, in the team to play the Wallabies. He told John Dawes that he felt he could cope with the positional change (though he had not expected it to be permanent), but was evidently alarmed at the need to throw in accurately at line-outs. After Wales's 19-16 victory in the Test the forwards pronounced favourably on his marksmanship, and Davies accepted a change which was to guarantee him immortality among other great Welsh runners and try-scorers. The price he paid, he has written, was "standing around for long periods waiting, as if for Godot. For that which may never come." A pass, that is.

As it was, along with Dai Morris and John Taylor, Davies scored a first try in his new position at Sydney to seal a rare away victory on a major rugby nation's soil. The win was nearly forfeited when Richards gave referee Ferguson some lip for allowing a dubious last-minute try by Arthur McGill which cost Wales a penalty attempt at the re-start on halfway. Skinner's shot at goal was short and the tourists were home and dry at 19-16.

Lastly on 31 May came an uninhibited engagement with Fiji at Suva, where the visitors found themselves trailing 8-11 well into the second half. A rousing rally turned the game around allowing Wales to finish her tour on a triumphant note. The six tries of the day included a hat-trick by Dennis Hughes, while JPR dropped an astonishing goal from the halfway line.

"The two end-of-tour Tests were actually a valuable experience," recalls John Dawes. "It would be another two years before Wales began playing 'super-rugby', but our displays against Australia and Fiji showed that we had the capacity to re-build morale and hit the field running."

We have noted his view that the tour was not unsuccessful; and indeed, since it highlighted the way the 1971 Lions would need to play in order to win Tests in New Zealand, it was useful. However, neither in Argentina nor Australasia had the Welsh Rugby Union put its players into pole position, and its ignorance about thorough pre-parations for major tours was exposed.

The other feature of the month-long tour to which Dawes gave much thought in its aftermath was the management. Despite the urbane presence of Handel Rogers and the constant galvanizing of Clive Rowlands there were a few too many senior citizens who were allowed to move around at their own pace. Brian Price was a man who had captained Newport to their 1963 win over Whineray's All Blacks; but the main card he played now, as tour skipper, was the setting of an example rather than dealing out roastings for tourists who gave less than a hundred per cent of effort. Says Dawes, "Brian is a genial man who has never known how to hurt people. There were occasions in 1969 when his team needed a talking-to by a nasty man."

At this time John Dawes had been in the top echelon of Welsh rugby for nearly one decade. A second was about to start, and from his standpoint it appeared to be full of challenges and mountains to climb. Just like that evening when he had first reported to Old Deer Park for training.

SEVEN

New Zealand rugby fans and the media chose not to excoriate their guests as Wales left the southern hemisphere. 'We expected a stronger challenge' was as far as the criticism went – in public at any rate. You almost felt that, deep down, these ancient rivals felt sympathy for their Welsh visitors, a feeling that deepened in the succeeding decades. But as the All Blacks cruised on to a seventeenth (at the time of writing) successive win over Wales even that emotion has evaporated, and in 2004 doughty opponents turned media pundits like Sean Fitzpatrick settle for congratulating the Welsh on winning a line-out.

In his autobiography *Number Eight* Mervyn Davies has echoed John Dawes's comment on the "senior citizens" who under-exerted themselves in 1969: "It seemed as if they had decided that, as they were nearing the end of their careers there was little to be gained from going flat out and taking a battering during the remaining fortnight." That was a reason why, back in Wales, ugly rumours gained credence about the disciplinary problems Handel Rogers was facing. But the whole party suffered on its return to the northern hemisphere, and no player could avoid the scornful barbs of mortified supporters. A tough time to be a player-celebrity.

For everyone, that is, except the other London Welshmen who made the trip with Mervyn Davies, the three Johns – Dawes, Taylor and JPR. Their Welsh-based team-mates could be recognized and button-holed in their home village and suburbs before being subjected to home truths about their performances Down Under. In 1969, besotted with Arsenal, Chelsea, Tottenham Hotspur and their like, London was not terribly impressed by the rugby game and its male leads. The stars of Old Deer Park could stroll down Oxford Street without fear of being recognized or pressed for autographs. Only in their own HQ were the quartet put under the cosh.

The flight bringing the Welsh party back from New Zealand arrived at Heathrow on the last day of June 1969, and when John Dawes reported back to work Spring Grove Grammar School

93

was about to close down for the summer holidays. The Head of Chemistry remembered to express his gratitude for time off to Headmaster Lister, who in turn advised him to thank the Hounslow local authority's Education Department. In the old days of amateurism players wanting leave to undertake high-profile sporting commitments for maybe months at a time could by no means count upon a favourable response from their employers and it paid to keep them sweet.

So now the tourist could enjoy again his family, from whom he had been separated for just over four weeks. Michael was now scooting around the house in Sunbury on Thames at the tender age of two and a half while his small sister Catherine was just six months old. Their father could spend prime time with them, and also create opportunities to work at maintaining his fitness. As he comments, "acquiring fitness is pretty hard. Losing it is too easy".

After the sustained progress made at Old Deer Park under the Dawes regime, the 1969-70 season fell far below the heights of the two or three leading up to it with a success rate of just 58.8% But London Welsh did not lose too much sleep over this, since part of the reason lay in the regular absence of eight or ten star players on duty for Wales or Wales B or the Barbarians. Dawes was among that number.

Meanwhile, a Test against the Springboks at Cardiff on 24 January 1970 was the next challenge awaiting Wales. The WRU staged two Trials, in November and early January, when the selectors drew encouragement from the Probables' comfortable victories. John Dawes was on the winning side twice, though the captaincy on each occasion went to Gareth Edwards. Among the numerous withdrawals was John Taylor, who had made clear his principled decision not to play against a nation whose racial policy was apartheid. In fairness to the genial flanker, he had travelled in the Republic with the 1968 Lions and seen the system at close quarters. He was therefore unwilling to play against representatives of South Africa's white community who "were party to the suppression of the millions of blacks and coloureds relegated to second-class citizenship" and asked the 'Big Five' selectors not to choose him.

The other absentees from the Trials were now out of commission permanently. In particular Dawes would miss the company of Maurice Richards, whose dazzling twelve months of Test rugby had brought approaches from Rugby League. The wing accepted the £7,500 offer made by Salford, where he would link up with David Watkins who had gone there two years earlier. Dawes greatly admired Richards as a rugby player, but the man's personality and character intrigued him too. "He was a bit of a Bible puncher, and often on my return of an evening to the room we shared I would find him busy reading the good Book. He never took alcohol, and his conversation off the field contained no swear-words. But in a match he bristled with aggression; and if things went against him or the team he would let fly with a short, sharp outpouring of vivid and original bad language. But – that footwork! It matched anything today's Jason Robinson could deliver. We would miss him."

Like his contemporary Richards, Keith Jarrett was a wanted man up North, though his famed goal-kicking expertise would be less relevant to the professional game of Barrow, whom he joined, than it had been to Newport and Wales. The pair's joint points contribution in the 1969 Five Nations triumph had been 47 out of 79; and their departures lifted the total of Welsh International players who had turned professional during the twentieth century to seventy, or one a year. League rugby was for long a leech consistently sucking away the best talent in the Welsh game

Two other men now out of contention were Brian Price and Norman Gale. The former, a superb line-out jumper and sound scrummager was cast in the traditional mould of the day, when forwards' attitude to their role was, 'We will win possession – it's up to you backs to use it'. People knew what a fine Sevens player Price had been with St Luke's College and, early on, for Newport, but little of his gifts in that respect seemed to surface in the 15-a-side game. Gale, who captained Wales a few times, never appeared happy meeting the demands of leadership, perhaps because in Dawes's judgement he is basically a man who found it difficult to order people around. When two penalty opportunities came Wales' way in the 1967 Test against New Zealand, Gale clearly had difficulty in identifying someone willing to kick at goal. In the end he shrugged his shoulders, placed the ball, and collected six points. His hooking skills would have been valuable to Wales at this particular time, but he, and Price, were now in retirement.

Curiously, these two great servants of the nineteen sixties were easier to replace than their fleet-footed team-mates from the back division. At Llanelli Barry Llewelyn was making a big impression as a prop who was endowed with muscle and great presence, while Geoff Evans was doing a vital job in London Welsh's second row. Nevertheless, the challenge confronting the selectors (until John Taylor's return) was a hard one: to replace thirty three per cent of a Welsh side which had looked to be maturing steadily until the second half of 1969.

As things turned out the Sixth Springboks' tour record against the three Home Countries and Ireland turned out to be by far the worst since the first visit to Britain of South Africa in 1906. Oxford University at Iffley Road were supposed to be a soft touch to give the invaders a first taste of British opposition, pitches and refereeing. Instead, the undergraduates won a remarkable game on 5 November by six points to three, and by the end of the month, though victorious at Swansea, South Africa had also been beaten by Newport and by Gwent at Ebbw Vale.

There can be little doubt that the tourists' capacity to concentrate on their game and cruise smoothly to top form was fatally undermined by the activity of a stop-at-nothing anti-apartheid faction. Ordeals that had to be endured included pitched battles at a number of venues between demonstrators and police, twenty thousand of whom were called upon at the different stadia in order to ensure that games could take place. The protesters hounded the players, setting off fire alarms in their hotel rooms to cause them loss of sleep. Eggs were thrown at the team in Dublin. Sometimes members of the touring party out for a stroll or to do some shopping were spat upon by their tormentors.

At Swansea some forty demonstrators burst onto the field of play, sat down on the pitch, and prevented the game from continuing for almost ten minutes before the police and stewards rounded them up and ejected them, sometimes very roughly. Men dressed up as bus drivers sought to hijack coaches used by the tourists. When the Springboks played Western Counties at Bristol a saboteur got onto the pitch at half time and scattered large bagfuls of nails along the touchlines. The late, sorely-missed

Introducing the
recently invested
Prince of Wales to
team members on the
opening of the new
London Welsh
clubhouse,
October 1969.
(*Western Mail*)

Dawes makes a break for London Welsh on the open field of the Old Deer Park, in 1971.

Although universally for renowned for his passing Dawes was also a good tactical kicker from the hand, watched here by Dai Morris and the England defence, at Twickenham in 1970.

The next four pages feature players who Dawes brought to London Welsh, and who went on to play for Wales and the British Lions, with or for him.

Here, wing forward John Taylor bursts through the French defence for Wales, in 1970.

Voted Wales' greatest wing, Gerald Davies dives in for a try against Ireland, at the Arms Park in 1970.

The ever dynamic JPR Williams dives past Martin Hales for the third Welsh try against England, in 1970.

Hugely admired by Dawes and just about everyone else, Mervyn Davies leaps above the rest in a line out at London Welsh, in 1972.
(*Associated Sports Photography*)

Coaches of successive Lions tours to New Zealand. Carwyn James had fought for Dawes as captain of the 1971 Lions, and had been rewarded with a series win. Six years later Dawes (seen here at a training session with Bill Beaumont) was unable to emulate this success. Their paths crossed several times: Dawes was preferred as Wales' coach in the seventies but was in close contact with James during his period as National Coaching Organiser. (*Colorsport*)

International flanker and rugby humorist Dai Hayward sternly accused the demonstrators of tin-tactics.

In Britain there had been a hardening of public opinion against South Africa, so that the presence of the Springboks in Britain was eagerly grasped as a heaven-sent opportunity to blast the Republic's regime by making life a misery for the young 'Ambassadors of Apartheid' as they were labelled. What is certain is that the hard core of agitators who turned up ostensibly to watch rugby football were not supporters interested in the game or knowledgeable about it. The All Black scrum-half Chris Laidlaw, who became the Dark Blues' captain when doing a degree course at Oxford, wrote an article for the New Zealand *Sunday Times* in which he said, "The alien world of Britain is closing in on the Springboks in a number of ways... the whole of white South Africa is on trial in the dark mud of Britain's rugby fields."

What mainly prevented the young tourists from focussing on their rugby priorities was the security that surrounded them, which in turn contributed to the nervous tension constantly in the air. Players selected for matches were smuggled into the grounds well ahead of kick-off time and spent hours waiting in changing rooms for the action to start. Police were always on duty outside hotels and on the touchlines of pitches used for practice. Sometimes there would be chanting and shouting into the early hours outside hotels where the team was staying. On police advice, players ventured out only under escort and were instructed to wear overcoats to hide their tour blazers. "Things have come close to breaking point," skipper Dawie de Villiers admitted to reporters at one stage.

Wherever they went that November, and through to the end of January, the tourists were front-page news for the discomfiture they suffered and the hostility they engendered. On the field, too, life was miserable and by Christmas they had been beaten five times. Two of these reverses were at the hands of Scotland and England, but after the two early defeats in Wales they pulled themselves together and recorded wins over Aberavon & Neath, Cardiff and Llanelli.

John Dawes declined to align himself with the moral stance taken by John Taylor (who he thinks may have been influenced by recently-made friends who worked for *The Guardian* newspaper) and his basic position is the orthodox one adopted by many who put rugby before politics. What it boiled down to was that he felt it was not his job, or his right, to interfere with other people's views or policies.

But in South Africa six years previously he had seen the restrictions under which blacks and coloureds lived out their lives – the bleak suburbs full of shacks, the sometimes brutal police surveillance, the 'whites' toilets where a black could not have a pee or, emphatically, sit on a seat. Did not such first-hand experience demand an attitude from him, and maybe actions by which people might be influenced against apartheid?

Dawes prefers to think back to advice given by South Africa's High Commissioner in London to the Welsh party before they flew to Johannesburg in 1964. "What he told us was: 'South Africa is our country. Yes, we have a problem. No, we are not ignoring it, we are trying to solve it. You may not necessarily agree with our methods. However, when you reach there please remember that you are our guests. We are not asking you to turn a blind eye to what you find; but don't react to it'. In 1969 the Springboks were our guests, and ought to have been treated as such."

Dawes adds, "As tourists, the young South Africans undoubtedly suffered from demonstrations and other forms of harassment which, by the time Wales were due to meet them, had been going on for three months non-stop. It should be remembered that, as prospective opponents, we too had experienced pressure from certain elements in Welsh society who wanted the International match to be cancelled. This was unsettling, and a constant topic of concerned conversation for our players when we met up for squad training. Rather than rugby players, it was easy to feel that we were pawns in a political confrontation which none of us wanted."

None of them wanted the Cardiff rain either. Sadly, it began on the Friday afternoon before the Test and by two-thirty the following day Cardiff Arms Park was a sopping playing surface on which no skills, no style, no finesse could thrive. The Welsh pack was a big one, selected to match the heavyweight South Africans for whom the conditions, though unpleasant, would suit their basic game-plan: "We will grind you into the mud – after which we may play a little rugby", as John Dawes puts it. "Power is an elixir of rugby that Boers, an uncompromising race, find much to their taste." On this day they manifested it to the full. To the chagrin of new Welsh caps in the pack – Barry Llewelyn, London Welshman Geoff Evans and hooker Vic Perrins – five strikes went against the head in South Africa's favour.

The rain was relentless, and the muddied oafs were soon a uniform brown as they churned through what quickly became a swamp. Nevertheless the scorers in the first half were place-kickers H.O. de Villiers and Gareth Edwards, who each managed somehow to project the ball up out of the slime and over the crossbar for 3-3 at the interval. With Jarrett and Richards departed for League and Stuart Watkins injured the Welsh three-quarter line bore an unfamiliar appearance, featuring Raybould as Dawes's partner in the centre and midfielders Bennett and Ian Hall as wings who, it had been hoped, would thrive in dry conditions. But on this wretched day nothing positive went their way, especially with Barry John preferring not to move the ball but to make progress with grub kicks aimed at forcing handling errors by the defenders.

The second half was notable mainly for its protracted forward battle along the south stand touchline, and for an unconverted try by each side. Jan Ellis's game for South Africa touched great heights in the conditions, and it was he who broke the stalemate by racing from a ruck on the Welsh 22 to link with De Villiers and Lawless, who put Sid Nomis in for a slick score. Soon, with just five minutes to go, Wales appeared to be lasting the pace better than the visitors, who came under huge pressure from line-outs and scrummage ball. But the home side was still in arrears.

Now the captain came to the rescue. With referee Larry Lamb prepared to blow for time at the next stoppage the Springboks made a mess of a clearance near their 22 where Llewelyn drove into the resultant ruck to ensure Welsh possession. Edwards made no mistake in handling the cake of brown soap which was the ball, glanced at a gap which had opened up behind South Africa's forwards and went for the line, over which he dived fending off a desperate cover tackle. Even he found the conversion too big a challenge, but 40,000 spectators hailed a dash which had enabled Wales, at the seventh time of asking, to avoid defeat by the Springboks at last.

The players trudged from the field, but John Dawes recalls no feelings of elation, or even satisfaction. "To 'not be defeated' left participants with a somewhat empty feeling and awareness of a job not done," he says. Although South Africa had improved through the tour, managing to draw with Ireland a fortnight earlier, their defeats by Scotland and England had led the Welsh to think that hopes of a victory were realistic. Disappointment was in the air, and the mood in the Valleys for the next few days was down-beat.

My freelance work took me to games played in Wales by the Sixth Springboks, at which my brief from sports editors was to describe the rugby and leave politics alone. However, there are observations that seem worth making at this juncture that readers who are too young to remember the tour and its political implications may find interesting. One concerns a visit I paid to Cardiff Arms Park a couple of mornings before the Test. I stopped short as I came into the stadium itself at the top of the terraced steps. There was something different about the outlook. Ah: the railings which encircled the pitch in the post-War years were festooned with roll after roll of, would you believe, barbed wire, black and sinister looking. The Park had become a fortress.

Secondly, the nature of the rugby game at all levels has bonding at heart between players in each and every ethnic group, something with which John Dawes undoubtedly agrees. This made it very difficult for those who had played against South Africans and their provincial sides suddenly to suspend personal friendships in favour of a political principle, however compelling. At Oxford British players, including myself, had participated in student rugby with South African Rhodes Scholars and found them for the most part to be decent guys. It went against the grain to blame them for right wing, even fascist, policies of which they by no means necessarily approved. Here was a genuine moral problem which many British friends and I found beyond us to solve. To turn your back on rugby pals was a hard thing to do.

Thirdly it has to be conceded that, for those bent on social and political reforms, the targeting of rugby football and the pressurising of South Africa's rugby community was tactically the correct path to tread. For most of a century rugby had been their national game, and the Springboks were better at playing it than the rest of the world. They could put up with demonstrations and aircraft dropping sacks of flour on the foreign fields which they visited. But when rugby's World Cup tournament arrived in 1987, and South Africa's traditional opponents no longer wanted to play with her, it was more than her rulers – political and sporting – could take. Their white population's passion for rugby was also their Achilles heel.

In 1990 Nelson Mandela, leader of the African National Congress and the champion of black opposition, was released from his long incarceration on Robben Island. Between them, he and the liberally inclined Prime Minister F.W. de Klerk worked on concessions which gathered momentum, reassured the white population about a future under a black majority and were enough to persuade world opinion of the Republic's new respectability. Hey presto! – the venue of the 1995 competition was to be Johannesburg. And few who viewed the South African XV's triumph will ever forget the joyous interaction between their winning captain Francois Pienaar and Mr Mandela as the latter, in a Springbok jersey with number seven on its back, handed over the Webb Ellis Cup.

A fortnight before Wales tangled with South Africa, France had kicked off the Five Nations tournament with a Murrayfield victory over the Scots. In those days it was extremely rare for two Tests to be played during the same weekend, and hence the tournament would stretch out for just over two months. John Dawes recalls the interspersed midweek matches played in Wales during the winter which not only put heavy pressure on players but carried a high risk of injuries incurred on frosty surfaces under floodlights which in those days were far inferior to those in place at most venues today.

Now it was Scotland's turn to visit Cardiff, where the Welsh would start defending their hard-won title of 1969. Considering that they romped home with tries by himself, Barry Llewelyn, Dai Morris and Laurie Daniel against a dropped goal and try by Ian Robertson and a penalty goal by Lauder it is surprising that Dawes remembers next to nothing about a game that was full of action. What sticks in his mind was the fate of Newport's Daniel, who also contributed one of the three conversions (Edwards kicked the other two) but never played for his country again. However, the overall verdict is, "It must have been a satisfactory start to our campaign and gave us a boost ahead of our next match, away to England."

Many Welsh International players of the mid-twentieth century will confirm that Twickenham was a forbidding fortress in that era. Entry to the stadium, whether on a team bus or after parking the car, took visitors past picnic celebrations featuring throngs of super-confident England supporters in brass-buttoned blazers or duffel coats. Up would go their car boot-lids and out would come the pork pies and pâté de foie gras to be munched, accompanied by veritable symphonies of popping corks. Inside the stadium, with its twin East and West stands, 'Swing Low, Sweet Chariot' was not yet adopted as a major anthem. Military bands played stirring music, not loudly enough to drown the animated buzz of analysis and prediction that pre-occupied the grandstands and terraces.

This all amounted to a Twickenham atmosphere which could unnerve the most hardened campaigners and get under the skins of contingents from the Celtic nations and France. Not until the players stood to attention while the anthems were played did the visitors feel that their men were in with a chance – and even then God Save the Queen's ponderous nationalistic chords were full of menace.

The Welsh team of the day knew that only five previous visits to Twickenham (since the ground was opened in 1910) had yielded victory to their predecessors. After a first success in 1933, nearly twenty years went by before the two great Grand Slam years under John Gwilliam's captaincy. The other Welsh wins came in 1956 during the heyday of Cliff Morgan and again in 1966. But now, in 1970, with just twenty minutes to go, Dawes and Co had leaked tries to David Duckham and Mike Novak, both converted by Bob Hiller, while laboriously lifting their own total to six points through unconverted tries by Mervyn Davies (his first for his country) and Barry John. To make matters worse, skipper Gareth Edwards limped from the scene rubbing a strained hamstring. Denzil Williams took charge and immediately whipped his pack up to fresh peaks of endeavour.

Out in the centre, John Dawes was trying to lift morale in the back division and enjoying a wide-angle view of action which now centred on England's 22. What he saw was unforgettable, and he still speaks fondly of 'Chico's match' – which the absence of the captain made possible.

"Gareth was more than just injured when he went off," he recalls. "His whole demeanour was one of head-down dejection. There is no doubt that the England back row of the day, Northampton's Bob Taylor and Bryan West plus Richmond's Tony Bucknall – three big, tough guys – had targeted Gareth, doing a major job on him and stopping him playing to a degree that few opponents had ever done, or later did. As they passed each other at the touchline it was all the captain could do to wish good luck to his replacement, Maesteg's 'Chico' Hopkins, the short, stocky scrum-half who had played against the provinces the previous year with Wales in New Zealand.

"The three men in England's back row could be forgiven, I suppose, for thinking that their afternoon's work was now over. Public enemy number one had been eliminated. By the way they packed down at the next scrum you could sense that they were awarding themselves a breather; they simply lost concentration. Of course, swanky London clubs have never been regular visitors to the Llynfi Valley, and they knew little at that time of our little Mr Hopkins.

"Almost immediately Chico made them pay for such ignorance. First he veered away to the blind side of a ten-yard scrum and gave a scoring pass to JPR who was up to full speed and could not be stopped. Then, five minutes later a rather deflated England pack failed to take the ball in safely at a line-out on their own goal-line, allowing Hopkins to pick up and slide over for Wales's record fourth try at Twickenham. JPR kicked the conversion, and Barry John dropped a goal to seal a notable victory."

Hopkins had seized his opportunity to grab twenty minutes' worth of fame. If it is true that players in the other Home Countries had scarcely heard of him, well, that was how it was during the Edwards reign. The latter's availability had kept perhaps a dozen other very able scrum halves out of International Rugby or on its margins through his brilliance behind the Welsh pack. Billy Hullin, Clive Shell, Brynmor Williams, Allan Lewis, Glyn Turner, Martyn Davies and Gary Samuel were all highly-skilled victims of the Edwards factor. But performance in the limelight is what counts, and John Dawes is fairly sure that Chico's masterclass-in-miniature on that Saturday at Twickenham was what won him a place with the 1971 Lions. Nigel Starmer-Smith, Roger Young and Duncan Paterson were in the frame to travel, but the Welshman's aggressive nature saw him hold off rivals. Incidentally, analysing the 1970 season the Welsh Brewers *Rugby Annual for Wales* named him its Welsh Player of the Year.

John Dawes has mixed feelings about Wales's next stop on the Championship trail. The wreckers of Dublin had put paid to successive Welsh title aspirations in recent years, and now the gremlins struck again. "For a start, at that time it was unusual for us to get a nil," muses Dawes as he thinks back to 1970.

"Though pointless, we were still in contention with over half an hour to go, when McGann and Duggan scored with a dropped goal and a try. Then came a tremendous solo run to our line by Ken Goodall from forty yards out where he slipped through our back division. It was a score that ranks with Ian Kirkpatrick's try against the Lions in the following year, and a blow from which we were unable to recover. A major setback for us – and the French challenge had still to be met in Cardiff."

After the win over Scotland and a hard-fought 8-0 win over Ireland the French still had hopes of a Grand Slam. They needed to win in Cardiff on 4 April; but even if the home side won, they could deny Wales an outright Championship title by beating England at Colombes a fortnight later. The stakes were high, and an uneasy 'Big Five' Welsh selectors swung the axe. Yet again the three-quarter line was reconstructed, so that John Dawes found himself down to play with three new caps. Jim Shanklin and Roy Mathias were selected on the wings, while Ebbw Vale's Arthur Lewis – Mr Dependable – was brought into the centre. The three newcomers were players in form, but Dawes grins as he thinks back: "I don't think any of the four of us could get near ten seconds for a hundred yards. There were props playing in Wales who were quicker than us!"

Changes up front included the selection of the big Llanelli lock forward Stuart Gallacher, while John Taylor came in from the cold to join Mervyn Davies and Dai Morris in a back row that would serve Wales admirably over the coming seasons. The

French were "full of fliers", explains Dawes, "and we needed speedy flankers to get amongst them. Sadly, that meant that my good friend Dennis Hughes's International career was at an end."

Gareth Edwards was retained at scrum-half but now the captaincy was taken away from him for a couple of seasons and given to Dawes for the first of five successive matches in charge. "Though I think most of us were aware that Gareth liked the job," recalls the new skipper, "it was also felt that he sometimes took too much upon himself and didn't always consider the help support players could give. What I can affirm is that there was no evidence of pique at his demotion; Gareth could get upset if we were losing, but he never sulked on his own account. It always helped if he declared himself a hundred per cent fit – because otherwise his team-mates had to guess."

From his own point of view Dawes believes that the game against France had a decisive influence on his credibility as captain. First of all, he knew better than anyone in his team the threat France posed (and always do) when casting caution to the winds. He was also aware of the blistering pace men like Lux and Bonal could turn on in attack, supported by the elegant Pierre Villepreux. So, though it went against the grain, he decided on a tight tactical plan for the day: his pack had to conquer their opponents so that Wales could turn the French backs with kicking from half-back to make counter-attacking difficult.

This brought a vigorous difference of opinion with Phil Bennett, down to play in his club position of stand-off half for the first time since the previous year's Suva Test against Fiji. There was no doubt over the twenty-two year old's kicking ability (though JPR took and succeeded with the two Welsh penalties); but his preferred game was a running one providing opportunities to employ his king-sized side-step and change of pace. "All through the game," says his captain of the day, "he moaned about my orders to kick and begged to be allowed to move the ball. But we had to keep it tight. Dai Morris scored a decisive try for us, while Bonal and Cantoni got one each for France.

"Inevitably there was criticism of a win that was less than entertaining. But from my point of view it cemented my position as a pragmatic captain with selectors who may have perceived my approach hitherto as that of an Old Deer Park ringmaster.

Further, I would submit that a fortnight later my tactics were fully justified by the fate of England who went to Colombes for the last game of the Championship. On paper the visitors looked powerful, but they cut no ice with a French XV in a murderous mood which ran up six tries in a 35-13 victory affording them a deserved share of the title."

A season which had promised a Grand Slam, then, had been flawed by the failure in Dublin, and on reflection Dawes felt that Welsh rugby at the top level had stood still. The team's patterns of play were not setting the world alight, and Wales had yet to show the continuity and flair which would eventually characterize the second of the Dawes decades. However, there were grounds for cautious optimism. A key player, Gerald Davies, was now about to return to the colours after his gap-year; the speedy and powerful John Bevan was emerging as the successor to Maurice Richards, though not cast in the same mould: he was one who liked to run through defenders rather than around them. And Dawes now held out high hopes that a worthy partner for himself in the midfield had been identified.

That man was the Ebbw Vale centre Arthur Lewis, at twenty-nine not exactly wet behind the ears. He had given a number of loyal seasons to his club, and in November 1969 was in the Gwent XV which defeated South Africa. In the lead by just 9-8 with five minutes to go, the home side badly needed to make the game safe. This was when Lewis's power took him almost beneath the tourists' crossbar, where a ruck formed. When the ball reached him again Lewis sighted Roger Beese unmarked on his right and delivered an overhead scoring pass. The display won him two Trial appearances followed by a first cap in the successful match with France.

Dawes remembers his colourful Monmouthshire patois, featuring syntax like "We'm going to do this" and "You'm going to do that". But more importantly, he recalls special gifts on the field. "Rather like Chico Hopkins," he says, "Arthur's rugby profile was not high – opponents, and even some team-mates, didn't know what he was capable of. He struck me as a versatile player, who didn't grumble if we used him for a crash ball move (which came to be called an 'Arthur'). Equally he possessed hands that were 'quick', that is, capable of a high-speed transfer of the ball to his wing, or to JPR coming into the line. Arthur was a good team player, in the special sense that he would fit into a tactical pattern."

Soon after the 1970-71 season began Welsh rugby's morale and pride received a big boost with the opening of the first sector of the new Cardiff Arms Park. In 1967 Glamorgan had played their last season on the turf next door to the rugby ground which the Third Marquess of Bute had presented to local cricketers a century before. The County retreated to Sophia Gardens on the other side of the River Taff, leaving the cricket field empty for the construction of a compact new arena for Cardiff RFC. In the early summer of 1968 construction workers moved on-site to the main rugby stadium to demolish the North Stand and erect a new one with 12,000 more seats, a task which would take two and a half years. Cardiff's new stadium was built to accommodate 15,000 spectators, and both complexes were ready for use in the autumn of 1970. It was the WRU's earnest hope that the much reduced match play on the pitch within their giant new complex – The National Ground – plus new drainage would see the end of the mud-bath rugby which had been a feature of the old stadium whenever stormy winter weather struck.

The opening of the main new grandstand was marked on 17 October by a showpiece game between an RFU President's side full of European International players led by Ireland's Tom Kiernan and a Select Welsh XV captained by John Dawes – evidently still in the good books. To Gareth Edwards fell the honour of scoring the first try at the face-lifted stadium before forty thousand spectators.

"What pleased us about the concept, I remember," says John Dawes, "was that the WRU sought to preserve our Ground's unique atmosphere by keeping the rows of terracing beneath the huge new grandstand. It was on these that impromptu choirs used to harmonise for all they were worth in the expectant hours before kick-off, and the terraces (including those on the other three sides of the stadium) were also where standing spectators made most noise.

"That is a big difference between the old Ground and our all-seater Millennium Stadium. Nowadays the latter is close to empty half an hour before matches start, and the bustle and activity beforehand is all about people making for seats. In its predecessor the terraces and the standing room they afforded – first come, first served – were packed with colour and music from as much as ninety minutes before a match started. Players, at least those in the home team, used to love such expressions of support; we were keyed up to produce great performances. And I'm certain the passion got to the visitors.

"Partly, I think, because unlike other great rugby stadia it is at the heart of a city, I think our players love performing at the venue, whatever the stadium happens to be called. It is still 'home' to Welsh rugby football. Similarly, Twickenham's nickname, to the whole world of rugby, is a somewhat stern 'HQ', but occasionally you detect the affection the English have for their venerable old base-camp: before Sir Clive Woodward's team of 2004 played its first home game since winning the World Cup, Lawrence Dallaglio, as captain, said that his side were 'coming home' to Twickers. Which seemed to me a nice way of putting it and, to be honest, unusually candid coming from an Englishman."

EIGHT

As the 1970-71 season moved along Europe looked forward to another engrossing Five Nations tournament, but long-range conversations were about the next British Isles tour to New Zealand scheduled for the following summer. There was a deep-seated desire to wipe out the memory of 1966's whitewash when Campbell-Lamerton's tourists were ill-prepared for All Black fury and had little to offer in exchange. The Lions had modernized their approach with the appointment of Welshman J.D. Robins as their first-ever coach, but he was unable to construct a Test side that could compete with the hosts' ruthless approach. There were, too, management and leadership problems which could not simply be overcome by a man in a track suit, however conscientious. The new coaching concept pioneered by the Welsh seemed unable to work at this highest level of the game. In 1968 an Irish coach, Ronnie Dawson, was hardly more successful in South Africa, drawing one Test but losing the other three. Would another Celt ever be chosen to coach a Lions tour?

The answer was, Yes. After an exhaustive selection process during 1970 the Four Home Unions' Tours Committee offered the job to a relatively unknown man of many parts, a certain Welshman called Carwyn James. He would serve under a Scottish International wing who had won eight caps twenty years earlier and was himself a Lion on the 1950 tour to Australasia. Dr D.W.C. Smith was chosen to be the Tour Manager of the 1971 British Isles.

By many expert observers, James is rated among rugby union's best two or three coaches to emerge in the twentieth century. His qualifications at this critical point in his career included two Welsh caps in the midfield plus a wealth of experience with Llanelli, Devonport Services (as a National Serviceman in the Navy), London Welsh and the Barbarians. He had been a schoolmaster at that great Welsh rugby nursery, Llandovery College, exposed to the coaching know-how of the legendary maestro in charge of rugby, T.P. Williams, and had recently moved to the staff of Trinity College, Carmarthen.

Altogether this added up to a potent pedigree in Welsh sport and academe.

But as the selection process moved along, with the emergence of James as a leading candidate whose intellect and persuasive personality surprised and charmed the committee-men who interviewed him, the man from Cefneithin in the Gwendraeth Valley was vacillating. As a member of Plaid Cymru, his first priority in the summer of 1970 was to fight the Llanelli seat in the General Election. Had he won it, instead of losing to the Labour candidate Denzil Davies, all thoughts of touring with a rugby side would have gone with the wind. It was the British game's good luck that Labour took the seat and James was back on the market. Despite winning some 8,500 votes – about the fortnightly gate at Stradey Park – he could not emulate his revered Party leader Gwynfor Evans, the first-ever Plaid Cymru MP.

His brother Dewi, who was the first outsider to know of his selection as Lions'coach, says that James was tested to the full by the Four Home Unions' Tours Committee, who wanted to know whether it was safe to appoint "a narrow-minded Nationalist" to an important rugby job. Carwyn, a master of dialectic, reassured them: "Though a Nationalist I am also an Internationalist. Besides Wales I care about England, Scotland and Ireland." He got the job.

At this time John Dawes's reaction was one of mild surprise that strong challenges from well-established coaches with higher profiles than that of James had been beaten off. But the appointment as he perceived it had small relevance to his own career for, in truth, he could not imagine being even selected for the 1971 Lions, let alone being given the tour captaincy. However, he was aware that his fellow countryman had begun the hard work as soon as his role was confirmed, was travelling tirelessly to monitor the form of tour candidates and was already making crucial, confidential decisions about which players were in the frame and which were not. For example, James was at Gosforth on 24 October to see the Barbarians' defeat by Fiji. One of six Welshmen in action that day was Phil Bennett, who unfortunately had a wretched game. Dawes thinks that it cost the mercurial stand-off his place on the Lions' tour, for James was to put faith in Mike Gibson, who could play at centre or as second stand-off half to Barry John.

Months later Doug Smith revealed how Dawes's qualifications for the tour captaincy nearly took a dive when he led the Barbarians against East Midlands in March 1971 at Northampton in torrential rain which fell throughout the game. Dawes knew that the Baa-Baas had influence on the FHU Tours Committee, but he was still puzzled when a group of Baa-Baas' committeemen – "alickados", as they are known – visited their side's changing room before kick-off. "They wanted to know how you delivered a team talk," Smith told him. "What they heard from you was, 'In these conditions we'll just go out to enjoy ourselves.' I guess they had expected to hear a harangue approaching that of Henry V before Agincourt. Your economy of words nearly cost you the captaincy of the British Isles!" As it turned out Bob Hiller of the Harlequins kicked a huge penalty goal out of the mud near the end to ensure victory for the Baa-Baas, so that ultimately there were smiles all round.

As the 1970-71 season progressed, London Welsh were back to top form. Up front, the first XV had powerful, mobile forwards who saw off most opponents at club level. Behind them was a back division featuring both men who could create openings and speed merchants able to finish scoring movements like Terry Davies, who would end the season with eighteen tries. Exhilarated by the style of play that he had preached and that others had now embraced, a relaxed skipper himself crossed for eleven tries. In short, there were no problems to solve at Old Deer Park, and Dawes was free to think seriously about the International prospects that beckoned to him in 1971.

Having led his country to victory over France in 1970, and skippered the Select XV in October, it looked as if he would continue in charge, something that was confirmed with his appointment as captain for the first Five Nations game against England on 16 January (five other London Welshmen also getting the nod). Dominating this tournament was clearly a priority. And yet, inevitably, he found himself speculating whether there would be a place for him in the Lions' party for the southern hemisphere tour in the summer. His regular encounters on the first-class circuit with Messrs Smith and James suggested that they were at least considering him as one of the centres they would take.

Nothing specific was mentioned, however, especially by James who contented himself with an occasional 'Well played' after the final whistle. Nor did Doug Smith give much away. There was no 'nod, nod, wink, wink'. But often, once the Five Nations was gathering momentum, Dawes could not help being aware that at after-match dinner occasions the Scotsman would button-hole him for a few minutes with words that seemed encouraging. "Keep up the good work," he would counsel. "Keep winning. Then we'll see what happens." Dawes was still cautious about his chances, but he remembers feeling that such random remarks by Smith were positive. He counted no chickens, however. He was certainly not aware that he had in fact become the preferred captain, and that the two managers were fighting his case against the reservations of some members of the Tours Committee.

The pack chosen by Wales to take on England was full of seasoned campaigners who were not only strong and street-wise but also able to cover the ground at speed. Behind the scrum, Gareth Edwards and Barry John would build upon careers that already shone with brilliance, JPR and Gerald Davies were potent attacking weapons, while Arthur Lewis would continue as a midfield partner for Dawes. But the selection which caught the fans' imagination was that of John Bevan, a native of Ferndale in the Rhondda, who was a student at Cardiff College of Education. He had turned out a few times for Cardiff in the autumn, played in the Final Trial and, ten days before the match against England, was loyally in action with his student pals. Dawes recalls his great maturity for a twenty-year-old – which would see him touring New Zealand in the summer and nearly breaking Tony O'Reilly's record of seventeen tries.

John Spencer and David Duckham were back for England in the usual threatening line-up whose trigger was the clever scrum-half Jacko Page of Bedford. Powell, Pullin and Fairbrother were a tough front row and Neary a quick open side wing forward. But the visitors included eight new caps, who were seven too many to compete with a Welsh side which was within reach of greatness.

Nevertheless, the visitors still enjoyed the bookies' confidence as favourites, and John Dawes admits that the Welsh mind-set was a cautious one: keeping them out was the game-plan for the first fifteen minutes. If that proved successful, then he would put his side on a looser rein and allow them to think they could win.

With their coach, Clive Rowlands, content with the vital role of motivator, Dawes would attempt to allow the back division to express itself with tactics that he had taught his London Welshmen to use. To take an example; thirty years before England and Wales were launching attacks through the back three, that is, two wings and the full-back, the Exiles were doing so through J.P.R., Gerald Davies and Terry Davies. If opponents missed a penalty shot at goal, these three would interact to run at the attackers from defence. The man who caught the ball called the move – for since almost every player on the field was in front of him he had the best view of the options that were on. Support runners would have posted themselves at corner flags so that scissors or dummy-scissors moves could be developed.

Dawes knew that such free thinking worked. If London Welsh thrived on it, then so in due course could the Lions, and now Wales. Once such counter-attacks had been launched continuity was well-nigh guaranteed by the skill of the wings. Gerald Davies could be checked or cornered, but he was not one to die with the ball. Invariably it would be unloaded inside by him to rampant flankers who broke the gain line, thus heightening the other forwards' morale. This was progress in every sense of the word.

England were hoping against hope to mark the RFU Centenary with a European title. But although their performance was brave, and by no means the unconditional surrender of Paris in the previous season, when half time arrived they were out of the hunt. Among the Welsh scorers in a 22-6 victory was young John Bevan, while Gerald Davies on the other wing went over twice. Taylor, Barry John and JPR shared the goal kicking, and Wales had gone eight matches without defeat at England's hands.

John Dawes has no hesitation in naming the game which followed, against Scotland at Murrayfield, as the most exciting International match he ever played in. The lead changed hands six times before Wales finished 19-18 winners. Some of the scores resulted from well-planned, even inspired, attacks; others resulted from minor errors by one of the teams, onto which their opponents latched ruthlessly. A third, unlikely category featured the Scots' captain, Peter Brown, who contributed four penalty goals: his approach involved hacking a divot out of the turf, dumping the ball in it, turning round, retreating four or five paces, about-turning to sight the posts and rubbing his nose with a sleeve, before finally sidling in to strike the ball. A wobbly routine – but one that yielded twelve precious points.

The usual army of Welsh fans was in Edinburgh, many of whom – ticket-less – would put their feet up in a comfortable hotel without ever making the trek to the city's western suburbs and Murrayfield. Colour television had been around for a couple of years and, with Bill McLaren's sonorous commentary to complement the pictures, was becoming a more than satisfactory way of watching big rugby. Nonetheless, not a seat stayed empty in the giant grandstand, while the huge terraces on three sides of the pitch were a seething mass of voluble supporters waving Red Dragons and the Cross of St Andrew.

With five minutes to go the Welsh were trailing 14-18. They had scored tries through John Taylor, Gareth Edwards and Barry John, to which the last-named had added a conversion and a penalty. But their captain's penalty goals and a Sandy Carmichael try had kept the Scots in touch, and they went into what seemed a terminal lead after a mistake by Bevan allowed Chris Rea to snap up possession and turn on electrifying pace to score near the posts. Alas, the conversion attempt by Brown, which could have decided the result, hit a post and bounced the wrong way for his team.

Dawes insists that, even at this late stage, the thought of defeat never crossed his mind. As they went back for the re-start he told his men, "Let's get to their 25, win the ball, and move it quickly." This was a moment when self-belief counted above anything else.

And now, the game soared to a towering climax. Delme Thomas took fast, clean line-out possession which was smartly delivered by Edwards to the three-quarters. Ian Hall (a replacement on the day for the injured Arthur Lewis) was missed out, the ball being sent straight to JPR whose angle of running caused the Scottish cover to hesitate. Thus when the full-back's well-timed pass reached him, right wing Gerald Davies was in the clear and sped on an elegant curve across the goal line. Scotland's full-back Ian Smith arrived too late to prevent the score, but he did force Davies to ground the ball a mere five yards from the corner flag on the Welsh right.

So Murrayfield was to stage one of the great tests of nerve in rugby's history. The conversion demanded a left-footed kicker, and John Taylor meekly accepted what would prove to be either a poisoned chalice or what came to be called "the greatest conversion since St Paul". Many of his team-mates simply could not bear to watch what happened, and coach Clive Rowlands in the grandstand was another who turned his back as the ball was being lined up. But to Scotland's dismay and grief the kick was a beauty. The captain remembers how, even before the crowd began to roar, Taylor turned away to run back to half way, eyes blazing and pumping the air with his fist: "I congratulated him and told him not to feel too pleased with himself because if he had missed there was no doubt that we would have scored another try! As a matter of fact Gareth Edwards did attempt to drop a last-minute goal, but by then it was a case of time-wasting by us and sitting on a 19-18 lead.

"Within myself, of course, I was incredibly pleased and satisfied. We had gone back to basics, and they had proved as reliable as ever. It would be nice to think that my show of confidence had rubbed off on the team. rugby's history is peppered with instances where, when time is running out and their team is trailing, individual players become the opposite of 'cool'; they tell themselves 'If nobody else can save this game, I will' and take ridiculous, individualist decisions which are doomed to failure. At Murrayfield in 1971 my men preserved their composure and were playing fifteen-man rugby up to the final whistle.

"A moving tail-piece to that afternoon came as we were leaving the changing rooms to get on our team bus. Through the home team's door there suddenly emerged Peter Brown. He extended a hand, and said to me, 'John, your guys deserved that. Well done.' I am not noted for being an emotional person, but I was slightly choked. I am not sure that I could have voiced those sentiments if our opponents had won. There is a place in rugby for gentlemanly words and sincere sentiments."

On paper Ireland's 17-5 win at Murrayfield at the end of

February appeared more convincing than that of Wales. But the men in green left ambition and confidence on the aircraft that brought them to Cardiff a fortnight later, and John Dawes thinks that their mood on the day was negative and pessimistic. His team conceded a couple of penalties to the boot of Mike Gibson before Denzil Williams and the Welsh forwards began asserting themselves. Their dominance meant that the strike runners could be let off the leash, and Gareth Edwards and Gerald Davies responded with a couple of tries apiece. Barry John contributed eleven points with the boot to clinch a win by twenty-three points to nine and a twelfth Triple Crown for Wales, with Gibson kicking a third goal for the visitors.

Once again then France in Paris, on 27 March, stood between Wales and a first Grand Slam since 1952. Brian Price's side had had to be content with a draw in 1969 which robbed them of a clean sheet, and at squad sessions in Cardiff the message hammered home by Dawes and coach Clive Rowlands was that not a grain of complacency should creep into the their team's preparations.

However, there were distractions. An announcement was to be made on 22 March by the Four Home Unions' Tours Committee naming the thirty players to tour Australia and New Zealand in the summer. Wales were currently in the ascendant, something that would surely be reflected in the tour party's make-up.

The Welsh selectors had returned to John Dawes as their captain a year previously, and he had delivered handsomely. In 1971, there had been three victories on the trot, and the team he led was poised for a Five Nations triumph. The FHU Tours Committee would now eliminate rivals like John Spencer and Mike Gibson from the frame – and Doug Smith could hint to Dawes, "I'll have some news for you personally some time on Sunday, and the other tourists' names will be released to the media on Monday" (that is, less than a week before the crucial clash at Colombes). Though astonished, the Welsh captain knew what the Manager meant, and looked forward to the promised phone call. He had one reservation: on hearing of their selection for the tour, would the Welsh Lions-to-be (thirteen of them as it turned out) give less than a hundred per cent in the Paris encounter for fear of incurring injuries which would keep them at home? This was a genuine risk: the Northampton centre Chris Wardlow was injured in England's defeat by Scotland the previous afternoon and, after failing to recover, had to be replaced in the Lions' party by an opponent, Chris Rea.

On Sunday, 21 March, the telephone at the Dawes home rang forty or fifty times. Mainly, the callers were London Welsh members who knew the possibilities and were hoping to hear good news from the man of the moment. Without exception the answer to eager questions was, "No comment". As it happened, the selection meeting lasted well into the evening, so that it was not until after midnight on the Monday morning that Doug Smith came through, with the laconic greeting, "Congratulations, John. You're the captain. Well done. Carwyn and I will enjoy working with you."

The choice was a momentous one – if only because no Welshman had captained a British side in the southern hemisphere since A.F. Harding (of London Welsh RFC and Wales, though born in Lincolnshire) who led the Anglo-Welsh tourists of 1908. The down-side was the omission from the party of veteran Welsh prop Denzil Williams and flanker Dai Morris. Dawes was sad at the former's omission but not surprised at that of Morris; "He was never a good traveller, especially when flying was involved. He always went by rail and ferry to venues like Paris and Dublin. I also recall his unease when we were in New Zealand two years earlier, and my guess is that he let it be known that he did not wish to fly to the southern hemisphere again."

The identities of the thirty men to make the tour were released to the media on 22 March. Given their outstanding achievement it is worth recording the names of the chosen Lions of 1971 managed and coached by Doug Smith and Carwyn James, plus replacements along the way: full-backs: J.P.R. Williams and R. Hiller; three-quarters: John Bevan, Alistair Biggar, Gerald Davies*, John Dawes (capt), David Duckham, Arthur Lewis, Chris Rea, John Spencer; halves: Gareth Edwards, Michael Gibson, Ray Hopkins, Barry John; forwards: Rodger Arneil, Gordon Brown, 'Sandy' Carmichael, Mervyn Davies, Peter Dixon, Geoff Evans**, Mick Hipwell, Frank Laidlaw, Sean Lynch, Willie John McBride, Ian McLauchlan, Ray McLoughlin, John Pullin, Derek Quinnell, Michael Roberts, Fergus Slattery,

'Stack' Stevens**, John Taylor, Delme Thomas. (*joined team after completing examinations at Cambridge; **replacement.)

Dawes reckons that a treasured moment in the wake of the announcement of his appointment to the captaincy came at breakfast-time on the Monday, when he placed a telephone call to North Celynen Colliery, where his father still worked as a black-smith. Great was the rejoicing at the pithead, where toasts to Reg and his son were drunk in an unofficial break for refreshments. Since alcohol was banned from coal mines Reg's butties made do with a glass of ginger beer; but rumour has it that Dawes senior enjoyed a celebratory bottle of Guinness, courtesy of the NCB.

On a morning with no match reports to fill columns and programmes the rugby media fall upon announcements about Lions' teams as manna. Thus the Tuesday sports pages and radio channels were full of analysis of the party. The captain received a telegram from Secretary of State for Wales Peter Thomas congratulating him warmly on his selection as the first Welshman to lead the British Isles. Not surprisingly – since a golden boy, John Spencer, had been captaining England through a series of centenary matches – the Anglo-centric Press had a go at the appointee. Writers listed no fewer than eight chosen tourists who could play at centre. So was Dawes doomed to be another Campbell-Lamerton, a captain whose presence in the Test XVs of 1966 was always in doubt? Today, he snorts at the idea: "I was the chosen skipper. Doug Smith and Carwyn James wanted me to lead. Unless I was to be in charge there was no point in my travelling at all. I lost no sleep."

He thinks that Carwyn James got the tourists that he wanted in the party, with one exception. Barry John's brother Clive (Llanelli) could have been a utility player in the back row or at full-back, taking some of the strain off Gibson who, besides play-ing at centre, was required to deputise for John at stand-off half if the latter was being rested. Dawes is also sure that, on mature reflection, James would have decided to include a second special-ist stand-off half.

Now, attention was re-focussed upon the Paris showdown. The visitors were proud possessors of a Triple Crown and would be playing for the last time at Stade Colombes before France's move to Parc des Princes. Their hosts were unbeaten but, since the opening defeat of Scotland, had been held to draws in Dublin and at Twickenham. For the third time in the Championship Wales were able to field the same fifteen players (a sequence broken only by Lewis's absence from Murrayfield). The French back division was sprinkled with relative newcomers, but their pack contained giants like the battle-hardened Spanghero brothers Claude and Walter, the immense Benoit Dauga and Christian Carrere, a worthy successor as captain to Michel Crauste. The conflict promised to be memorable.

Named as captain of the Lions, John Dawes had one outstanding achievement in the bag, and now he desperately wanted to show a sceptical rugby world the qualifications and ability which under-wrote his appointment. He also intuited that the nature of the Paris encounter would play into his team's hands. At Colombes, before their hyper-critical fans, the French side would not dare to close the game down, so that both teams would be setting out to play 15-a-side rugby. Under him, he felt convinced, were brilliant men who could make the Grand Slam dream reality in a fast, competitive match.

The initial twenty minutes saw Wales, not for the first time in the Championship, on the back foot. Although Lewis broke memorably up to their 22 at one point, the home team's heavy-weights were directing every probe, every thrust, at the cruiser-weights facing them. And inevitably, a blow came that put the visitors down for a count of nine. The huge but agile Dauga, at number eight for France, claimed loose possession inside the Welsh 22 and crashed across the goal line at the head of a rolling maul for a morale-boosting try which Villepreux easily converted.

Dawes, who was finding the action both exhilarating and exhausting, recalls that France could have doubled their lead a few minutes later. Once more it was Dauga in the van, but this time checked close to the Welsh line. Undoubtedly he would have scored again had it not been for the intervention of Barry John, who flew at the big fellow with just enough momentum to knock him off balance and into the corner flag. No try – but in the collision the Welshman broke his nose and spent some minutes having attention from Gerry Lewis beside the tunnel. "When he returned," smiles Dawes, "his first remark to me was, 'I want to know who pushed me into him'!"

Now came an inspired riposte to remind the French that they were in a match. Dawes recalls, "Their right wing, Roger Bougarel, was put into space on our ten-yard line and began to run slightly infield to try and pull JPR away from the support runner he sensed had got outside him. But John Taylor was closing in on Bougarel, so that I think our full-back felt he could afford to go for an interception when the pass was given. This was a risk which he seldom took, preferring to nail ball carriers.

"His lunge came at exactly the right split second, and the next thing we knew was that he was heading for the half way line at speed. The trouble was, several of us had corner-flagged, so that the only team-mate anywhere near JPR was dear old Denzil Williams, who was now being overtaken by the panic-stricken French backs and was not an option for a pass.

"This was when, partly through instinct or partly, maybe, through a quick squint over his left shoulder JPR realised that a team-mate was moving fast just behind him close to the left touchline. He therefore moved infield to check the French coverers and in the same stride gave a perfect pass to a man who just happened to be Gareth Edwards. Our scrum-half had the stamina to finish a 90-yard counter attack at France's corner flag. The conversion attempt failed but we crossed over only 3-5 down, instead of 0-5.

"Gareth has written affectionately about his early mentor, the late Bill Samuel, who gave him some fatherly advice after he started scoring tries for Wales by blasting his way across the line from short range. Apparently Bill told him, 'you're not a finished product until you start scoring from seventy or eighty yards out.' Well, Colombes 1971 suggested that Gareth had taken notice. Even though he had not been the chief ball-carrier, he must have sprinted all the way from our 25 to get the score."

The second half continued at an awesome, non-stop pace, punctuated by two more – rather less painful – moments featuring Barry John. First he kicked a penalty goal, following it up with a second Welsh try. Made possible by Jeff Young's strike against the head close to France's posts, it was a classic-in-miniature and a superb example of the spectral running which John could now turn on as his judgement matured. Just a dozen strides from France's line he ran at the opposing centres, showed Dawes the ball, and finally found an unguarded channel to the goal line. Unaccountably he mis-hit the conversion that could have put the result beyond doubt, but at 9-5 Wales were able to hold on for their Grand Slam and a first win in Paris since 1957. Nor had any of the visitors' Lions-elect been seriously injured as they put their bodies on the line – only Barry John was nursing a damaged nose. It had been the kind of gutsy play, laced with passages of sheer magic, that would be needed by the British Isles in New Zealand. Verdict – a good dress rehearsal, orchestrated by the captain-elect.

At the post-match banquet that night Dawes decided to respond to the toast 'Notre convives' – 'our guests' - by speaking in Welsh and French. Clive Rowlands edited the former composition while a kindly-disposed head waiter translated the latter. After the formalities Denzil Williams asked his captain what language he had used.

"Two – Welsh and French," came the reply.

"Oh," frowned the pack leader. "They both sounded the same to me. And I couldn't understand a word."

Although the nominated captain of the 1971 Lions had toured and travelled abroad more than practically any man on the FHU Committee, John Dawes's experience was ignored both at the selection and the scheduling stages of the Lions. Mere tour captains evidently had nothing of value to contribute. We have noted that the party was given a standing ovation at Twickenham on leaving the 1971 Middlesex Sevens which they had watched as guests. However, their immediate destination was not Brisbane or Sydney; instead there was to be a 'preparatory' week spent at a country club in Eastbourne. The young Lions were not at all impressed by the township's ambience. Remarked Mervyn Davies, "Every resident I see looks to be eighty-five. It's almost as if we're all here to end our days!"

In retrospect Dawes is sure that the bonding which is a prerequisite of successful touring could have been achieved on the Lions' arrival in Australia. This stop-off, incidentally, was a last-minute, added-on commitment designed to raise revenue for the

Australian Rugby Union, a body which was perennially broke in those days. Though training periods were frequent and vigorous the last thing any member of the group wanted was to be crocked and left at home. Caution was a priority.

Many aspects of the Eastbourne experience had to do with off-the-field concerns. Kitting-out took place, with blazers bearing the British Isles' crest along with the official ties, shirts and slacks to be worn at functions or off-duty. A posse of sales reps from boot manufacturers descended on the camp bent on persuading the Lions to wear their products. Some boots were indeed taken to the southern hemisphere, but many parcels left Eastbourne during the week for addresses in the British Isles.

Player relationships were cemented at an early stage by the permutations of room-sharing, which featured the attraction of opposites. It was deemed a good idea to pair the up-and-coming lock forward Gordon Brown with a true veteran in the position, Willie John McBride. With his wide open face and infectious grin young Brown loved to tell the tale for years after the tour: "McBride was a hero of mine. Just being spoken to by him was enough to make me weak at the knees. Before we put the lights off on our first night together the great man said to me, 'Do ye snore?' I stammered that I wasn't sure, but would try hard to refrain from doing so in order not to keep him awake. He grunted, turned over and nodded off. How could I be sure of not disturbing him? Would ye believe me, I sat in an arm chair all night reading a book!"

Intriguingly, the captain found himself billeted with Ireland's Ray McLoughlin. Far from being a donkey, the super-prop had attended several universities and, as Dawes considers, was a cerebral sort of player whose company, and intellect, were much to the liking of none other than Carwyn James. The downside of all this was that he unloaded onto the tour captain a selection of analytical papers written during an International career that had already lasted for nine seasons. What was more, he wanted to discuss them all during the evenings following training. After a few days' relentless exposure to this non-stop master-class on forward play Dawes felt slightly faint, and asked for a respite. He was replaced as McLoughlin's room-mate by none other than Barry John, whom the Irishman attempted to draw into protracted discussions on tactics for advanced rugby players. His overtures, however, met with the world-weary rejoinder, "Ray – just get the ball for me, and I'll do the rest".

But no-one had any doubt as to McLoughlin's technical know-how. Says Dawes, "He had the answer to every problem a pack meets on a rugby field, and indeed could probably have been a great captain of Ireland if only he had known how to motivate men, something that the Celtic nations need from a leader. Had Ray possessed that gift, or acquired it, then he might have exercised a long-lasting influence on Irish teams comparable with Martin Johnson's spearheading of England's 2003 World Cup triumph."

Other new team-mates who were impressing themselves and their capabilities upon the skipper included the uncapped Welshman Derek Quinnell: "Once, in training, he failed to take an easy pass from one of the half-backs, a knock-on by him halting a promising movement. 'Oh, Derek, that was absolutely *sloppy*,' shouted Carwyn James. Well, the word stuck and you can guess what young Quinnell was called for the rest of the tour!"

Eastbourne was also where delicate personality problems were met head-on and dealt with. In his early seasons John Taylor could be fiery in argument if he was mischievously wound up or teased – or indeed if a referee upset him during a match. He just about put up with the nick-name 'Bas' – short for the fox-puppet Basil Brush to whom Gareth Edwards had likened him; but the management trio decided that he now needed a job offering a measure of prestige. What should it be? – maybe pack leader of the mid-week 'dirt trackers'? Objection: he was highly likely to be playing in the Test XV. OK; how about Choirmaster?

"It was an inspired choice," remembers Dawes. "Although JT wasn't a great singer, certainly not in Carwyn's league, at least he could wave a baton convincingly. Furthermore, he was responsible for introducing our theme-song to the lads – a sea shanty called 'The Sloop John B'. If the truth be told, it was a rather mournful ditty, to which a rival ensemble headed by Bob Hiller and John Spencer took a dislike. The diplomacy of our choirmaster-elect won the day as he decreed that Bob, John and Co could inject the 'boom-boom, be-boom-booms' in between the narrative lines. The verse which began, 'The captain's a wicked man' was my personal favourite."

There was another cultural *leitmotif* that needed to be firmly dealt with. The English (not just their rugby players) are strangely sensitive about usage of the Welsh language, even in Wales itself. If, for instance, it is being spoken in a pub which they enter during a visit to the principality they often imagine that they are being spoken about – disparagingly – by the natives. In the past this issue had contributed to perceived clannish attitudes in the Welsh which, allegedly, made them unpopular tourists.

In a short address to his players at Eastbourne, Carwyn James de-fused and demolished this canard. For five or six members of the party including himself, he explained, Welsh was the mother tongue in which it was wholly natural for them to converse with each other, switching to English when it was appropriate. There was absolutely no foundation for the English-speaking majority to imagine that the Welsh language was a code used by his countrymen to insult fellow Britons. There were nods of agreement all round, and a language barrier never became an issue.

Eastbourne, then, might not have seen the 1971 British Isles party training flat out. However, another kind of foundation for success was laid: the camaraderie and mutual respect which developed between the players – and also between the players and the two managers. Men who had never met (or possibly even heard of) Doug Smith and Carwyn James said to themselves and their team-mates, "These two know what they are about. We will do it their way."

NINE

In Australia Dawes's 1971 Lions fell at the first hurdle, Queensland. A mere two years previously Wales's tour to this same part of the world had been undermined by maladroit scheduling; and now, evidently, the lesson had not been properly appreciated and acted upon by the FHU's Tours Committee. The last-minute agreement to play a couple of provincial fixtures in Australia, thus improving the ARU's cash-flow, was well-meant but played havoc with the Lions' plans. At Brisbane the British Isles team members who took the field had stepped from their aircraft a mere forty eight hours earlier, and went down by fifteen points to eleven. In the limelight immediately, Dr Doug Smith attributed the result to his men's "cyclical disrhythmia". If that meant "jet-lag", the Manager's diagnosis was spot-on.

Back in the UK the critics nodded sagely. The whitewash suffered by the 1966 Lions was still fresh in the memories of rugby people everywhere, and now it looked as if their 1971 successors were heading for a fate even worse than that. As a matter of fact, they were explicitly branded as "the poorest Lions ever to travel to the southern hemisphere". By none other than the Queensland coach, Des Connor. His verdict could not have been more premature!

Carwyn James had hoped to give all his players a run-out before the tour moved on to New Zealand. However, Gerald Davies was still in the examination halls of Cambridge and another three-quarter, Chris Rea, suffered a slight injury in training so that John Dawes found himself in action for a second time. New South Wales, the other great exponents of rugby union in Australia, were the Lions' next opponents on an absolutely wretched day at the Sydney Oval, which also stages Test cricket. This time the British Isles got away with a 14-12 victory. The skipper remembers the game for two positive reasons:

"Firstly, on a sopping wet playing surface upon which incessant rain bucketed down I was a try scorer. Barry John chipped ahead, the ball crossed our opponents' line, and after a thirty yard sprint through the mud I just got the touch-down ahead of the opposition. I made absolutely sure of grasping the ball tightly as I landed on it, because letting it go would have provided a golden opportunity for the referee to disallow this score by alien Pommie invaders of whom he disapproved.

"Anyway, in the cuttings which reached us from the British Press I was amused to read J.B.G.'s account of the try, which finished by stating, 'Dawes outstripped the New South Wales defence and showed the antipodes his new-found speed'. New-found! – at the age of 30! I thought that was rich. But I think that our kindly *Western Mail* critic was sending a corrective signal to some rugby people's view that I might not make the Test team. In fact, most of this speculation originated in the New Zealand media and, after a week or so in their country it died away.

"Mention of my age prompts the comment that, like the Queen, I have a natural birthday, 29 June (and was to celebrate my thirty-first at Invercargill) plus an 'official' one. The latter is enshrined in the lists of 'celebrity' birthdays printed in the broad-sheet newspapers and is always noted on 29 September. As far as I can tell the original error was made by John Reason, lifted from him, and never corrected.

"I hope, however, that Her Majesty will not be too upset to learn, as I have from research connected with this book, that I actually have a third birthday! Terry Godwin's masterly volume, *The Complete Who's Who of International Rugby* (1987), says that I was born on 29 April 1940. The result is that I am not quite sure whom or what to trust. Should it be my mother or the media?"

The other matter which was resolved in Australia concerned the Lions' pecking order of place kickers and the way in which Barry John exercised *droit de seigneur*. Until this juncture in his career the gifted stand-off had established himself as a kicker of conversions and penalties for Wales – but only from field positions on the left which favoured his right boot. He had shared the kicking respon-sibility with J.P.R., who sometimes kicked down the middle, and John Taylor, operating from the right hand side of the pitch.

"In that same match against New South Wales," recalls Dawes, "the most treacherous area of all was the cricket square, right in the middle of the stadium and on the half way line of the rugby pitch. Here the surface was composed of very fine soil which dried quickly in the wake of rainfall – but during a downpour had the consistency of liquid mud. Anyway, right there the Lions were awarded a penalty, and I tossed the ball to Barry saying, 'Put it away. Kick for touch'. Then I turned my back and re-joined the three-quarter line.

"A second or two later I turned round again – to see Barry completing preparations for a place kick at goal. 'Cheeky so-and-so,' I thought to myself. 'He won't kick that'. But he did. Not only on that Sydney afternoon in the mud but throughout New Zealand – as he worked his way 'around the corner' to an astonishing 180 points from sixteen appearances. He never asked for permission to kick, just proceeding with his preparations. Nobody sought to challenge his right to do so. Actually, of course, his decisiveness made my job easier since I never had to worry about who should take kicks. Only when he and Bob Hiller happened to be in the same team did Barry defer to the full-back's orthodoxy and great experience."

The Australian leg of the tour, albeit short, was a distraction which irritated the Lions. In 1971 the Wallabies' accommodating of inward tours (as Wales had found two years previously) left something to be desired. There is no doubt that they have worked tremendously hard on their game since that time, and are currently the sole nation to have won the Rugby World Cup twice. Partly, this has been accomplished as a result of the centres of excellence where the final glitter is put on Australia's rising stars. In the Australian psyche, however, there is also a ruthlessness which means, in the opinion of John Dawes, that their sportsmen and women will go overboard to win and, if a serious injury to an opponent should occur – then, too bad. Their international sportsmen and women grow up being told by their coaches that they are the world's best. Therefore, in every match and every contest they have to prove this belief to be correct.

New Zealanders, on the other hand, are stronger on fair play. However, they too desperately want to win, and they compete ferociously to that end. Just how ferociously the 1971 Lions were about to discover. They landed at Auckland Airport on 15 May.

The Kiwi Press pack rushed off to headline Doug Smith's forecast of a series victory for his men in the Tests while the Lions travelled the short distance to Pukekohe, some miles south of Auckland. The weather was much to the tourists' liking, and it remained dry and mild throughout a schedule lasting until 14 August and containing twenty-four fixtures. John Dawes under-lines the importance of this factor, claiming that it is important for preparatory work as much as match play. In a game, men will put up with eighty minutes' rain, however heavy, because there is something at stake. But, if it is raining as training starts, everyone quickly becomes wet through, cold and dispirited – and a return to the changing rooms and a shower cannot come too soon. The captain remembers only one spell of unpleasant weather, at Greymouth for the match against West Coast-Buller. The Lions would take that in their stride.

Certainly in Thames Valley, whose select XV would provide the Lions' first opposition, the sun shone on the practice sessions conducted by Carwyn James. Senior players like Delme Thomas and Willie John McBride recalled how in 1966 training took place in both mornings and afternoons – which they recalled was boring and counter-productive. James in contrast made it clear that normally his men would work hard during mornings, after which they could please themselves what to do. Often there were visits to race meetings, where the Lions were well looked after by tipsters and returned to their hotel satisfied with generous capital gains. Such refreshing expeditions meant that the players' atti-tudes were very positive when they reported for training the following morning.

Carwyn James, Doug Smith and John Dawes met every day to review progress and plot forthcoming strategies, and in the very first week a difference in their attitudes to selection emerged. The latter two were used to naming a best XV every week – Dawes at Old Deer Park and Smith at London Scottish. But at Llanelli James had become used to 'squad-orientated' selection, 'horses for courses', 'mix and match' and other stratagems which he wanted his two colleagues to accept. They did so, and assisted the coach to ink in teams for the first five matches against Thames Valley, Wanganui-King Country, Waikato, NZ Maoris and Wellington – the last of which would be a best-guessed team for the First Test. The permutations of personnel that emerged made almost every player think he was in with a chance of a Test place and kept ambitions on the boil. The danger of division and discontent was minimised.

Nobody, therefore, thought or spoke of 'first teams' and 'dirt trackers', certainly not at the outset. It took the appointment of Bob Hiller to negate the strategy when he was named captain for one of the midweek fixtures. Immediately he invited the members of his team to take tea and scones with him, stressing archly that 'Saturday personnel' were not welcome. By now there were no thin skins left in the party and no harm was done. 'T&Ws' (Tuesdays and Wednesdays) became part of the Lions' vocabulary.

Dawes says, "From an early stage I had realized that working with a pair of talented, self-assured colleagues like Carwyn and Doug promised to be the experience of a lifetime. Our Scottish boss (who died a few years ago and is sorely missed by all his Lions) had emerged as a master of man-management and discipline. He was the one who kept an eye on the kit we wore in public. It was simple enough: white shirts and a Lions tie were always worn, along with grey slacks. When travelling or at informal events, we donned sweaters; blazers were worn to matches and functions such as civic receptions.

"Doug was also hot on punctuality. If the team bus was scheduled to leave our hotel at nine-fifteen – that really meant 0915. The Manager never lost his cool; instead, heavy sarcasm was his main disciplinary weapon. 'Merry Christmas' he would intone as a late-comer scrambled on board. He could sense if one of his men was upset, and we knew that the key to his room would be made available to any Lions who wanted to get something off their chests. If Doug's presence was required he would make sure of being at hand to lend a friendly ear.

"In public and at speech-making he could also hold his own. As captain, I spoke at post-match functions whether I had played or not, while Doug always said a few farewell words to our hosts before we left for our hotel. All in all, counting the public appearances we were committed to, he must have given about a hundred speeches. It was his practice always to finish with a joke – and I remember that he never, ever repeated one. The only chore that he lumbered me with was Keeper of the Campari, a drink to which he was particularly partial. It was my job to make sure that, among our effects at social or formal functions attended by the team, there was always a bottle of this bitter Italian aperitif at hand in case our hosts didn't have any or had run out.

"So to Carwyn, whom I was now getting to know properly after seasons of casual encounters. Now, contact with him was focused and purposeful. As we met and talked at the daily meetings I swiftly began to realise that in a rugby context, he was an out-and-out elitist. That is, he was an ideal coach for a top flight team full of top-flight players, preferably personnel who had been selected by him. Certainly it seemed to me that he had little or no patience with the ordinary. Therefore having, as it were, chosen his Rolls Royce all he had to do was keep its tank full of petrol, start it, rest a finger on its steering wheel and caress the accelerator occasionally. Maybe he didn't know how everything worked – but he knew the performance that such a car was intended to deliver.

"Occasionally he could get things wrong, but this stemmed from his concern for the players' welfare. He found out when the tour was well under way that Mrs Hiller was giving husband Bob a rather hard time for being away and out of touch on a mission that she hadn't realized would last so long. Carwyn decided to give Bob two days off to recover his composure. 'Don't fly with us,' he told the bemused Hiller. 'We'll hire a car for you and you can take your time unwinding and driving to our next destination'.

"The plan mis-fired. 'Good God!' came Bob's response. 'So, it's come to this! I can't even travel with the boys any more. I've been banned!' Carwyn had got it slightly wrong; but the episode proves how deeply he cared."

The captain remembers the coach as essentially a quiet man. In John Dawes's recall James scarcely ever raised his voice, either at work on the training pitch or when arguing a point with one of his players. He never used heavy swear-words, though an exasperated 'Dammo' might escape his lips if a promising move broke down. His motivation technique was not full of fury like that of Clive Rowlands, consisting simply of level-headed advice inviting his men to recognize their own ability and play up to it; and also to share such thoughts with team-mates. He himself enjoyed a superb rapport with every single player. Often, long after other Lions had left the dining room, someone who peeped back in would see the coach sharing the last of a bottle of Kiwi claret with a team-mate in need of an in-depth consultation.

As coach, the total commitment he gave is beyond question. He accepted that if unexpected on-field problems manifested themselves it was his job to solve them. Early on, although the Lions were winning games, rucking did not appear to be their forte. A day or two before the game against Otago at Dunedin (the seventh fixture) James took the bull by the horns and spent a whole afternoon in the company of rugby thinker and coach Vic Cavanagh. Now a veteran, this was the man who had more or less invented rucking and introduced it to All Black rugby as a means of winning second-phase ball at the tackle situation. What he had to say was absorbed and digested by the Lions coach and re-cycled for the benefit of Ray McLoughlin and the forwards. It soon yielded results on the field.

And the make-up of the man? Dawes says: "I think that within Carwyn there burned a love of his country that I've scarcely known to be matched. His use of the Welsh language, I am assured, was both beautiful and scholarly. He was steeped in the culture of Wales, and exceedingly well-read. He knew our music, its composers and hymn-writers; and his solo renderings on special occasions of Joseph Parry's love song 'Myfanwy' became the highlight of evenings when the Lions set out to repay the hospitality of their hosts with entertainment of their own. If he felt the need for a change of surroundings and tempo, he would accept invitations to visit *émigré* families at home, especially if the language of the evening was likely to be Welsh. For such engage-ments his hair was carefully combed and brushed and his dress would be a suit. Only fingers browned from holding endless Players Full Strength betrayed the bad habit of a lifetime.

"In short, I have to fall back on the word 'charismatic' to define the persona he presented to the world. Even the way he ate a meal was graceful; and to those sharing his table he appeared totally engrossed with what they had to say. My last word at this stage would be about Carwyn as a selector: he knew what each of his players could do and selected them with that in mind. Too many coaches these days pick players because of what they think they can do – and there is frustration when this turns out not to be the case. During the 2003 World Cup and the Six Nations Championship of 2004 the Williamses – Shane and Rhys – were enabled to do what they could do – in style."

Between them, it is clear, the Lions' triumvirate had created a family atmosphere before May was out. And as in families there was no jealousy, just mutual respect for siblings. For example, Dawes recalls the arrival of Gerald Davies after finishing his Cambridge exams, and its repercussions. Up until now the front runners for wing positions in the First Test were John Bevan, on the left, and David Duckham on the other side, where Davies also played. The latter immediately threw down his challenge with two good tries on his first outing. The captain decided to come clean with Duckham.

Dawes told him, "We have a selection problem with the Tests getting nearer. You're playing well. Gerald has hit top form straightaway."

"No problem," replied Duckham. "You must play Gerald. He's world class."

"It isn't as simple as that," was the reply.

"Not to worry," said Duckham. "I'll get my chance of a Test." And he did.

After a month or so, too, the players had come fully to understand the roles they were expected to play, on and off the field. Yet the rein that disciplined them was a loose one; they were treated as grown-ups. After matches there would be the obligatory exchange of pleasantries with their hosts before, without overdue delay, the return to their hotel. Here, team spirit was was cemented in a common-room whose door would be locked fast. This was the time and place at which the Lions let rip about the opposition, the referee, the crowd and anything else that had fired them up during the afternoon's sport. Sometimes the air was blue-tinged.

This cathartic exercise terminated with a sing-song and was followed by the evening meal. Then, if their hotel had a ballroom facility where a gig was being staged, those tourists who enjoyed a hop could take to the dance floor. Arthur Lewis played a vital role here as the 'Collector of Totty' – that is, making sure there were partners with whom his team-mates could foxtrot or quickstep. He would buttonhole young ladies in the hotel bars with blunt instructions like "You'm coming to enjoy the dance" or even "You'm not, 'cos you'm too ugly". One way or another, it seemed to work.

"The after-match time," recalls the captain, "was when we partied quite hard. Gins and tonic of various sizes were downed and large amounts of ale, but care was taken to ensure that none of us became a public nuisance. If that threatened to happen the offender would be ushered to his room by senior players with orders to stay there and sleep it off."

As the southern hemisphere winter deepened, the tourists still found themselves favoured by mild, sunny weather which certainly brought the spectators out. Record crowds piled into the smaller centres, while 47,000 watched the Lions play the Maoris at Auckland, 45,000 saw the Wellington game and 53,000 were at Lancaster Park to see the challenge of Canterbury. Lots more, too, came to watch them in training. But it was the quality of rugby being served up that really had the fans queuing at the gates. Up until the eve of the First Test the Lions won ten games on the trot, five in North Island followed by five in the South, scoring 282 points while conceding a mere 83.

From time to time Dawes was reminded of squad days back home on Aberavon sands where onlookers packed the promenade to look down on Wales at practice. Here the feeling of being welcome was palpable as was the acclaim from stands and terraces as the Lions teased and tormented opponents the length and breadth of the land. "In particular" recalls the skipper, "there was a short-range try by Barry John against New Zealand Universities which was greeted in astonished silence by the crowd. Our stand-off made as if to drop a short-range goal; checked and dummied; sped past forwards who were still disengaging from a scrum; and touched down under the crossbar. The lack of instant acclaim made Barry think he had done something wrong – until the stunned crowd woke up and delivered well-deserved applause."

Two of the early games, in particular, are worth reflecting on – and are certainly memorable for Dawes. The first of them indicated that Carwyn James's decision, taken during the first week in New Zealand, to field his likely Test side against Wellington had been valid. John Pullin appeared to have won his battle with Frank Laidlaw for the number two jersey, but otherwise the

133

names were as expected. In winter New Zealand's capital city is often stormy, and the Athletic Park stadium where top rugby was staged then stood on a low but exposed hillside, but on this day the weather for the province's clash with the British Isles was, yet again, perfect.

As, indeed, was the way the Lions played to secure their 47-9 victory. They ran in nine tries, of which John Bevan scored four with Gibson (2), Carmichael, Taylor and John getting the others. The last-named, plus Gibson and J.P.R., kicked the balance of points to leave Wellington out for the count. It is worth quoting J.B.G. Thomas once more, a writer who had seen more southern hemisphere rugby than any other British media person. What he wrote was quite touching:

> One can be carried away by spectacular play and perhaps over-praise it. But on the Sunday after this match I was still pinching myself to see if I had not been the victim of a dream in which a Lions side did everything right. For years I had waited to see the Lions dominate in such fashion by playing copy-book rugby at forward and running brilliantly behind. Everything they had done on this particular day was of a remarkably high quality.

John Dawes recalls, "Yes, it was a special afternoon, and the first thing to say is that once more we entertained the crowd and showed them the handling game at its best. However, there was also a long term gain. Rather as Welsh people like to tell a touring side, 'OK, you've beaten Ebbw Vale and Abertillery – but wait 'til you play Cardiff', so Kiwi supporters had been telling us, 'You've beaten a few combined teams – but wait until you get to Wellington!' So our win at Athletic Park was as if the All Blacks had put fifty points on Cardiff. It stopped the loud-mouths in mid-sentence and, more important, it both astonished and worried all the elements and strata that make up New Zealand's rugby fraternity. It was a statement that this British Isles party was made of stern stuff and had not come to their country to roll over obligingly and give up the ghost."

If such a theory needed to be tested to the full, that would happen a fortnight later, in the other game of which Dawes has vivid memories. A confrontation in Christchurch would determine whether the visitors were really lambs in lion's clothing.

Three days before the British Isles were due to play Canterbury they were busy in the rain mowing down West Coast-Buller opposition. In a more than satisfactory 39-6 victory David Duckham, with six tries, and Bob Hiller (twenty-four points) showed star quality; but the management's gaze was not entirely focused on the run of play. It had become clear, through rumour, gossip and media speculation, that Canterbury were bent on taming the Lions at Christchurch by fair means or foul. No punches would be pulled by a provincial side coached by two former All Blacks, wing Maurice Dixon and lock, A.J. Stewart. Was it directives given to their team by these two men which turned Lancaster Park into a battlefield on 19 June? In effect they decreed, "OK, Lions. You've had a nice little run so far. Now we are going to show you just how tough New Zealand rugby is. And anything goes."

"Clearly Canterbury would be out to soften us up," says John Dawes. "Our genuine concern about the sinister approach of these opponents was reflected in our selection. Given Barry John's sensational form, he would surely be targeted for 'sorting out' by Grizz Wyllie and the other members of the province's back row, while the slight frame of Gerald Davies would be at risk should he fall on the ball beneath the hooves of their front five. So Mike Gibson who, as an amateur boxer, knew how to look after himself off the ball, and the sturdy David Duckham were preferred on the day to the two Welshmen – but alas, it was not the Lions' back division that was destined to suffer grievously but our pack."

The game's brutality is well documented and began at the first line-out, when Fergus Slattery was punched in the face some twenty yards off the ball. This kind of activity punctuated the game, with the Lions exercising restraint under extreme provocation. Ironically, one of the two men they lost in the mayhem was their Irish guru, Ray McLoughlin whose thumb was broken by his own punch with which he sought revenge for dirty work by Wyllie. Sandy Carmichael's depressed fracture of a cheek-bone was suffered at a set scrum when a viciously-clenched fist came through from Canterbury's second row.

Says Dawes, "The sad thing about our opponents' approach was that, had they played rugby instead of laying about the Lions, they were basically skilful enough to have shown us, and their supporters, real quality. Perhaps they could have got within a point or two of us. But as it was, both of the game's tries were scored by us. Arthur Lewis crossed for one, while the really memorable score was John Bevan's. Confronted by three defenders near a Canterbury corner flag he must have said to himself something like, 'I'm going to show these so-and-sos', and, wallop, he ran through them to get the touch-down. A couple of penalties and a conversion saw us through to a 14 -3 victory. We had demonstrated our resilience, and New Zealand knew that we had taken everything that was thrown at us.

"And we won the match. But, in another sense, we were losers. Half an hour's havoc had robbed us of our two front-line prop forwards with all their experience and know-how. I wouldn't say that Carwyn or the rest of us were demoralized. But certainly we were gravely concerned."

It must have cheered the Lions to read the following day's newspapers which, without exception condemned Canterbury's approach and conduct. The local paper wrote of 'The Game of Shame'. Terry McLean had a go in the *New Zealand Herald*. "All Black rugby," said Truth, "has become as grotesque as a wounded bull." Without exception the London Press censured Canterbury's approach. And that might have been the end of it.

Instead the All Blacks' coach for the Test series, Ivan Vodanovich chose to fan the flames by warning at a Press conference, "If the Lions do not get off the ball in the rucks, the first Test at Dunedin will resemble the Battle of Passchendaele." This was a Belgian village on the River Schelde which gave its name to a World War I battle, graphically described by Britain's Prime Minister of the day, David Lloyd George, as 'the most grim, futile and bloody fight ever waged in the history of war'. On its first day British casualties reached 32,000. Vodanovitch's outburst was a reckless threat in the worst of taste made by a man who ought to have known better. It was swiftly ruled out of order by Jack Sullivan, Chairman of the New Zealand Council, who added: "There will be no battle at Carisbrook next Saturday."

As it turned out, not one of the wounds or blows which the Lions suffered at Lancaster Park resulted from the opposition's rucking. The essence of the ruck is that a pack (even in the mean mood of Canterbury's) needs to drive over and ahead of the ball, which is left for a scrum-half to use. Hence, stamping, or kicking a man who cannot get out of the way, are not useful actions. The tourists' injuries resulted mainly from punches or late tackles. Therefore the relevance, let alone the usefulness, of Vodanovitch's warning has to be questioned. Was it the fevered threat of a man who had suddenly realized the immensity of the challenge that faced him?

For Dawes, along with Doug Smith and Carwyn James, the immediate task was about plugging gaps and damage limitation. Both the other two props, Sean Lynch and Ian McLauchlan, had perforce been put onto the field as replacements at Christchurch and seemed well equipped to step into the boots of Carmichael and McLoughlin. But clearly two new back-up forwards for them were now needed urgently. The Cornishman 'Stack' Stevens, by now of Harlequins, was alerted and straightaway left Heathrow for Auckland. There was rather more discussion about the second replacement, and it is possible that the elimination from contention of a second British Isles prop forward had not been allowed for at the planning and selection stage.

Many years on, Dawes says that the emergency permitted James to argue the case for an extra lock forward to join the tour party: "He had this thing about jumbo-sized front row men able to match the first shove of the All Blacks' pack. So, if he sent for Geoff Evans it would free another Exiles lock, big Mike Roberts, to play at tight head prop. Of course, I could hardly argue with the idea of calling upon yet another London Welshman, and Carwyn got his way; but I did have reservations about putting a seasoned lock like Roberts into the front row. For a start, Ray McLoughlin had spent some time educating me about the role and techniques of prop forwards, including the considerable difference between the tight and loose head positions.

"A variety of different skills and applications is called into play, having to do with binding, angle of shove, timing of shove, placing of feet and ways of making life difficult for opposite numbers. In *The Lions Speak* Mighty Mouse McLauchlan and Ray McLoughlin contribute forty two pages of close analysis of the props' roles: the equivalent of a life-time at the coal face. To accommodate Geoff Evans in the second row, Mike Roberts had to absorb as much of this kind of props' lore as he could in next to no time, as well as playing world-ranking rugby in a position that was foreign to him. The result was that he was risked only four times in the second half of the tour, making one last appearance at lock and playing three games at tight-head. Effectively, he was denied the chance to show his paces as a front-jumping lock, a berth which I think he could have handled. Readers who remember how he saw off Bill Beaumont for Wales in 1979 may not disagree.

"Upon our two remaining front-line props there fell a heavy – and risky – work-load, Lynch and McLauchlan finishing the tour with fifteen and eighteen appearances respectively. Yet, happily, they avoided injury while rising to the challenge; we never worried that they would let us down as we sought vital parity at set pieces. Meanwhile Geoff Evans got only six outings. Yes, I think Carwyn gambled at this juncture in the tour, and we were lucky to get away with a misjudgement by him."

After the Christchurch mayhem there was the usual post-match social session, at which the temperature was a little more frosty than usual. "I contented myself with remarking that we were pleased that a doctor had been appointed to referee the game," recalls John Dawes. "That seemed to go down well with the Press corps! But, as usual we left Dr Doug to handle the tough talking. He sought to bring back common sense without inflammatory words, telling his listeners, 'We have lost two key players. But nothing changes within our ranks. We are going forward with the same free-spirited attitude that we have always cultivated'. Generous applause.

"With the first Test just a week away I gave some thought to my style of captaincy. To be frank, because of the collective calibre of the Lions a low-profile approach was both desirable and feasible. For example, with a man like Ireland's captain Willie John McBride in charge of the pack I never dreamed of shouting orders like 'Throw to the front' or 'Throw it to the back to get momentum'. Under him the forwards always knew exactly what they were supposed to do next, and did it well. Even now, without the departed pair of props, our scrummaging was pretty effective and beginning to show the dynamic that would be fully charged by 1974 in South Africa.

"So my remarks were usually addressed to Gareth Edwards or Chico Hopkins – usually a simple 'We don't want it' [possession] or 'Let's have it now'. If there was nothing on, the two scrum halves, or Barry John and Mike Gibson, would retain the ball and do the right thing. However, if the Lions were awarded a penalty we did use a stratagem which I had picked up some years earlier from the Wallaby Ken Catchpole.

"This put responsibility on the scrum-half's shoulders. He could wait for the stand-off half to arrive for a touch-finder or a shot at goal; or he could tap and go – *unless* I immediately shouted 'No!' This kept us all alert."

The T&Ws group excelled themselves on the Tuesday before the First Test, running in seven tries at Blenheim in defeating Combined Marlborough and Nelson. Carwyn James cracked the whip at the final training sessions, for once bringing his Test side back for an extra afternoon session on the Thursday. He himself was busy working on the Lions' mood: crucially the players' expectations and ambition needed to be brought to the boil, and yet an inner relaxation was imperative.

New Zealand, as it happens, is a wonderful country in which to relax. Except in the cities visitors to the North Island can always feast their eyes on dramatic scenery that features hot springs and volcanoes. Away to the south east in South Island (where the Lions were now based at Dunedin, the Test venue) the distant western horizon is bordered by the high and handsome range called the Southern Alps. And the country's inhabitants, some three million of them, believe in getting out into the open air to enjoy what the countryside offers. Golf courses dot the landscape; clay pigeon shooting is available; there is power boat-ing at river estuaries in the south. Here, the water temperature reminds you that Antarctica is not all that far away, while at places like the sub-tropical Bay of Islands lounging on a beach is the ultimate therapy. Or maybe not quite – for Chico Hopkins had discovered a marvellous healing routine which had rid his leg of a haematoma, or blood bruise. He climbed into a jacuzzi with a vacuum cleaner switched to reverse which, instead of sucking, directed pressure on the dead blood, which dispersed over a day or two. The operation blew bubbles all over the hotel gymnasium, which impressed the Lions who pitched up to applaud this miniature Neptune in action.

Chico's recovery allowed him to take the field and prove his fitness against Marlborough-Nelson. On the Thursday before the First Test the Lions experienced an eleventh-hour crisis over the fitness of Gareth Edwards, whose hamstring was wrenched when his foot slipped into a pot-hole. Immediately, he went on the table for attention from 'Doc' Murdoch, the physio in attendance, but self-doubt began to trouble him a during a fractious debate about selection which lasted until the Friday evening. Doug Smith was not sceptical about his condition and believed him when he said that the hamstring was 'not a hundred per cent reliable'. As Manager, however, the Scot had to look to the longer term and pressed Gareth to say just how serious he thought the injury was. Could he play in the Test? If so, would he last for eighty minutes? If not, when would he be fit again? Should the Manager ask for a replacement and send him home?

Edwards is on record as saying that he found this interrogation unsettling and upsetting. It was a huge relief when Carwyn James devised the compromise that saved the day. His first-choice scrum-half would play for fifteen minutes before giving way to Hopkins. It made sense; and the Lions could sleep easily on the eve of the Test.

They had come a long way for the examination to which the All Blacks would submit them. Tomorrow they had to deliver answers.

TEN

In April 1971 I shot material for a BBC Wales report on the Lions' pre-tour preparations at Eastbourne. It needed to be fleshed out back in the Cardiff edit-suite by in-vision comment from three 'princes of Welsh rugby', as we called them. Bleddyn Williams, an outstanding midfield player of the post-War game in Britain was joined at Cardiff Arms Park by one-time tearaway flanker Clem Thomas of the deep chest and twinkling eye and Newport's great lock forward Brian Price. Each man had in-depth experience of All Black rugby, Price in particular having captained the Welsh tour party Down Under just two years earlier.

Since World War II the British Isles had paid three visits to New Zealand, winning but a single Test match (in 1959) out of twelve and managing a draw in the opening Test of 1950. Most recent savage experiences at the hands of merciless All Black sides had been the four Test defeats out of four in 1966 followed by the two-nil defeat of Brian Price's Welshmen. On this spring day the atmosphere was anything but optimistic.

Price spoke harrowingly of New Zealand's awesome forward power and the might of likely opponents such as Colin Meads, Ian Kirkpatrick and Peter Whiting. Thomas thought that Dawes's Lions would be a tougher proposition than their predecessors of 1966 while warning that the Test series was bound to be lost. A Lion in 1950, Bleddyn Williams spoke of the New Zealander's fanatical determination to win on his own soil and concluded that this would swing the rubber decisively against the British Isles.

They were to be proved wrong – and what is more they were delighted at the experience. Not only did the 1971 Lions become the first to win a full series in New Zealand by two Tests to one; only two previous British Isles sides had managed to win a single Test in a series (those of 1930 and 1959). The achievements of Dawes's men turned the world of rugby inside out and upside down.

★

In the days leading up to the First Test Carwyn James was doing a crucial welding job. His two replacement props (whose tour outings had hitherto been confined to selection for the T&Ws) had to dovetail with the back five whom the coach had selected for his pack; this took much practice and adjustment. But secondly, the Lions needed to use McLauchlan and Lynch far more effectively against the All Black pack at the line-outs. New Zealand forwards, James had noted, had developed a technique which he christened 'compression'. It meant that at the throw-in the Lions' support forwards were separated from their jumpers by opponents who insinuated themselves on the wrong side, in space that strictly belonged to the tourists. This was when he delivered to his forwards one of the great rugby maxims of the twentieth century which was also a brilliant and original oxymoron. He told them: "Get your retaliation in first."

This was a command which caused media and administrative eyebrows to rise. Though not in the 'Passchendaele' league, it was nevertheless perceived as a coach sanctioning his men to look after themselves by laying about them. John Dawes is at pains to explain that James was simply urging his props to position themselves carefully and not to surrender a square foot of territory which was rightly theirs. Certainly, it was not meant to incite the Lions to violence. But James would surely have grinned quietly to himself at witnessing the brief consternation he had caused.

The two Lions targeted by him were very different. Dubliner Sean Lynch had made his International debut the previous spring at the age of 28, and would go on to win seventeen caps for Ireland. Dawes recalls him as a dutiful prop, a past master at doing the jobs that prop forwards have to do. However, given the ball in midfield with space in which to move he would probably have struggled. If he was a tradesman supreme, Ian McLauchlan was a technician. "He had to be," says Dawes, "since, although he was a very powerful man indeed, he was short – no more than five feet ten. The up-side of this was that the Kiwi props with whom he engaged were often three to four inches taller than him; to lock horns they had to come down, thereby losing straight backs and a forceful shove."

New Zealand's media were responsible for the nickname that stuck. It was thought to be a psychological weapon aimed at

'Mighty Mouse', and legend suggests that it found the target. His captain recalls, "What came to his rescue was tremendous self-belief. My guess is that he privately rated himself above both McLoughlin and Carmichael; when he stepped into their boots he thought it was simply a case of getting what he deserved."

In contrast to the three veterans quoted at the beginning of this chapter John Dawes had no doubts about the British Isles' ability to beat the All Blacks despite being robbed of two key players. You will recall that reservations about New Zealand's invulnerability had surfaced in his mind in 1967, and even more positively in 1969. He saw no reason to have second thoughts about these, taking the belief with him into the Carisbrook arena for the First Test. Two thoughts dominated his approach: one, that if a huge effort by his forwards could turn New Zealand from time to time and render their possession on retreat poor, this would undermine the morale of their pack. The second consideration was pragmatic: New Zealand were in a re-building era and by no means the mature side they had been in 1967, for instance, or even 1969. Lack of experience, in other words, could contribute to their downfall.

If any Lion had harboured doubts about the calibre of the captain, and his claim to lead his men into a Test series, these had been banished long ago. His understated skills were becoming apparent, to be saluted by his peers. Colin Meads has written that he "could not leave John Dawes out of an ideal contemporary rugby XV. His influence on team performance demands his presence". In his memoirs Willie John McBride says, "John Dawes was the most under-rated player of my era. His appoint-ment as captain in 1971 was absolutely predictable, absolutely right." Gerald Davies has written, "...each situation, whether in defence or attack, was one to respond to in a positive fashion." Doubters had been put to flight.

So. Came the man, came the hour. This was it. What about the other participants? These were the fifteen names released by the British Isles to the media on the Thursday before the Test: J.P.R. Williams, Gerald Davies, Michael Gibson, S.J. Dawes (capt), John Bevan, B. John, G.O. Edwards, J. McLauchlan, J. Pullin, J. Lynch, Delme Thomas, Willie John McBride, P. Dixon, Mervyn Davies, J. Taylor.

New Zealand: Fergie McCormick, B. Hunter, B.G. Williams, K. Carrington, W.D. Cottrell, Bob Burgess, Sid Going, B. Muller, R.W. Norton, R. Guy, Colin Meads (capt), Peter Whiting, A.M. McNaughton, A.R. Sutherland, I. Kirkpatrick. Seven of the team would be winning first caps. John Pring (Auckland) was to referee.

The British captain's team-talk around two thirty on a bright but blustery afternoon in Dunedin was short and to the point: "Forget about provincial games. These have been mere side-shows compared to the task before you. An All Black team is limbering up in the changing room next door, in all probability sharing the nervous tension. Beating them today is the start of the job we are in New Zealand to do," Dawes told his men. "And we are going to do it successfully." Then he stepped out into the corridor to shake hands with his opposite number Colin Meads and, correctly, call heads as Mr Pring flipped a coin.

Curiously, the veteran New Zealand writer Terry McLean states that Meads won the toss, but Dawes insists that he did, advising Pring that he would decide once his team were on the field whether to kick off or choose an end to defend. The teams had been incarcerated on a lower floor for fully ninety minutes since arriving at the stadium, and the current state of the weather was unknown to them. The Lions preferred to play against the wind (unless it was gale force). Now came a little gamesmanship.

Leaving the tunnel, the captain led his men to the windward half of the pitch and told the referee that the British Isles would start the game. He thinks that kicking off should be recognized as a great tactical opportunity, one which London Welsh exploited in Seven-a-side competitions. If done well it means that the opposition has to stay rooted to the spot, while the attacking team can rush at them with momentum to jump and catch or knock possession back to team-mates. Incidentally Dawes thinks that the steepling kick-offs of today's game, admittedly aided by size-able tees, are an improvement on those of his era, when they were often casually taken.

On this day, when Meads and the All Blacks appeared they naturally made for the empty half of the pitch, thinking the Lions had done them a favour. But Dawes's stratagem had worked: he had got the end of the field that he wanted, plus the kick off. Barry John carefully lined up the ball, but as the whistle blew John Taylor nipped in to drive the ball towards the Lions' right wing – a move called by the Lions the 'wrong way' kick off. At least the opening moments would not now feature the All Blacks running amok in a high pressure offensive on the Lions' 22.

However, with Chico Hopkins replacing Edwards early on as agreed, this was the last the Lions saw of a ball for all of fifteen minutes. Although they had kicked off, the fury of New Zealand's assault in the first quarter of the match and its concomitant monopoly of possession led the tourists to rub their eyes and wonder whether Mr Pring and his touch-judges had brought a ball onto the field or whether the kick-off had been a mirage. However, despite overwhelming dominance the All Blacks did not start accumulating points, one reason almost certainly being over-eagerness. Meads was guilty of this as he sought to justify his status as captain of New Zealand for the first time. What could have been scoring passes were not given, by him and others.

A second failure on New Zealand's part had to do with selection. At twenty years of age the hugely promising wing Bryan Williams was the rising star of All Black back divisions and had been tested to the full with outings against South African opposition. On this Carisbrook occasion he was selected at centre, where John Dawes and Michael Gibson found it straightforward to close him down. As was seen during the rugby decade that followed, on the wing 'B.G' could be brilliant but was also willing to come infield to look for possession.

Not to be overlooked in the way the game unfolded was the scrupulously correct refereeing of Aucklander John Pring. His control of the Lions' victorious game against Otago at this same ground a fortnight earlier had impressed the management and now, once again, his work was proving absolutely impartial. Many of the 1971 Lions had been on previous visits Down Under which featured 'homer' referees shouting "our ball" at scrummages or dancing jigs as New Zealand kicked a penalty, so that this man was a breath of fresh air. New Zealand's administrators sought to persuade Smith and James to allow them to appoint four different referees for the Test series, and the Kiwi media frequently highlighted what they saw as an unhealthy relationship with Mr Pring in that the Lions "liked him too much". But thanks to robust lobbying by their Manager, the tourists held onto their honest broker

The battering at the All Blacks' hands lasted for almost the whole of the first half. However, before the interval arrived the tourists had moved from no-hopers to pole position. After broken play during a rare period on New Zealand's 22 Sid Going switched a quick pass to Alan Sutherland who seemed well-placed to put in a big clearing kick. No way: 'Mighty Mouse' McLauchlan hurtled through to charge down an optimistic, flatly projected strike and bundle over the line for the Lions' opening score. The try stayed unconverted, but soon New Zealand equalized when John Dawes, of all people, was ruled to have failed to roll out of the way for the ball to be rucked, and McCormick, at his third attempt, kicked an equalizing penalty. "The ball may have been wedged somewhere next to my body," admits the captain, "but if it looked as if I was deliberately staying put – well, that was not the case. Readers who have not been at the bottom of an All Black ruck should know that it approximates to being run over by a tractor, and I had simply adopted the foetal position as protection. I survived, but McCormick scored from twenty-five yards."

Nevertheless the half-time oranges tasted delicious to the Lions. They had taken their opponents' best shots. In the huddles out on the pitch, as well as among the 45,000 spectators, the chat was all about the next forty minutes: could the Lions gain the upper hand? Three-three. Everything to play for.

A number of days before the Test Doug Smith had alarmed New Zealand with another of his provocative statements aimed at the All Blacks' nervous system. Even John Dawes was never able to find out from the Manager who was being referred to when he said there was a 'weak link' whom he and Carwyn had identified in the home side's ranks: someone 'ordinary'. The nearest the captain got was an admission that this person was not one of the new caps, and had been in the British Isles with Brian Lochore's team of 1967.

Three decades on many people are convinced that it was full-back Fergie McCormick, especially in the light of the wickedly-accurate torrent of tactical kicks now unleashed upon him by Barry John. The second half would see him disintegrate as a world-class full-back. Time and time again he was drawn to one of the touchlines inside the New Zealand 22 – only to see the ball roll out of play inches from his grasp. This was crucifixion of a once-mighty talent, and McCormick never came back from the dead. He had been a victim of John's "defence through attacking kicks from behind a beaten pack", as Dawes puts it, and never played Test Rugby again.

Barry John's place kicking had not been infallible during the first half, but sixteen minutes into the second he kicked a penalty to restore the Lions' lead. Finally, as this pitched battle of a game drew near its resolution, 'the King', as he would be known from now on, punished a late tackle upon himself by young Alan McNaughton with a penalty that put the Lions two scores ahead of New Zealand with only minutes remaining. All over, that is, bar the shouting. And generous applause.

The All Blacks have never been frequent losers, especially in this period of their history. But now they overcame the lack of practice, and applauded their opponents off the field. The British Isles stopped at the tunnel to return the compliment. Then, as, flushed and happy, they rested weary limbs in their changing room, there was a knock on the door and in came Colin Meads clutching a glass of lager which he lifted to John Dawes, following up his toast with a warm handshake. Then he spent a few minutes on a bench next to Willie John McBride who had been an opponent for donkeys' years in the colours of Ireland and the Lions. Finally New Zealand's captain spoke on air to Cliff Morgan, by now a top broadcaster who was covering the tour for the BBC. Gritted the stern giant, "The Lions beat us and deserved to win. We congratulate them." Today, Dawes says, "In these pages I have been, I think fairly, critical of Colin's some-times reckless approach to the playing of the game. But on that afternoon in Dunedin he swallowed his pride and saluted my Lions. As for us, we knew that he was charged with breaking in the new generation of All Blacks who, one day, might climb the heights scaled by predecessors – a major responsibility.

"We met again in the evening, at the one and only after-the-match dinner function I can recall attending throughout the tour. It was not a noisy, or even celebratory, occasion, mainly because of a reaction. We were just drained. There was little exultation – just relief that we had held on for the win. Carwyn James spent a good deal of time locked in conversation with his opposite number Ivan Vodanovitch. I remember that the T&Ws were quite lively, sharing our pleasure at the Test victory; but we players needed our early night."

Next day brought a series of short flights on board an eleven-seater aircraft which ferried the party over the mountains to Queenstown for a couple of days' relaxation. At one stage in the flight the Lions seemed doomed to crash into a vast cliff face which, with a last-second adjustment, the pilot just avoided. Unfortunately, in this most scenic of New Zealand holiday resorts, the tourists experienced a period of non-stop rain which confined most of the party to their hotel.

"To beat the boredom," Dawes recalls, "Derek Quinnell, Mervyn Davies, John Taylor and myself hired a car and drove twenty miles or so up towards the Southern Alps. After a while we drove into a village which had a small hotel that sold beers, wine and spirits (New Zealand doesn't have pubs; its bars are part of hotels). Soon the locals turned up for their lunch-time pint; we were recognized; and from then on we didn't have to put a hand in our pockets. It was pleasant to learn from 'ordinary' New Zealanders how much our rugby was being enjoyed. The following morning, at a not-too-demanding run-out we passed the news on to the others. Then we went southwards to Invercargill, the Commonwealth's southernmost city, where Southland were beaten by 25 points to three. Alastair Biggar scored two tries, and there were three more courtesy of London Welsh by John Taylor, Merv the Swerve and myself."

There followed wins over Taranaki and New Zealand Universities (the game in which Barry John scored his wonder try) before the management sat down to select a side for the Second Test. By pencilling in his team for the First Test early on in the tour and securing the agreement of his Manager and Captain, Carwyn James had so far managed to avoid tedious and time-consuming arguments about selection. Even the injuries to his front-rank props at Christchurch simply left no alternatives to succeed McLoughlin and Carmichael except McLauchlan and Lynch. Problem – with only one solution.

No prolonged argument, then, in the Lions' selection committee about fourteen of the players who had won the day down in Otago and deserved to be retained. To the triumvirate just one change to the back division seemed necessary. It concerned the twenty-year-old John Bevan, whose rise had been meteoric. He had contributed points regularly and heavily on the left wing, and was already odds-on to break Tony O'Reilly's try-scoring record of 1959. However, both on the field and from the grandstand it was noticed that he had developed a 'snatching' habit and often seemed bent on scoring tries before he had the ball. "He also had to be in the action all the time," says Dawes, "often as an individual and not always for the greater good of the team." Out went Bevan; David Duckham got his reward for being patient, named now as left wing for the Second Test. His scoring on tour was nearly as heavy as Bevan's, and as opposed to the Rhondda youngster's confrontational game he looked for, and created, space.

Within minutes of the Lancaster Park kick-off Sid Going slipped away from a set scrum near the Lions' line and sent Burgess racing to the corner for an unconverted try. Gerald Davies replied with a long run-in to equalize, but New Zealand's half-back would not be stopped and, swept on by his pack, got the All Blacks' second score which this time was converted by McCormick's successor at full-back, Laurie Mains. Barry John kicked a penalty from thirty yards and an interval margin of two points – 6-8 – did not seem a disaster to the tourists.

But like the non-stop pressure of Dunedin the home side's attacks kept coming in the third quarter – and this time they did not fizzle out. The next score was again sparked by Going, who was tackled by JPR as he arrived at the Lions' goal line and sent what he hoped would be a scoring pass to Brian Williams. The ball appeared to go forward, but as Williams stretched out his arms for the ball he was tackled by Gerald Davies, whose action conceded a penalty try. Mains's conversion meant that in a trice 8-6 had become 13-6 and the All Blacks were on a roll whose momentum was exploited by Burgess with a second try and Mains with a penalty.

There followed one of the dozen best solo Test tries of the

twentieth century. The twenty-five year old back row forward Ian Kirkpatrick, destined before long to captain New Zealand, burst off a maul just inside the Lions' half and picked up speed and momentum as he left the visitors' forwards in his wake. Dawes recalls being in a short queue of defenders who weighed up the pros and cons of taking him on: "But he put a big hand into Edwards's face, and brushed Barry John out of the way, soon followed by me and, I think, Gerald Davies." The final tackler to be left for dead was J.P.R., in whose defence it can be said that he was somewhat dazed from an earlier collision. The big flanker finished with a flourish, crossing for a try at the corner flag on New Zealand's right which went unconverted. That was 22-8 with twenty minutes still to go, and the Lions looking down and out.

But Dawes recalls that the tourists now rallied and actually dominated the final quarter. The All Blacks' lead was highly unlikely to be overtaken, prompting New Zealand's fans to show their true feelings about the visitors' style. Generous applause greeted the scoring by Gerald Davies of his second try. Barry John could not convert it but in the closing minutes managed to drop a goal from thirty yards out. That was 12-22 and time was up. New Zealand had squared the series.

"We finished on a high," recalls John Dawes. "You have to remember that at Carisbrook we had really been whipped up front, and had never managed to dominate the match. We were able to do this at Lancaster Park for the last twenty minutes. The first thing I told Carwyn as we came off the field was that if we could carry on as we had finished here – and why not? – we would win the Third Test. Also I think our display had impressed New Zealanders, many of whom felt that we had been lucky to win the First. Now they had seen that we were able to import into Tests the free-ranging style which had brought our series of provincial victories."

These continued against Wairarapa-Bush at Masterton, where the former All Blacks skipper Brian Lochore made a surprise appearance at lock forward – keenly watched by New Zealand selectors since Peter Whiting was injured and would be unavailable for the Third Test. The Lions ran in seven tries in a 27-6 victory and were equally impressive at Napier where 25-6 was the final score against Hawke's Bay. This game, though not as violent as the Canterbury encounter, was rated as 'thoroughly disagreeable' by the tourists and their captain. As a spectacle it was redeemed by the wonderful running on the right wing of Gerald Davies. His great speed and dazzling footwork brought four tries and those who tried to defend against him probably remember to this day how much time they spent empty-handed on the deck.

The Lions were not allowed to run rampant in the two games immediately before the next Test. A record crowd of fifteen thousand was at Rugby Park, Gisborne, to see a robust challenge by Poverty Bay & East Coast XV. It took a last-minute dropped goal by Dawes to put the Lions two scores clear and finish at 18-12, while 19-12 was the final score at Eden Park against an Auckland side that had really prepared hard for the game, including viewing films of the various tour matches played by the visitors. John Dawes made yet another appearance, heading for his nineteenth game and setting a noble and tireless example to his men. For the second time running he put the result to bed, with a try set up by Edwards and converted by John. After a job well done, the tourists headed off to the Bay of Islands for some more rest and leisure before flying to Wellington for the Third Test. During the week radio news bulletins reported that Lochore was indeed being recalled by New Zealand, Richie Guy was brought in at prop and Keith Carrington was reintroduced to cover for the injured Bryan Williams.

Now, the Lions had selection problems too – or perhaps one in particular – which needed to be discussed in detail. Sid Going had been in wonderful form at Lancaster Park: always a threat, both when creating opportunities for his back row and midfield players, and in his own right. Stopping him, in truth, demanded a re-think of the Lions' defensive strategy.

From the start the tourists had fallen in with fashionable opinion concerning the use and role of flank forwards. Hence Peter Dixon and John Taylor played right and left on the sides of the scrum at Dunedin and Christchurch. Sensibly Willie John McBride had been co-opted by the three selectors, and now offered his strongly-held view that containing Burgess, and especially Going, demanded the presence of two specialist flankers, retaining Dixon on the blind side. He then put forward Fergus

Slattery's claim to be given an outing at number seven. In retrospect this may have been a little hard on John Taylor who, playing in an unfamiliar role, experienced the worst of both worlds: that is, he never got totally on top of Going, but equally was unable to give Burgess the kind of attention he would normally hand out.

James agreed with the Irishman in principle, and accepted his proposal to play Slattery at open side. However, he felt that the 22-year-old Derek Quinnell (uncapped as yet) had the physical presence to bar any break the short, stocky Going might attempt down the blind side. Also, he would give the Lions an extra jumping forward at the end of the line-out to compete on terms with Wyllie and Kirkpatrick. The giant Llanelli blind-side flanker had fully recovered from a knee problem and was raring to go. With his selection went an uncompromising message: he had to attach himself like glue to 'super Sid' and police every move made by the elusive New Zealander. Another change saw Gordon Brown brought into the second row at the expense of Delme Thomas.

One interesting reaction to the re-structured back row was that of John Taylor, definitely not a happy flanker at his omission. In his book *Decade of the Dragon* Taylor contents himself with admitting "I was naturally disappointed" at being dropped. But his captain grins and says, "That's a masterly under-statement! For a couple of days 'Bas' was not friends with anyone. On the management side none of us was too miffed, since it really showed how passionately JT felt about performances by the team."

Only when Slattery had to pull out on the Saturday morning suffering from tonsillitis was Taylor restored to favour – to give an outstanding display. In his book, incidentally, he quotes Carwyn James as telling his forwards that they had become so preoccupied with scrummaging that they were simply not wholly alert to the threat of New Zealand's half-backs. It was real, and had to be dealt with. That was the rationale behind the selection process.

Yet another fine day dawned at Wellington, where the previous two fixtures played by the Lions had been in weather that was surprisingly pleasant for New Zealand's wet and windy Capital. Again, John Pring had been given control of the match, and the Lions' mindset was comfortable as they took the pitch.

The tourists lost no time in throwing down a formidable gauntlet. Their commitment and physical effort were probably at a peak during the first thirty minutes of the game, when the All Blacks reeled before fury that New Zealand rugby has seldom experienced, before or since 1971. The scoring was opened by Barry John, whose dropped goal resulted from a brilliant sortie down the right touchline by Gerald Davies. He was tackled inside New Zealand's 22 but the rucked ball was gratefully accepted by Gibson and transferred to the stand-off half. Three-nil after only three minutes – and the Lions' appetite had been whetted.

The next score saw Gareth Edwards changing his mind after receiving line-out possession close to New Zealand's line. Instead of sending a pass to his left and the three-quarter line he turned towards the corner flag. He had chosen a risky route, since short cuts to the goal-line in this sector of the pitch are usually barred by brawny forwards, a wing, a full-back and possibly, a scrum-half's opposite number. Edwards drew at least three such defenders onto him before stopping abruptly in order not to invade the space Gerald Davies would need at the corner. The ball transfer was magical and mysterious, and the wing's dive over the line brave and decisive. Davies, in truth, had all the virtues of a deadly finisher. It is no wonder that his name regularly comes out on top in polls for the greatest wings of the twentieth century.

Nine minutes gone: eight-nil to the British Isles as John kicks the goal. All around Athletic Park people blink in disbelief. But there was more to come. Kiwi jaws would drop from dismay and chagrin.

At eighteen minutes Dawes's men struck the last of three lethal and demoralising blows. Once again the forwards were lined up on their right touchline and inside the New Zealand 22. Again the tourists' jumpers delivered quality possession which was right up Edwards's street. He headed for open country, his acceleration taking him beyond the All Blacks' back row of Kirkpatrick, Wyllie and McNaughton. Suddenly only an alarmed Bob Burgess stood between him and the opposition's goal posts. Despite the large, unfriendly hand-off that knocked him off his feet, Burgess half-checked the scrum-half's progress, and Edwards looked for support. Who should be there but His Majesty? 'King John' took a short pass and cruised beneath the crossbar for a try that he effortlessly converted.

A mere quarter of the Test match had gone by; a purple patch in the history of British rugby in the twentieth century had been witnessed by the crowd of 50,000. The short, sharp fireworks display was over and the remainder of the game turned into a war of attrition. New Zealand contrived just a single unconverted try by Laurie Mains in reply to the Lions. Ten minutes from time Burgess was taken from the field concussed, but even before his injury Meads and Co were not looking likely to get on terms. Did the Lions sit on their lead?

"You have to remember," says their captain, "that, although they were trailing, the All Blacks continued to go through their disciplines faithfully. They were (and still are) supreme at carrying out one particular pattern, which boils down to securing possession at forward; driving it; when stopped, rucking it; drive again; repeat cycle – or maybe give the backs a run. Usually this sequence eventually brings victories.

"So their traditional tactics were still being employed by Colin Meads. We had already showed in the Tests how we had learned to soak up this conventional pressure; and I suspect he and his lieutenants were unable to work out another way to take us on. However, on the other hand they were not actually playing badly, and we spent a lot of time defending. It was never the case that we expected to put an avalanche of points onto them.

"I can tell you, we were happy enough at the final whistle. 13-3, on top of 9-3, with only one Test left to play, meant that we had out-performed all our predecessors of the twentieth century. Never had they won more than a single Test and consequently there had not been a series victory either. We still had that to aim for, but even if we lost the final clash at Auckland (which we were determined not to) we would never be remembered as the 'defeated Lions of 1971'. Rather the reverse – for Colin Meads, of all people, called us 'the greatest touring team that he had played against'. Big words from a big man.

"Gerald Davies has received a fair share of compliments from me, and at this stage I want to record my pleasure at the input of three other young men who had helped Wales to her Grand Slam in Europe and were now assisting the British Isles to make history in the southern hemisphere. First and second, were the partners at half-back who positively sparkled on that afternoon in Wellington. The first impression made on spectators of Barry John was his laid-back demeanour. But not only did this cover superb skills with hands and feet; it also disguised terrific concentration and wide-angle vision which told him unerringly where the openings were.

"At scrum-half Gareth Edwards had played his game of the tour. He put not a foot wrong in this vital Third Test and, after the final whistle, was almost forgiven for his recently-developed fetish for drop-kicking at goal from anywhere in the opposition's half (usually missing). It was as if, on this day, he wanted to tell New Zealand, 'I know you don't rate me – well watch this!' He delivered two scoring passes under the noses of the All Black back row.

"I found myself reflecting how, when they had come to New Zealand with Wales two years before, he and Barry had been boys in the game. Now they were men"

The other relatively young tourist singled out for his displays by Dawes was the gangling Mervyn Davies. "I cannot resist quoting the veteran journalist Terry McLean's colourful pen-picture of our young number eight:"

> Thin as a rake, with long legs that made him look rather like a praying mantis, Melanesian-type mop of hair and a not-very-interested look. Appearances deceived. Not many internationals put as much conscientious effort into their play.

More seriously, McLean adds:

> His great height assured him of a measurable degree of superiority when the ball was thrown long at the line-out. His jump was higher and better-timed than that of Ian Kirkpatrick. He handled and tackled soundly.

Davies's captain adds, "I rated him as the second most important Lion, after Barry John. He had attributes in abundance, which were missed and caused us concern when he was obliged to drop out of a few games before the Third Test. He wasn't afraid of hard, dirty and thankless work and as a tall man – for whom getting back on his feet is a chore – he was ready and willing to go to the floor to tidy up. What did he do in the Tests? Tackle, tackle, tackle."

The Lions let their collective hair down in ceaseless partying that, says Dawes, lasted "until Monday". Early on the Sunday the party took a short flight from Wellington to Palmerston North, where they were greeted by a fleet of vintage cars, one for each player. The tourists climbed aboard to be joined by a driver plus a competitor in the early rounds to choose New Zealand's entrant for Miss World – most agreeable, thought the boys. The vehicles were driven in procession round and round the town square, to the acclaim of an army of admirers put at 25,000 strong.

A first function in their Victorian-style hotel was a meeting of the 'Sunday Club', a totally informal and random mix of team-mates who fancied a pint or two in relaxed company. Barry John recklessly agreed to play barman, a role which the Lions thought he carried out with laudable generosity. Cliff Morgan joined the party again and, not satisfied with re-christening the gathering a 'Sunday School', he presented each Lion with a tie for whose gaudy pattern he claimed to have searched New Zealand. Dawes still has his – but is reluctant to reveal how often he wears it.

The Lions trained hard to flush out their systems on the Monday morning, a large proportion of the previous day's welcoming throng turning up again to watch them at practice. James and Dawes thought the fans deserved something special to watch and devised an off-the-cuff spectacular which incorporated endless scissors moves between the players. This was played out for a full forty minutes – in which no participant dropped the ball. More thunderous applause; the British Isles were really winning over the hearts and minds of New Zealand's people.

They were not doing too badly with the media, either. New Zealand's Pressmen and broadcasters were half a decade behind the coverage common in Europe. The organization of basic Press conferences scarcely existed and, in practice, the media had to button-hole men to whom they wished to speak at the post-match unwinders held in 'sheds' beneath the grandstand. Here, as the waitresses circulated with sandwiches and shandies, reporters and men with microphones had to compete with fans for a few words with players who had been on the park that afternoon. But the fear-nothing approach of James and Smith always ensured that the Kiwi writers and interviewers got a sound-bite or two, while the tourists could be approached by the British media at any convenient times during the day.

In the Lions' camp, incidentally, there was a spicy element of subterfuge which, ultimately, enhanced TV coverage of the tour. Although the BBC had done an exclusive deal with NZBC for (black and white) coverage of the Tests, HTV, the Cardiff-based channel serving Wales, had decided this was not good enough. It sent former Wales wing Dewi Bebb and a single-camera unit to film the tour – in colour.

The significance of this was that colour TV had taken the UK by storm in 1969 and New Zealand's monochrome footage was less than attractive to viewers able to receive the new, enhanced output. However, because of the contract between NZBC and the BBC, the presence of an alien crew was not strictly legitimate. It seems that Dawes's Lions were only too ready to assist a former rugby-playing pal, and smuggled Bebb's crew and kit past the scrutiny of stewards. Their usual vantage-point might be on a terrace where heads would bob into shot and great moments might be missed. But the end-product was, literally, colourful, and vibrant.

Three provinces remained to be taken on, beginning at Palmerston North where the Lions ran in eight tries (five of them converted) in a 39-6 win which showed a relieved Carwyn James that his men's attitude and keenness for the fray remained on a high. This game, against Manawatu-Horowhenua, was memorable for John Bevan's seventeenth try of the tour which brought him level with the record set by O'Reilly twelve years before. Could he break it? He failed to score in the next match, a hard one against North Auckland (Going country) where the tourists were held to 11-5 and the ball failed to run his way. In the knowledge that he would not oust David Duckham from the Fourth Test team, the youngster was selected for his third game in a row, against Bay of Plenty, again without managing to score. Dawes thinks that when running in his try Mike Gibson left defenders a long way behind him and had time to put Bevan in: "But then, in the heat of the moment and especially in a closely-fought game – which we won 20-14 – you don't think of things like records." Perhaps Gibson preferred that his distinguished Irish predecessor's name should not be deleted from the record books; and perhaps John Bevan was happy to be a joint record holder in such august company.

And so to the Fourth Test and the clinching of an historic series victory. Earlier John Dawes recalled a certain lethargy which accompanied the approach to the game and manifested itself on the field – the *ennui* blended with *hiraeth* which Carwyn James had feared from the outset. The outcome, a 14-14 draw, was suspected by many New Zealanders to have been orchestrated by the Lions to validate their Manager's prediction back in May of a 2-1 victory in the series with one match drawn.

"Even if such things were at all feasible in a rugby match, the way the All Blacks played at Eden Park left no margin for any such jiggery-pokery," smiles John Dawes. "They had put the Third Test result behind them, and we found ourselves using the boot as we had weeks before at Carisbrook to stay in contention. Colin Meads noticed. Afterwards he grumbled, 'You've always claimed that your Lions are the ball-handlers in this series – but we did that today and all your guys did was kick!' I have to admit, he was right. But, to secure our place in history, we simply had to play winning rugby. Otherwise our mission was doomed to be less than historic."

Conditions in Auckland favoured a running game on 14 August 1971. The sky was overcast, but the playing surface at New Zealand's principal stadium was firm and the rain was forecast to stay away. The All Blacks struck first when Cottrell rounded off some intricate passing in the Lions' 22. Mains converted the try and added a penalty, to which Barry John speedily responded. Then Edwards broke into midfield from a line-out, releasing the ball in the tackle. The support forwards included Peter Dixon, who dived over for a try converted by John. Eight-eight at the break.

Eleven-eleven was the next joint landmark to be reached, with a second penalty by John and a try for the All Black Lister from a close-range line-out. Then came a strike which, arguably, would have itself proved a noble and definitive end to the tour. It resulted from poor possession at a line-out which Duckham tidied up before slinging a soaring pass to J.P.R., who was just inside New Zealand territory. The full-back gathered it, steadied himself and, perfectly poised, dropped an immense goal. As he trotted delightedly back to the Lions' half he was seen to wave towards the grandstand, where he knew that his recently-arrived parents were seated.

Some reporters were moved by the gesture, saying that he must be a very devoted son. The truth was that during the week JPR had told the T&Ws, plus anyone else who would listen, that on the tour he had scored a few tries, kicked a conversion or two, and put over some penalties. Now, before they all left for home, he felt like adding a dropped goal to complete the set – a promise that was greeted with cat-calls and general derision. Therefore, immediately the referee signalled the goal, J.P.R.'s gesture was one meant for his fellow-tourists amounting to, 'Eat your words, you guys!'

At that stage the narrow lead looked conclusive. But, ultimately, the spoils were shared when Dixon fell offside at a scrum, conceding a penalty which Mains placed. There were seven minutes left, during which John and Edwards peppered the All Blacks' posts with penalty attempts and off-target drop kicks. From the crowd there rose the sad farewell chorus 'Now is the Hour' – and indeed, it was. The British Isles tour of Australasia, 1971, ended with the final blast on John Pring's whistle. Having defeated New Zealand by two Tests to one and getting the draw at Eden Park they had achieved what no previous Lions tourists could do.

"But we hadn't given of our best in the final encounter," asserts Dawes. "On the day we lacked spark. Some of the tactical decisions made by our half-backs could have been improved upon: they both dropped for goal when scoring passes, in particular to Duckham, could have been given – that wouldn't have happened when the Test rubber stood at one-all. However, it was not just those two. The whole team lacked the urgent desire to win; it seemed to be a case of, 'Let's get this game over and then we can go home.'

"I went up to the VIP box at the close and gave a quick squeeze to Carwyn and Doug. Then, picking up a handy microphone, I thanked this particular crowd – and the whole New Zealand rugby fraternity – for the warmth with which they had treated my Lions over the last four months. What I said seemed to lift the throng around the tunnel to a fresh level of acclaim and applause which drowned me out. I settled for waving to them.

"They knew, and I knew, that history had been made."

ELEVEN

After an evening of quiet rejoicing, with newly-made friends and admirers joining the victory celebrations to wish them godspeed, the British Isles players rose early on the Sunday morning to get into the shops for some final souvenirs. Maori carvings of little mannequins with large heads and frowning faces were popular and still decorate exclusive mantelpieces around the Four Home Unions. But especially treasured are the giant scrap-books containing Press cuttings of the tourists' progress through New Zealand compiled by pupils from numerous high schools who had each 'adopted' their own Lion. Much of this memorabilia was stowed away in crates to be shipped back to Britain but, even so, there were suitcases galore to go on board the big jet which would transport the team from Auckland to Heathrow.

The reactions of conquerors and conquered were strangely similar at the end of it all. Early in these pages John Dawes admits to a sense of anti-climax and his "lack of jubilation" after a job well done. Mike Gibson, too, is on record as admitting, "Now that it has happened I feel flat. No elation. No nothing. Just flat." He could, I suppose, have added, "Drained".

The New Zealand players felt even flatter. Although they attended the end-of-tour farewell function, they sat out the speeches in an anteroom. Furthermore, wrote the veteran rugby writer Terry McLean:

> None of them turned up later to say goodbye to their guests at the airport. These were not All Black attitudes as one had known them. In the past they took their lickings and rejoiced with their opponents. They did not as a rule sulk.

But the Kiwi media put in an appearance at the airport, and their presence was welcomed by the Lions as they gave their last interviews. This was the final act of New Zealand 1971; and now the team slotted themselves, not without a squeeze, into seats which had not been designed for hulking frames like those of Mervyn Davies, Gordon Brown, Willie John McBride and the other large men. For much of the journey the tourists snoozed or talked quietly, re-living great feats of skill and resolve and also the fun and companionship that had characterized their progress from strongpoint to strongpoint in the lair of the All Blacks. The route home was west-to-east, and Dawes remembers the short break at San Francisco where he and a few of the team piled into a taxi to see sights such as Alcatraz and China Town.

His respect for his men's conduct and deportment was already profound, but they had one card still to play on the journey across the Atlantic. As the aircraft neared the Irish coast its captain left his cockpit to introduce himself to Doug Smith, offer congratulations to the team, and warn the party that a crowd of around 2,500 fans was congregating at Heathrow to greet the heroes' return – thought to be the biggest since the Beatles had come home from one of their tours. Soon Dawes recalls movement along the aisles and Lions pulling items out of the baggage compartments. Spontaneously his tourists were donning their 'number one' dress, featuring blazer, ties, and white shirts. They would show any welcoming party that Doug Smith's men were a well-drilled and properly turned out rugby squad fresh from a great mission – and not just any bunch of guys coming back from a jolly. Dawes was moved, and their gesture sticks in his memory.

As it turned out, Heathrow's public relations people had not got it quite right. On arrival the Lions were ushered away from the fans to a private lounge, and only after some delay could the players locate families and friends who were on hand to welcome loved ones, and wave to a crowd simply dying to celebrate and acclaim the victors. Somehow information was relayed to nearest and dearest that the tourists would adjourn to one of the hotels that had begun springing up around the terminals for a luncheon hosted by the Chairman of the Four Home Unions, former England International John Tallent. It was here that many joyful, and tearful, re-unions took place. Then, without further fuss or ceremony, the players dispersed to Dublin, Belfast, Edinburgh, Cardiff and the regional airports of England.

John Dawes had only the short journey to London's western suburbs to make – in the company, now, of Janette and the two children. Their father recalls how Michael was overjoyed to be hugged though Catherine may have been a bit unsure of this man whom she had not seen since the spring. For Mrs Dawes there was an element of relief built into the joyful welcome back. She had given an interview to the *Western Mail* during the tour saying that three months away was more of a strain, and seemed much longer, than she had expected.

"Sure," agrees Dawes. "I was very conscious during my absence what a load of responsibility was upon her. There was running the household single-handed and time-tabling baby sitters. Although by this stage she had perforce set aside her ambitions to sing professionally, Janette also had her own priorities. She was committed to rehearsals, as a soloist, with amateur operatic societies, which in their own way were more than comparable with the demands my rugby schedules made upon me. Not only did the tour take me out of the domestic reckoning, it had followed a winter of squad training with Wales, the travel involved in my Five Nations appearances and evenings spent training and selecting for London Welsh. This freedom and flexibility for me came partly from her willingness to make sacrifices and shoulder the running of the household. I was constantly in her debt."

Soon after his return Dawes was beginning to give thought to his future, in the game and out of it, at home and in his teaching career. He describes the period following his return from New Zealand as a kind of limbo. For the second half of August he decided to award himself a well-earned rest and re-discover his family, delaying pre-season training with London Welsh. There was also his professional career to be considered, for the teacher of chemistry was aware that the demands made by all this rugby had tested the tolerance of a headmaster whom he liked and respected. It was also a factor that, secretly, he had grown tired of laboratories and classrooms.

Fate now took a hand in the shape of Roy James, his old teacher and friend at Pengam with whom he had also played for Newbridge. That October James called in at Old Deer Park, telling Dawes over a pint of his career position at North London Polytechnic. This was an establishment enjoying status roughly between that of a university and a training college, at which James was head of PE and recreation. He mentioned a new course in which graduate students could study the principles

162

and techniques required to administrate the 'recreational centres' which were springing up all over the country at this time. It needed someone to run and control it.

'That sounds interesting,' observed Dawes.

'Well, why don't you apply,' came the reply. 'Write in.'

Dawes did, and got the job, resigning from Spring Grove school at the end of the autumn term of 1971. The new position carried director status, forty per cent of which had to do with PE, and the rest, course management. The new recruit slotted in well, coping well with the broader aspects of the work as well as minutiae such as devising time-tables and programming tutorials. He missed the camaraderie of the staff room at school, but compensations included frequent travel around the UK and in Europe to absorb new thinking in the recreational field.

Roy James acknowledged the nature of his rugby commitments and was generous in giving his recruit time off. This would become even more critical in due course when Harry Bowcott stepped down from his position as London Welsh representative on the Welsh Rugby Union, to be succeeded by John Dawes.

Now, besides the calls made upon his time by rugby football, there were also 'celebrity' occasions which ate into Dawes's time. Breweries organized high-profile congratulatory evenings at which, certainly in the London area, the Lions' captain was top of the guest list. Local education authorities were eager to hear Dawes's views on the schools system in New Zealand, in particular their PE policies. The Four Home Unions held a post-tour Dinner which was honoured by the presence of Cabinet Ministers from the Heath Government who could hardly wait to hear from returning heroes, beginning with their captain.

Because of Janette's teaching commitments in September the family had been unable to take a holiday away from London, so in the early autumn Dawes decided to start playing himself back to a decent level of fitness. No pressure to get back into the colours came from London Welsh (now under the captaincy of Tony Gray), but finally there arrived an afternoon at Old Deer Park when the Lions were well enough rested to play competitively again. A long injury list meant that Geoff Evans and Mike

Roberts had to go straight into the first XV which fought an honourable draw with visitors Newport. But it was decided that the first outings by Dawes, JPR, Gerald Davies, John Taylor and Mervyn Davies would be with the 'Dragons' (the Exiles' third XV) in mid-November. However, Dawes maintains that the touchlines of the number two pitch were where the majority of spectators chose to be that afternoon, to welcome back the first-magnitude stars who had defeated the All Blacks.

It was probably on that early-winter afternoon that the Wales coach of the day, Clive Rowlands, was buttonholed in a quiet corner of the clubhouse by Dawes and told that his Grand Slam captain of 1971 was calling it a day: there would be no more International Rugby for him. It was a decision that he had never expected would be necessary to make as long as he could run, catch and tackle. No wonder that the first reaction of Top Cat was, Why?

Dawes respected the furious motivational skills of the National Coach and to this day cannot understand why the WRU offered two men as candidates for Lions coach – Rowlands plus Carwyn James – to the Four Home Unions Tours Committee when the normal procedure was to put forward one name only. "Clive was a rough Welsh diamond," he says, "without the intellectual presence, and refinement, of Carwyn – which presumably influenced the 'old guard' of Englishmen to give him the job. So I wondered if he would treat coldly anyone perceived to be in the James camp. I was also aware of Clive's sadness at never having been picked to play by the Barbarians. No doubt his success as Manager of the Lions who beat Australia in 1989 cheered him up no end. But: in 1971, was Carwyn the better choice? All I can say is that our results proved that no-one could have improved upon his record."

Dawes continues, "As it turned out I needn't have worried. Clive questioned me hard without hectoring me. All I could enlighten him about was my mind-set and the absence of enthusiasm or appetite to play more International Rugby. In the end he nodded and told me that, very reluctantly, he would accept my decision. He thanked me for my contribution to Welsh rugby over the last decade or so and also expressed his gratitude at being first to be told of my exit from contention – giving him plenty of time to think about a successor to the Wales captaincy." The news was released to the media on 17 November 1971. It could be said that Dawes had gone out at the top.

For both London Welsh and Wales there were gaps to be filled as the older generation began to follow Dawes's example, curtail their responsibilities and leave the game's top level. No cause for alarm at Old Deer Park; newcomers arrived. Keith Hughes (Llanelli G.S. and Cambridge University) came to Westminster Hospital to further his medical studies and used outings at Old Deer Park to attract the attention of the 'Big Five' and make a sprinkling of International appearances. Another welcome recruit was the versatile Cardiff H.S. and Cambridge product, Tony Pender who could play back row or as a speedy prop. Alan Richards was a young wing who began delivering a heap of tries each season in the early seventies, while Jeff Young added to his haul of Welsh caps after joining London Welsh's pack. John Vaughan, too, was a newcomer of whom the club thought highly.

Despite the myriad other commitments and his late start to the season John Dawes still managed to make twenty-five appearances for the Exiles under Gray, going in for six tries. By April the team had run up thirty-two victories, suffering just eight defeats, for a highly satisfactory 79.3% success rate. London Welsh became *Western Mail* champions of Wales and super-league winners in addition to capturing the coveted *Sunday Telegraph* pennant. The winning ratio dropped under John Taylor in 1972-73 to 66.3%, with thirteen defeats suffered as the team addressed its re-structuring.

Before the opening of that season, and what was to be his last active winter at Old Deer Park, Dawes went with the Exiles – accompanied this time by Janette – on a happy-go-lucky visit to Sri Lanka (then Ceylon). The club had visited Hong Kong, South Korea and California on its Centenary world tour, and would subsequently play in Malaysia, Singapore and the United States. But Ceylon was a mis-match.

The visitors played six matches on the island, and at first John Dawes and his team-mates thought that nobody was going to turn up to watch them in their first game against a Ceylon XV at leafy Havelock Park, Colombo (where the returning British Isles side of 1950 had played a courtesy game). With five minutes to go before kick-off there was practically no-one on the terraces.

Then, suddenly, colourful, smiling fans began literally dropping out of the palm trees surrounding the stadium to applaud the visitors onto the pitch.

"However, sadly, we were far too strong for the Ceylon Select XV in the opener," recalls Dawes, "which was won by seventy points to three. Thereafter we passed 100 points in three games, won one 96-3 and finished back in Colombo with a 66-3 result. We conceded only twenty-points, including just two tries."

Only hours after their return to the UK London Welsh were travelling westwards into Wales to open Llanelli's centenary season celebrations at Stradey Park, a mission which they found flattering but on the day beyond them. The glory-hungry Scarlets scattered Taylor's side to the winds and delighted 12,000 supporters with a 31-0 victory. "Jet lag," gritted John Taylor afterwards, and people commented that 'Bas' was going to find it hard to follow John Dawes and Tony Gray. But the following Saturday brought a 48-9 demolition of Saracens at the Athletic Ground, and through the remainder of the season the words of critics often had to be eaten.

Dawes accepted an invitation from Crawshays Welsh to go on the West Country tour of September 1972, where he was put down by a late tackle and broke a collar bone – that most painful of injuries since the bone cannot be stabilized to mend. Nevertheless, by the end of the London Welsh winter he had still managed to make twenty-five appearances for the club. It was half way through this swan-song season that a career pinnacle was scaled. Not with Newbridge or London Welsh. Not with Wales or even the British Isles. Rather, it was the farewell match which the Barbarians used to play against major touring sides at the end of their visits to Britain. At the beginning of this book Dawes recalls his exhilaration at the winning display given by the last team he captained.

The tradition had been established back in 1948 when the Third Wallabies' need for funding was met by a Barbarians side which beat them 9-6 in front of a capacity crowd of 46,000 at the post-War, bomb-damaged Cardiff Arms Park. Once or twice subsequent matches had been staged at Twickenham, and usually touring sides had edged their way to victory (a notable exception being the 6-0 defeat – the only one – of Avril Malan's Springboks in 1961). But Cardiff was where the fixture belonged, and now Ian Kirkpatrick's All Blacks would be on show, fresh from a draw in Dublin after defeating the other three Home Countries. Even more strongly than their desire to see the Baa-Baas win was the crowd's eagerness to see the All Blacks humbled. They were tourists whose mien was surly and sinister, wearing black bandit-style sombreros above frowning faces. Since their early defeat at Stradey Park (as Llanelli's Centenary season gathered triumphal momentum) the Seventh All Blacks had marched unbeaten through to 27 January 1973 and the farewell match at Cardiff Arms Park. Making few friends.

Clearly, in the minds of the Barbarians' selectors was a dramatic scenario featuring a frolic re-uniting of the 1971 Lions. To that end they asked Doug Smith, Carwyn James and John Dawes each to pencil in a Barbarians' XV that would reflect this aim. Originally the XVs offered for consideration by each member of the triumvirate abided by this criterion (with the exception of choosing as token uncapped player the Cambridge University lock Bob Wilkinson, who had played well for the Light Blues early in the tour against New Zealand). The late withdrawal of Gerald Davies triggered a telephone call by the Barbarians' secretary Geoffrey Windsor-Lewis to Old Deer Park, a re-shuffle of the back line and the inspired selection of John Dawes to captain the side. On that same Saturday, 27 January 1973, his club was to play London Scottish in a vital cup-tie, and the Exiles showed great magnanimity in releasing their erstwhile skipper to join the Baa Baas' squad preparing in Penarth for the big game. Mervyn Davies went down with a heavy cold and Barry John was now in retirement, so that the team which eventually took the field looked like this: JPR; Duckham, Dawes (capt), Gibson, Bevan; Bennett, Edwards; McLoughlin, Pullin, Carmichael; McBride, Wilkinson; David, Slattery, Quinnell.

New Zealand selected the side which had just drawn with Ireland, leaving out only Sutherland and Norton: Karam; Williams, Robertson, Hurst, Batty; Burgess, Going; G. Whiting, Urlich, Lambert; MacDonald, P. Whiting; Scown, Wyllie, Kirkpatrick (capt). In control was to be France's Georges Domerq, who knew a healthy amount about refereeing the advantage law.

Once in charge of the team Dawes decided that it would be a good idea to invite Carwyn James back to address the twelve Lions (plus Bennett, Wilkinson and David) and give his team's morale a boost on the afternoon before the game. The Barbarians' old guard took umbrage at this suggestion, and vetoed it; the club's tradition was to play it the old-fashioned way without the need for pep-talks by coaches. James's initial response was to keep his distance, perhaps out of embarrassment – which did not suit the Dawes book. He invited his coach of 1971 to pay an 'unofficial' visit to the Baa Baas' team room on the Saturday morning, from which alick-ados were banned. Carwyn attended, and delivered words that made the team's hair curl. It was quietly inspirational stuff; but the main detail Dawes recalls – vividly – was the coach's final words, addressed to the relatively inexperienced Phil Bennett, Barry John's successor. Said he, "Phil, don't waste any time. Soon as you like – take them on!" Which was, as it turned out, prophetic advice.

The January day was kind, the atmosphere at the National Ground was expectant, and there had been an agreement, albeit tacit, that the tourists would loosen the chains on their sombre style to match the Barbarian ethic of an uninhibited handling game. This meant that, although they would be unwilling to aban-don their essential power game up front, New Zealand's backs were cleared to run the ball and take exciting risks.

The ingredients, then, were all present and the banquet served up was fit for the gods of rugby. The video of a great match commemorates a superb display of skills by every one of the thirty players involved (thirty-one when Colling replaced Going). Dawes has spoken earlier of the pride and exhilaration he felt at his men's display, and the perfection of their support play and handling. They began firing on all cylinders just two minutes after kick-off. Phil Bennett had taken Carwyn James's advice to heart, and detonated a series of extravagant side-steps past three All Black forwards who were set to exert pressure within the Barbarians' 22. Next came the near decapitation of JPR as he linked and fed Pullin. With Edwards hovering behind, Dawes bore the movement on with the subtlest of dummies and a pass to David, who rode the tackle and found Quinnell's large hands ready for his slung transfer. All the while Edwards had been steadily accelerating, and now he reached top speed to cut out a pass meant for John Bevan, sprint the remaining yardage, and dive in close to the corner flag. "What a score!" exclaimed Cliff Morgan commentating on BBC television. It was curtain-up on a command performance, and a try that has probably been played and re-played on TV and home videos millions of times.

New Zealand found it impossible to get quickly back into the game, looking jittery and uncertain. Worse was to come as Bennett first kicked a penalty and then converted a try by Slattery. John Bevan was next to hurtle over the All Blacks' line and the interval was reached with the tourists' trailing by an incredible seventeen points to nil – shades of Wellington, 1971. Then, at last, Kirkpatrick's men found a second wind. Karam's penalty was followed by the first of Grant Batty's tries after Bryan Williams came in from his wing. When Batty crossed again, his side was back in contention at 11-17 and poised to draw level. At this stage, Dawes remembers a detail overlooked in many accounts of the game: "For some unaccountable reason the accomplished New Zealand skipper Ian Kirkpatrick put down a pass near our posts. Had he held on and scored a try, a straightforward conversion would have tied the game at 17-17 and we could have found ourselves fighting to survive."

The final quarter of an hour, then, was reached with New Zealand still within striking distance. Some calming words to his men from the Baa Baas' captain at this stage were probably among the most valuable he ever spoke on the field, encouraging them to stick to their guns and keep moving the ball. Thus it was that Cardiff Arms Park was to witness a climax that featured one of the all-time great sequences of combined play, different from the single-phase opener but in the same league of excellence. Nigel Starmer-Smith describes it in his book *The Barbarians*:

> Duckham counter-attacked, running and jinking diagonally upfield at full speed leaving the All Blacks trailing in his wake like some bewildered sheep. Quinnell, as ever, was in close support. Dawes continued the move, Williams took it further, then Gibson dodged a tackle and fed Slattery; finally, a combination of brilliant support play by men from all four Home Countries was completed by JPR, who hurled himself over in the right-hand corner for a decisive try converted by Bennett for 23-11. The capacity crowd entered a seventh heaven.

Give or take the odd South African or Wallaby, Dawes could reflect quietly on a record against New Zealand opposition that was second to none. In 1967 he was in the East Wales side that held Brian Lochore's team to a 3-3 draw before playing in a Wales touring side which went down to New Zealand 33-12 at Auckland. Then came the 1971 Lions tour with its Test series victory; and now he had master-minded victory over an All Black side by – to be frank – a scratch team. No other British player could lay claim to such a track record.

At the end of the season John Dawes informed London Welsh RFC that he was following his retirement from the international game by opting out of club rugby. He would continue, in the short term, as the Exiles' club coach, preaching his personal gospel to the players; but Old Deer Park would see no more of that unique midfield generalship which identified opportunities and spread the club's basic game to the wide open spaces. To watch, the Exiles were still good value; but supporters had to re-learn lessons about how to lose graciously.

Consider, then, the mind-set of a man who has moved along rugby football's Himalayas and conquered their Everest. How can one possibly build on, and enhance, a career record of such quality? True, another mighty peak awaited an assault by the British in 1974; but there was no way John Dawes could be considered for, or would consider, a 22-match tour of South Africa and its heavyweight opposition at the advanced age of 34.

But he had by no means waved goodbye to rugby, and the next career moves open to him were crystallising in his forward planning. It is true to say that, in the old amateur days, the work-load of administrators was heavier than that of players. While the latter simply had to turn up at the right time to practise or play, running a club meant a huge investment of time and different kinds of decision-making. This Dawes was prepared to be part of, willingly, for a couple of years. But a next, major, step was about to be taken. On the grapevine came the message that Clive Rowlands would soon step down as Welsh coach, and in due course he announced that the 1974 Five Nations campaign would be his last in charge of Wales.

Beginning with the handling of the Argentine tour, his had been a good six years, during which the Welsh Rugby Union's acceptance of change and new ways of doing things had yielded generous dividends. But, in different ways, the last three seasons were unsatisfactory by the high standards of Top Cat. Firstly, the 1972 tournament was marred, and uncompleted, as a result of decisions by Scotland and Wales not to play Ireland in Dublin because of increased violence in Ulster and possible repercussions in the Republic. As a result, Ireland were deprived of valuable gate money; and, moreover, since they won both their away matches at Colombes and Twickenham, could have been dreaming of a Triple Crown and even a Grand Slam. But the Welsh also had cause for regret, too, having won all three games they played – one short of a back-to-back Grand Slam.

The following year produced a freak final table after all five nations won their home games and lost the away ones. A 'quintuple tie' was how some described it; but the title was awarded to the Scots by dint of their scoring the most match points. Then, in 1974, Ireland did finish on top, though Wales could have shaded them had the draw in Dublin been turned into a win. However, Rowlands's period in charge had shown how creative coaching could pay off, and the WRU duly invited invitations from qualified candidates to succeed him as national team coach. For Dawes the post seemed to be a natural progression and a challenge which he could meet, if not immediately, then after Carwyn James had done a stint. He would have a go.

His application to be considered was among a number received by the WRU's coaching committee, which predictably included Carwyn James (and also David Harries, Dawes's Newbridge pal). But, considering that in James and Dawes the list of applicants contained, arguably, the best coaches of the day in both Wales and England, the job of narrowing the field down to a short-list of two was straightforward. The sub-committee's recommendation about the best of the bunch would no doubt be accepted by the general committee after its members had studied the case for each man.

While pleased to be short-listed, Dawes thought James was the likely lad – until he found out, many months later, about the stringent conditions which the former Lions coach had set out in a memo accompanying his application. It proposed that autocratic powers should be conferred upon Clive Rowlands's successor (i.e., himself). If he was appointed he would wish to be a supremo who had the last word on the selection and preparation of the national team. Alas for him, he found himself ahead of his time. What is taken for granted in 2005 was revolutionary talk in the third quarter of the twentieth century, when a 'Big Five' selection committee (at that stage comprising Cliff Jones, Rees Stephens, Keith Rowlands, Clive Rowlands and whoever was National Coach) were the unit which watched, assessed and finally chose players to represent the nation. Like any self-respecting coach of the twenty-first century, James would have been obliged to put in place a group of advisers to help him identify candidates for caps, and mention of this might have eased the impact of his proposals. As it was, they went a bridge too far. Dawes got the post. James licked his wounds – and found that the media were only too glad to take him on board. And they paid fees.

Still more travel and other demands upon his time were the new loads which had to be borne by the successful candidate. Around about this time, too, Dawes was sitting on the RFU's coaching advisory panel and taking time off to prepare London Counties for the high-profile games they played periodically. All this activity was strictly not compatible with his work at the North London Poly to which, not without some reluctance, he tendered his resignation in order to work instead for a property developer called John Rendall. The job gave him independence, plus a car, and the freedom to determine his own timetable. However, far from the hanging up of his boots, the pace of coaching which he set himself was, if anything, accelerating rather than slowing down.

TWELVE

The Welsh victory of 1971 in Paris came at the end – and possibly caused the end – of a period of French dominance in Europe. Despite the continued availability of Villepreux, Lux, Dauga and Spanghero, and the emergence of such as Maso, Skrela and Fouroux, France spent some seasons at or near the bottom of the Five Nations table. The ultimate indignity was the 1975 trip to Parc des Princes by a Welsh side with a new captain and six new caps. Five tries, the highest number ever by registered by Wales in Paris, figured in the visitors' 25-10 winning score-line, helping to bring two wins in four years.

Now, the French were spitting blood. Just as they had thought, after their successes of the sixties, that they were now major players on the European scene, here were these wretched Celts cutting reputations to shreds and bursting defences at will. No wonder the FFI supremo of the day, Albert Ferrasse, called for sterner measures and a tougher approach. Suddenly the tearaway Jean-Pierre Rives, man mountain Gerard Cholley, Robert Paparemborde and the immense Jean-Pierre Bastiat were new flavours of the decade. Their presence in the second half of the seventies meant that the Third Golden Era of Wales, with its Grand Slams, needed tenacity and resolve. It was dented once by a *Grand Chelem* for the French plus their 14-13 Paris win of 1979 which denied Wales a fourth Grand Slam of the decade.

Sometimes the battles for supremacy in Paris and Cardiff were little short of barbaric. In his book *Price of Wales* Pontypool's Graham Price has recalled the unbridled ferocity which he experienced – and responded to – in the front row:

> At the first scrum Cholley tried a bit of gouging... So I bit his thumb as hard as I could... Cholley took reprisal. In went his fingers at a maul, and I felt his nails scratching hard at my eyeballs. It was murderous. By his sheer physical size Cholley could do such things and defy you to do anything back at him... I did not go to the dinner that night because I was blinded. I had to be driven home and helped to bed.

173

Under Rives's captaincy such brutality was methodically eliminated. Neverthless, for the second half of the nineteen seventies
Wales was the team everybody wanted to beat. The men in red
had to battle their way through the Five Nations fixtures for the
full eighty minutes before opponents gave best. This is well illus-
trated by the four winning scores of the 1978 Slam: 9-6 (v
England), 22-14 (v Scotland), 20-16 (v Ireland) and 16-7 (v
France). Such margins meant that no laurels could be rested
upon for a moment. Not a runaway victory was to be seen.

There were, of course, disappointments, none greater than the
defeat by New Zealand in the WRU Centenary Test. Yet as the
seventies ended, with a fourth Triple Crown in successive
seasons, the National Coach could reflect with satisfaction on the
impact he had made. But, back at the start of his reign in 1975,
he had known that Clive Rowlands's act was a tough one to
follow. Where should he begin?

First there was the problem of where the newcomer should be
based. Clive Rowlands had operated from Cwmtwrch in the
Swansea Valley (*Upper* Cwmtwrch, as he once insisted to the
Princess Royal) which was centrally located in the South Wales
rugby hot-bed and less than an hour's drive from Cardiff Arms
Park. There was a lobby on the WRU's General Committee which
felt that John Dawes's headquarters, too, should be in Cardiff. By
now, however, his roots in western London were firm, and he
could argue that he had his own power-base at Old Deer Park
with its strong complement of top-flight Welsh Internationals. He
won the argument to stay put, although it meant taking on board
endless hours driving the M4 (by now complete from Middlesex
to Newport). As often as not his passengers would include key
players such as Mervyn Davies, JPR and Gerald Davies, and their
informal conversations kept him well primed about the mood and
morale of his squads. In these early days he would be in and out
of Wales perhaps three or four times a week, either for meetings
or for the vital groundwork of talent spotting at big club games.

Next was the matter of allies and confidants, who included the
'Big Five', of whom he was a *de facto* member. Dawes names his
predecessor Clive Rowlands as a sturdy giver of support, along
with the latter's namesake Keith (destined to become in due
course one of the game's most powerful figures as Secretary of the

International Rugby Board, not to mention succeeding Sir Tasker Watkins as WRU President in 2004). Other selectors who now worked with him included the former Llanelli lock forward Rhys Williams, Rod Morgan, a high-ranking police officer who presented a dour front to the outside world, and later the fiery Jack Young. The Chairman at this time was Cliff Jones, a brilliant stand-off half in the immediate pre-War years whom Dawes recalls as an enigma – but one who shouldered the responsibility of announcing selected teams to the media and fielding awkward questions. Doubtless influenced by his good friend J.B.G. Thomas he conscientiously made himself available for interview to journalists from the *Western Mail,* for example and the BBC's *Good Morning Wales.* This meant that a grateful National Coach was not shackled until the early hours before being able to depart along the M4.

In the mid-Seventies meetings took place close to Cardiff Arms Park at the Angel Hotel, where two to two-and-a-half hours' debate were followed by dinner at which less formal chat continued. When phase one of the then new stadium made rooms available, the selectors altered their meeting place to the Air Space Lounge overlooking Cardiff RFC's ground.

The selectorial agenda comprised the choice of a team for the next match, preceded by discussion and in-depth reports from members on the games they had attended and the players whom they had watched. Selectors' commitments were worked out and submitted by the National Coach with the object of securing maximum critical input; that is, for Saturday matches one or two assessors would be detailed for the top fixture with a single selector at three other games (John Dawes could often monitor form displayed by his London Welshmen). Midweek activity was a little more random, with selectors free to go where they chose. Broadly, this was the routine worked out by Clive Rowlands, which his successor now found satisfactory. The selectors would be advised by Dawes which men, and their current form, the National Coach wanted to know about.

Players bidding for selection, and hopeful outsiders, were on their mettle knowing that one of the 'Big Five' was in the grandstand. Sometimes they would be chagrined to know that a misdemeanour or a poor on-field judgement had been noted by these spectators. Dawes remembers meeting Tony Faulkner after a Pontypool game and drawing the burly prop's attention to a lapse of discipline on his part. "Damn!" was 'Charlie's' response. "Damn. I just knew that you'd have spotted that!"

"I found this monitoring business pretty hard," recalls Dawes. "Harry Bowcott had warned me that you had to concentrate very, very hard on the man under observation. What can happen is that you get carried away by the ebb and flow of the game, and suddenly have to admit to yourself that you've lost sight of him. It's then that you have to remember that you're not there to enjoy the match; you have a job to do. But at the end of the day creative spectating could give you food for thought to share with a player and made for a meaningful exchange of views with him.

"What were we looking for? The International player, or a potential one, is marked out by a number of characteristics. His skills-level is higher, he is fitter throughout a game, his strength is well above average, and his attitude or hunger for excellence is stronger. Also, whether we are talking about a prop or a full-back, it should become clear that your man is thinking and reacting more positively than others to what is going on around him. These things tended to reveal themselves positively, and defined the selectorial process.

"And that was absolutely vital. Our aim as a group was to agree upon a long-list of outstanding players by mid October. We would then concentrate for a couple of months on this elite, before feeling able by Christmas to narrow our choices down to a squad capable of competing well in the Five Nations tournament."

Dawes cannot remember major arguments or stalemates in selection. There was not even an occasion during his time in office when a vote was necessary: "I grew to trust my four colleagues implicitly and to accept their opinions, while trying to be flexible myself. Sometimes I might admit to a slight uncertainty about a certain selection, but if a couple of the others felt strongly about a certain player's inclusion I would be willing to back down. Our meetings' atmosphere, in other words, was cordial."

There was one figure in the WRU whose counsel, it is clear, Dawes valued equally with that of his fellow selectors. Since August 1967 Ray Williams had been the (paid) Coaching

Organiser to the Welsh Rugby Union, the first man in the wide world of rugby to hold such an office. A native of Wrexham, his track record included many games for Northampton RFC and, most recently, a post as senior representative of the Central Council for Physical Recreation for the West Midlands specializing in rugby. He had also assisted the RFU, sitting on their coaching advisory panel. In the bracing company of men like Ian Beer, Jeff Butterfield and Mark Sugden he attended discussions at which elements of the rugby game were taken apart and then put back together in the shape of a manual and coaching pamphlets. He found the experience exhilarating.

This was the legacy he brought back into Wales where, before long, he was winning over the most reactionary clubs to his ways of thinking and finding time to assist the new National Coach. Although some die-hard members of the WRU found it hard to accept the presence of a track-suited 'professional' with the National Coach at squad sessions, the charm and palpable dynamic of Ray Williams put their doubts to flight. He can claim to have modernised rugby-speak, introducing crisp new phraseology which included 'ruck', 'the gain line' and the 'QP [quality possession] Factor'.

"Ray was definitely a man before his time," is Dawes' verdict. "I was fortunate in having at least as much practical contact with him as with my fellow selectors. At squad sessions we would vary our roles, one of us working with the forwards while the other oversaw the backs. Afterwards Ray would participate in sharp, no-nonsense exchanges of views with our players. It was great to have him on strength."

And so the Welsh knuckled down to shaping a side to contest the Five Nations tournament. There were autumn commitments to be met, stemming from the new Four Home Unions' initiative of constructive contact with rugby's 'evolving nations'. Japan had been in Wales the previous winter, losing four of their five games and going down 62-14 in the single Test. With a grin, Dawes recalls their dismay on encountering long grass for their game with East Glamorgan at Penygraig, which didn't favour the playing style of light-weight, fast-moving tourists.

Now, in late 1974, Tonga were the visitors, coming off a recent victory over the Wallabies. Like the Japanese they could manage only a single win, over East Wales at Cardiff. They were notable for a somewhat scatter-brained approach to matches and, sadly, for reckless head-high tackles which did not endear them to spectators. But they held Wales to 7-26 at Cardiff Arms Park before a 28,000 crowd – and could always drown their sorrows with deep-chested choral singing after their matches.

Dawes and his Welsh hopefuls were brought down to earth with a thud in late November, when the All Blacks under Andy Leslie called in at Cardiff following a short tour of Ireland in celebration of the IRU's Centenary, where they had won six games on the trot including a Test in Dublin. Though fielding a sprinkling of the unbeaten Lions of 1974 (in South Africa) the Welsh could not master New Zealand's traditionally powerful pack in what was an 'unofficial' match for which no caps were awarded; Ian Kirkpatrick scored the game's only try, Karam added eight points with the boot, while Bennett kicked the home side's penalty. Dawes admitted afterwards, "We have to admit that New Zealand were the better team. But be patient; you will see progress and achievement in the Welsh side by next March."

An intriguing sub-plot was emerging as the year neared its end. Although Phil Bennett's contribution to the British Isles' successes in South Africa had been immense, it was clear that back in Wales he faced competition for the number ten jersey. Aberavon's John Bevan, who played in contact lenses, had won selection against Tonga (while the summer's Lions enjoyed a break from the game) and also against New Zealand at centre when Roy Bergiers was injured. The All Blacks' final match was at Twickenham against a Barbarians XV containing five Welshmen, one of whom was Bevan. Mervyn Davies scored the try which gave the Baa Baas a draw.

It is clear that for a major period at the outset of his job Dawes believed that Bevan was the better man for the style he wished Wales to play. He says, "There are two kinds of stand-off half. Bevan was in one category; his awareness of opportunities and what was 'on' meant that match-winners in the back division saw plenty of the ball in space, rewarding their half-backs with tries like the hat trick J.J. Williams was to score against Australia in 1975.

"In contrast Benny's game was always instinctive, reacting like lightning to the ghost of a chance to make breaks himself. It was noticeable too that he disliked being on the bench with the prospect of having to take the field as a replacement. When Bevan was injured at Murrayfield, Phil came on to play in a wholly unconvincing mood. His captain on the day, Mervyn Davies, confided to me that he even declined a request to take a penalty kick at goal. So the selectors took the view that, rather than being named as a replacement, he should be left out of the squad completely. This, of course, was drastic thinking that would lead to a rather regrettable saga early in 1976.

So, in January 1975 Bevan got the nod for Paris, winning a first cap along with five other debutants who would serve Wales nobly in the coming years. As if six such men were not enough, the team had a new captain – Mervyn Davies – by now the holder of thirty-two Test caps but not yet hailed as a leader of teams. The man himself has written:

> Although I knew what was coming [from John Dawes] it was still a startling and moving experience actually to read the word 'captain' after my name in the newspapers... my model would be Willie John McBride, a non-stop worker whose own play was a constant example to others. I decided too that, also like McBride, I would cultivate a certain detachment and command status to underwrite my authority... However I was also tormented by doubts which lasted until the kick-off.

The National Coach, however, had every confidence in 'Swerve'. Dawes had decided that Gareth Edwards should be relieved of captaincy responsibility, which would allow him better to remember that there were team-mates, such as Gerald Davies, who like himself could win matches. In his role, there needed to be a senior figure in charge whom everyone would respect and obey. Mervyn Davies harboured doubts, but in his side were men who could banish them.

The most eye-catching choice was that of a front row containing the three Pontypool hard men Bobby Windsor (hooker), plus newcomers Graham Price and Tony Faulkner. A fourth player from the club, the experienced Terry Cobner, was picked at flank forward along with another debutant in Trevor Evans. At centre the newcomers were Ray Gravell of Llanelli and Bridgend's Steve Fenwick. The media found the selection bizarre and high-risk, especially for a major examination in the French capital. But Dawes dismisses their alarm: "A storm in a tea-cup and very much a media thing. As selectors, we were confident that the new men would show the steel necessary at Parc des Princes. And my senior players, who'd been in Paris in 1971 and 1973, knew the priority: the French had to be stopped from playing their tricks. That is not to say that all the boys were calm before kick off – when no-one was more jittery than Ray Gravell.

"After I had given my final words of encouragement and left the changing room, I am told that Grav vanished into the toilet, or the *ty bach* as he would put it, where he sat for a quarter of an hour quietly singing to himself songs by the inspirational folk entertainer Dafydd Iwan. In the end his club-mate Derek Quinnell, a replacement, had to tip-toe to the door and instruct Ray to come out to do battle. He finally emerged to contribute a big game for us next to the unflappable Steve Fenwick. Grav may have been akin to a cat on a hot tin roof, but he was to become a major presence in the midfield with 'soft' hands that dropped passes once in a blue moon."

Although Dawes himself was not directly involved, London Welsh had crossed swords with Pontypool occasionally over the Gwent side's uncompromising forward play. But on this day at Parc des Princes the PFR (Pontypool Front Row) were just what was wanted, wading into the French from the kick-off and brandishing an eighty-minute whip-hand that never permitted Vacqerin, Paco and Azarete to deliver smooth possession to their menacing back line. The Welsh attackers, too, were rampant, with Gerald Davies, Cobner, Edwards and Fenwick getting breath-taking tries and the last-named contributing five points with the boot.

But the *pièce de resistance* was the fifth Welsh try. France's Gourdon had scored a try and Taffary two penalties, and play was fast and furious around the visitors' 22 as the French strove to save the game. Suddenly they spilled possession, allowing Graham Price to boot the ball upfield and pursue it with J.J. Williams close at hand. The latter forced a handling error from Lux, and Price was up with the play to seize the ball and roar in for a try that had come seventy-five yards and sealed a magnificent 25-10 victory.

The National Coach was in no doubt about the immense quality of the try and its value: "It was scored in injury time, and put the match out of France's reach. JJ deserves praise for getting across from his wing to the right touchline, but even that pales as a feat compared with Pricey's effort. I think it was momentous. He was twenty-one; and just to have survived in the Paris cauldron was remarkable, let alone finding the stamina to get a try like that. It was one of the plus-points which vindicated our selection, and Graham was set to spend nearly a decade anchoring the Welsh scrum in his tight-head position."

At Cardiff England were put down by 20-4, but after leading 16-0 at the break the Welsh were criticized for not hammering home their advantage and allowing the visitors to share the second half scoring: "We seemed to run out of steam," was the Dawes verdict. Nevertheless he made just one change for the March visit to Edinburgh, forced on him by Geoff Wheel's injury, introducing Mike Roberts in the second row. A world record crowd of 104,000 crammed Murrayfield on St David's Day, to see a clash in which the Scots stood up to be counted against the pace-makers of world rugby, winning by twelve points to ten. For Wales it was a performance to forget, undermined by the dislocation of John Bevan's shoulder which forced his replacement by Bennett. The Llanelli man never got into the game: rugby historian John Billot described his performance as "the worst game of his life".

An estimated 40,000 Welsh camp followers saw a disjointed effort by the Championship leaders, but one which could have been redeemed by Allan Martin's last ditch penalty attempt that drifted past a post and enabled Scotland to clear just before the final whistle. "Our senior players made too many elementary errors," commented Dawes tersely.

With France, Scotland and England falling by the wayside the Championship title was up for grabs when Ireland came to Cardiff for the last match of the Five Nations games. McBride, McLoughlin and Kennedy would be making their final International appearances and were out for blood-letting. Phil Bennett had been given another chance at stand-off for Wales, and now won total redemption for unleashing a back division which ran in four tries against the elderly visitors. Tony

Faulkner (almost as ancient as the Irish) scored another while Bennett contributed three conversions plus a couple of penalty goals in Wales's biggest home win over Ireland which secured her ninth outright Championship title. Dawes had warned that the best of his side "would not be seen until March". He must have had meant 15 March, not St David's Day.

But, at the end of a first season in charge, the new National Coach could look back with satisfaction. The Welsh Brewers' *Rugby Annual for Wales* congratulated the team for its fourteen tries in the Five Nations which contributed to a post-War record of eighty-seven points, adding "Nominated as Welsh 'Player of the Year' Mervyn Davies enjoyed a masterful and memorable season in which his consistent standard was better than anything he has produced previously."

There was to be no resting on laurels, and in the late summer of 1975 the selectors named twenty-five men to play in Hong Kong and Japan with what Dawes called a 'developing' side. Tongues wagged when it was learned that the party would be managed by a former lock forward called Les Spence, uncapped but a man who had made 267 appearances for Cardiff in the pre-War years. The intriguing aspect of his appointment was that he had been captured and interned by the Japanese during the Far East war, where he endured cruelty and a starvation diet for nearly two years. When challenged about his readiness to visit Tokyo and fraternize with Nippon's rugby hierarchy he responded, "There comes a time when you must forgive if not forget."

John Dawes remembers Spence as a man with charm and a dry sense of humour. After a Hong Kong Colony XV had been brushed aside 57-3, the tourists flew to Tokyo and booked in at a big central hotel. Its windows had vertical sun-blinds and many of them looked out on a red-brick multi-storey car-park which was only yards from the hotel in the densely crowded Japanese capital. After half an hour Dawes decided to visit the manager to see if he was comfortable. He found him pacing up and down his room, clearly somewhat distressed.

"I can't stay here," he said.

"Why not?" asked the concerned Dawes.

"It reminds me of my days as a POW in a cell guarded by

Japanese soldiers," said Spence, gesturing at the blinds, which evidently bore a resemblance to iron bars, and the red-brick façade outside which looked like the walls of a compound.

"We'll get you moved," said the Coach. "Come on, now."

Spence made for the door, where he abruptly came to a halt.

"No," he gritted. "No. I must tough it out. I'll stay put."

A small incident, Dawes recalls, but one that vividly brought home to him, and the senior members of the party, the suffering that Allied prisoners had experienced at the hands of an earlier generation of Japanese. The young Welshmen thought that a modicum of revenge would be highly desirable. The Spence composure had evidently recovered itself when he took his players for introduction to the Japan RU's hierarchy dominated by Shiguru ('Shiggy') Konno, who had been his country's tour manager in Wales in 1973. Konno named his committee before asking Spence to introduce his players. "My coach will do that," was the response. "This, gentlemen, is Jack Daw."

"Rather like 2004, when a Wales side full of second-stringers and new recruits went down to South Africa and her heavyweight pack of human bulldozers, Shiggy's men lacked the physique to give the visitors a run for their money," recalls Dawes. "Although the Japanese really believed they could win, the stark truth was that they succumbed by fifty-six points to twelve in the Osaka Test and by eighty-two points to six in Tokyo. Les Spence had warned us that though our hosts could be charming we should watch their eyes, which narrowed when they were angry or felt they were being worsted. There was plenty of that as their skilful but under-weight hopefuls conceded such record points totals. Konno himself was shattered at what he saw as the humiliation of his players – and, indeed the Japanese nation.

"Without serious pressure from opponents (though I worked them hard in training) our players enjoyed themselves and were usually well behaved. The only minor crisis was when two or three of them 'borrowed' bicycles from a nearby car park which they rode back to the hotel. Phil Bennett was last to arrive, spotted by a police sergeant and his constable who had come post-haste to investigate the thefts and immediately alerted me, ordering the miscreant to be handed over by us for removal to the local station. Nobody could find the elusive stand-off half but the sergeant, determined not to be humiliated in front of his assistant, insisted that he must make an arrest. We decided to hand over the captain, and the giant 'Swerve' meekly accompanied the officers to their HQ for a grilling. After writing out a 'confession' (in pidgin Welsh) he was released with a warning from the sergeant who said as he left, 'You not look so big on bike.'

"When he heard about the incident Shiggy was far from happy. He expected our high-spirited young tourists to conform to Japanese standards of behaviour in public. He also displayed arrogance; when, trying to be helpful, I suggested that in view of the exhausting heat he should change his team (as I did mine) for the Second Test he took no notice – a stubborn response which cost Japan a world record Test defeat."

Though a one-sided experience, Dawes looks back on the visit as worthwhile. Although their small physique is a handicap which means that they are never likely to win the World Cup (despite importing mercenaries of European extraction), Japan made his players work very hard for the spoils. He regards the tour as a launch-pad for the remainder of the seventies. His players' fitness was as high as at any stage during his rugby career hitherto and, as he is fond of saying, "Get the fitness right and the skills will do the rest". That slogan, in his view, contributed to a series of great displays in the 1975-76 Home International season.

It began with the heavy pre-Christmas defeat at Cardiff of an Australian side which, though hardly the best ever, included world class players like Paul McLean, Greg Cornelsen, Garrick Fay and the skipper, scrum-half John Hipwell. J.J. Williams's hat trick of tries, alluded to on an earlier page, came at regular intervals in the second half, Gareth Edwards scored a neat try, while Martin, Fenwick and John Bevan contributed goal points. The sole response for the Wallabies was McLean's penalty.

Secretly John Dawes was delighted, and now looks back on the game as part of a progression of excellence which had begun in Tokyo and would continue. However, he had no intention of letting his men know of his satisfaction and remarked at his Press conference after the match, "There was a tendency to over-kick by our backs, and we have to find a better balance between kicking and passing." However, the team which took the field against England for the first Five Nations fixture of 1976 showed only two changes: his pulled hamstring having mended, Gerald Davies returned to the right wing and Bennett came back as Bevan cried off with an injury (as it turned out he had played his last game for Wales). But the build-up for Twickenham was fraught with controversy and ineptitude.

What happened was this: sticking to his guns, Dawes's original selection for the January opener was John Bevan at stand-off half. The uncapped 21-year-old Swansea number ten David Richards was summoned to the bench – with Phil Bennett out of the frame altogether, something that astounded and mystified both the media and the fans. They did not have the benefit of the rationale outlined earlier in this chapter by John Dawes, making clear the selectors' perception of the Bennett psyche. However, looking back the coach concedes that he ought to have picked up the phone and explained the thinking of the 'Big Five' to Phil. He is right; and a substantial coterie of Welsh International players who learned from the radio or in the Press that they had been dropped will applaud his admission.

As it was the Welsh selectors had to eat humble pie and invite Bennett to play at Twickenham after all. John Bevan hurt an elbow and young Richards pulled a hamstring. Despite his some-what shabby treatment 'Benny' agreed to come in out of the cold. For him it would be the first time to be on a winning side in a major International match outside Wales; furthermore, he would not be left out of his country's team again. Since Fenwick and Martin were at this time the established goal kickers his name was not among the Twickenham scorers, though he was part of a scissors move with JPR which enabled the full-back, on red-hot form, to claim a second try. To the fans the 21-9 win seemed a good start to a title campaign.

However, the coach and his captain were bent on excellence and not adequacy. Now in his second winter of captaincy, Mervyn Davies commented, "By our high standards I don't think it was a very good win." Dawes chose to be critical too: "We must buck up," he told the media. "We were far too loose in various situations and I expect more control. We will not win the title if we continue to play like that." What did please him, however, was a welcome tendency towards introspection and self-analysis on the part of his players. He had introduced the '71 Lions' habit of spending a 'happy hour' after matches at which the squad locked itself away in their hotel and got true feelings out of the system. His men's willingness to criticize team-mates and themselves seemed healthy and constructive.

But the outside world learned little about such private acts of catharsis. The National Coach would spend another couple of years upsetting the media with his ban on the interviewing by journalists of any players except new caps and the team captain. What triggered his decision may have been the widespread public excoriation of the WRU over the treatment of Bennett, but understandably writers and broadcasters found it an irritant and a shackling of their right to ask questions. Dawes defends himself by maintaining that, while some of his players were happy to be interviewed, a number disliked the experience. He felt that there could not be different rules for different squad members, so that the only course was to impose his blanket ban. Shame that a record-breaking try scorer or goal kicker could not get to say his piece on air. But team captain Mervyn Davies backed the ban, observing laconically, "It was in the team's best interest. We were not disturbed by phone calls throughout the week."

However, the show was on the road. Thirteen points kicked at Cardiff in a 28-6 win over Scotland demonstrated that Bennett had overcome his private demons and made him the highest Welsh scorer in Welsh rugby history with a total of 92 points that overtook Barry John's 90. Later in February came the Dublin trip despite an intensification of the terrorist extremists' campaign and death threats to a number of Welsh players in letters posted in the Irish capital. But a superb display by Wales brought a 34-9 victory, and a thirteenth Triple Crown in Mervyn Davies's thirty-seventh consecutive game, when he became the most capped of his country's forwards. Bennett's 19 points in the match equalled the individual record held jointly by Jack Bancroft (1910) and Keith Jarrett (1967). Ireland's management admitted frankly, "Our boys couldn't live with all that."

There was no end to Welsh record-breaking. In the clash of titans at Cardiff, France met a 19-13 defeat which lifted the Welsh aggregate to 102, the highest for a season by any country.

Bennett, Martin and Fenwick kicked five penalty goals between them; J.J. Williams got the Welsh try. Romeu scored with the boot for the French, whose try-scorers were Averous and Gourdon. The match is remembered for a match-winning tackle by JPR. Gourdon, speeding for the line in search of a second try, was taken out by the full-back's ferocious shoulder charge just short of the corner flag. (It was about this time that, driving home one evening, JPR's car was in collision with a jumbo-size petrol tanker. The Press reported that Wales's champion escaped unhurt, while "the tanker spent a comfortable night".) JPR's appearance against France saw him overtake W.J. Bancroft's record thirty-three caps for Wales at full-back while Gareth Edwards edged Ken Jones of Newport out of the record books with a forty-fifth game for Wales.

The partying began in earnest after the completion of this seventh Grand Slam by a side which had learned to compete for a full eighty minutes at the highest level. Dawes recalls how spectators watching, perhaps, a slow start by their heroes used to comfort each other with the assurance, "No need to worry. We'll win the game in the second half". He says, "A top tennis player may start well and hit some good shots. Such a player does not lose that capability – but he can only continue to play them if he has the fitness to keep doing so."

His Grand Slam men knew they had every reason to be pleased with themselves and overjoyed at the grandstand finish which gave them four wins from four. But the Dawes discipline made sure that they ate a snack during the 'happy hour' which would ensure that the alcohol – champagne on this occasion – which they enjoyed at the formal reception and dinner would not be drunk on an empty stomach. Afterwards the wives and girl-friends were brought in to share in the merriment, and their presence probably helped to negate any suggestion of a booze-up. After their games at Parc des Princes the Welsh enjoyed late-night visits to Parisian night-clubs accompanied by opponents whose star presence was welcomed by the managements.

John Dawes's second term in charge of the National XV ended sadly when Swansea's Mervyn Davies, who had proved to be an outstanding leader, suffered a brain haemorrhage in a Cup semi final against Pontypool at the Cardiff RFC ground. There was no suggestion of blame upon anyone; the video tape shows the big number eight pitching to the ground in open play as he sought to support his back division. He underwent a major operation which, said surgeon Robert Weeks, had left him "fighting for his life". After his recovery 'Swerve' sadly announced that he was taking Mr Weeks's advice and would be retiring from rugby with immediate effect. John Dawes wrote a foreword to his captain's autobiography:

> He still has much to contribute to the game. When one has to recommend someone for young players to try and emulate it would be easy to mention other great names, especially the 'prima donnas' as Mervyn would call them, but there could be no finer model than 'Merv the Swerve' himself. It only remains to say that I personally had the great fortune to play with him and even better luck not to play against him!

Now Dawes recalls, "The tragedy cost Mervyn two or three final seasons as Wales's number eight and – I can reveal this now – a certain appointment as captain of the British Isles in New Zealand twelve months later. Knowing his passion for the game, and for playing it hard and fairly, I felt huge sympathy for the big fellow and his new status as a spectator when he watched former mates like Edwards, JPR and Gerald Davies continuing to cover themselves with glory while he sat in the stand. I think he felt a wee bit better when his contemporaries had all hung up their boots."

Dawes's men were not up to speed when Argentina arrived in Wales for a first-ever Test at Cardiff Arms Park on October 1976. True, the home side were leading at the break, but five minutes into injury time at the end of the game were, astonishingly, trailing their 'evolving' visitors 17-19. It was then that the "battle within a battle", as John Dawes calls it, between the burly Pumas' centres and JPR, ended with a last gasp win for the reigning European champions: "JPR came into the line in a desperate attempt to swing the game, but was taken out high and hard by Adolfo Travaglini, the tackle conceding a penalty to the home side forty yards from the crossbar. The crowd held its breath, before erupting with delight and relief as Phil Bennett scored with a match-winning last kick of the game."

The captain on the day was Terry Cobner, leading his country for the first time – a man who would retain Dawes's trust as a pack leader and organiser of combative forward play. Meanwhile Phil Bennett had re-entered the National Coach's good books, not simply as an attacking number ten but also as team captain, a role which he would play until the final game of his International career.

As the New Year opened the coach was busy plugging gaps caused by injury or retirement. Names like Glyn Shaw, a Neath prop, Newport centre David Burcher and his back row club-mate Jeff Squire began to appear in the match programmes. Although Ireland were beaten at Cardiff by 25-9, the Welsh forward effort for Paris was weakened by the dismissal from the field of Geoff Wheel (along with Kilkenny's Willie Duggan). The burly lock forward would have contributed powerfully to the contest with France's big bruisers the following month but suspension kept him side-lined from a Welsh side that went down 16-9. His return stiffened the pack's resolve when tested by England at Cardiff, where Clive Williams was a debutant in the front row. There was praise for the forwards from Dawes, who recalls: "Our possession in this game was the best we have obtained. An outstanding feature was our scrummaging – which is where success begins and ends."

Continuing their recovery in March Wales were impressive in an 18-9 victory at Murrayfield. J.J. Williams went in for one of two tries for the visitors, while skipper Bennett contributed two conversions and a couple of penalty goals. But the try he finished ranks as one of the two or three greatest counter-attacking tries ever scored.

It came when Wales were reeling under furious Scottish pressure which threatened to wipe out their narrow 12-9 lead. The Welsh tackles were going in, only for Scottish attackers to arrive in strength competing wholeheartedly for 50-50 balls and driving possession majestically and ruthlessly towards the Welsh line. Spectators on tip-toe, cheering themselves hoarse, wondered which side would crack first. Would it be proud Wales or would Scotland run out of steam?

There came an uncomfortable moment when the great JPR was caught in possession on the Welsh 22. But upper body strength allowed him to feed Fenwick, who had to start running since a touch-kick might be charged down. Gerald Davies, mirac-ulously, came off his wing to the midfield acting as the link by which possession reached Bennett and, again, Fenwick. Now it was Wales's turn to attack imperiously, with Burcher at hand to keep up the momentum. Finally, the ball was in Bennett's hands again and, beating a last-ditch Scottish tackle, he went hard to the posts, flopping down beneath the crossbar for a try that boasted every ingredient of counter-attack: ambition, vision, persever-ance, continuity and finally a killer instinct. The conversion went over, and Wales were out of sight. Their reward for the season was a second Triple Crown: despite France's booming *grand chelem*, not a bad consolation prize.

For John Dawes personally there came a more than satisfactory reward with his appointment as coach in 1977 of the British Isles side in New Zealand. His club record at Old Deer Park plus his manifest capability to coach match-winning Five Nations Test rugby put him head and shoulders above the competition. The tour Down Under, though, was a bridge too far as we shall see.

The Welsh thirst for success was unquenched as the 1978 Five Nations campaign got under way, though a gutsy display by England at Twickenham kept the victory margin down to 9-6. In a steady downpour and on a greasy surface no tries were scored and the visitors had skipper Bennett to thank for the three penal-ties which stopped England in their tracks. But the third successive defeat of a spirited Scottish side at Cardiff saw Edwards, Gravell and Fenwick snapping up tries with Bennett adding a dropped goal and a penalty. The match is remembered for Derek Quinnell's first try for his country, when he handed off three defenders as he strode his way to the corner flag. The father of Scott and Craig made the number eight position his own for a series of thirteen appearances there, while Dawes used big Jeff Squire on the flank.

Next came a thriller in Dublin, with the super-confident Welsh allowing fired-up Irish opponents to claw their way back into contention at 13-13 in the second half. The home team also levelled the scores at 16-16 before a J.J. Williams try made the game safe for Wales. Mike Gibson had led Ireland onto the field to win a world-beating sixty-fourth cap, but JPR did not stand on ceremony as he took his British Lions mate out with a palpably late try-saving tackle. Candidly the full-back owned up to the foul afterwards, saying "I've done it before and I'll do it again". Booo, roared the Dublin crowd every time he touched the ball up to the final whistle. But the Welsh were well satisfied with the completion of a third Triple Crown in successive seasons, something none of the other four nations had ever managed.

The point has been made earlier that Wales were made to fight every inch of the way along their road to yet another Grand Slam. At Cardiff there were two tries from Phil Bennett, but the other points against the French, defending their Championship title, were from the captain's conversion and two dropped goals by Gareth Edwards and Fenwick. If not a pretty game, the encounter was full of sound and fury and it was the determination on the day of Bennett's team which brought Wales a third Grand Slam of the decade.

Dawes said at his media conference, "This team deserves to be recognized as one of the greatest of all time." So: better than 1976? Now, over a quarter of a century later, mature judgement prompts him to award his personal accolade of the decade to Mervyn Davies's team: "You would have to say that the captaincy was in the best possible hands. And there was the way Mervyn's players contributed to discussion and debate about how to win. But that is not to take anything away from Phil's team, against whom the opposition was always hell-bent on winning. But two or three of my players were at the end of their International careers and Wales spent a lot of time on the ropes."

The day after the game Gareth Edwards told a Sunday newspaper that he would no longer play International Rugby. Dawes now pays him a generous tribute: "His career lasted from 1967 right through to 1978. That is eleven years of hard labour, not forgetting that through three summers he was overseas with the Lions. Gareth could moan sometimes about aches, pains and pressure; but if he was prepared to take the field in a major game (which he did on 53 occasions for his country) you could take it for granted that he was fully fit and finely tuned. He looked after his personal fitness better than any other player I know. What a contribution! What a glittering decade. An era was over, with Phil Bennett, too, calling it a day."

*

The closeness of the scores in the Grand Slam season of 1978 prompts Dawes to conclude that the other big players in world rugby at the time were now bent on analyzing the contemporary Welsh style the better to counter it. Video tape had arrived, making it possible for coaches to study its attacks in depth and see how Wales exploited space. Thus defensive frameworks were put under the microscope with the objective of snuffing out the Welsh genius at source. Certainly the coach became aware of this when he took his Grand Slammers to Australia for a nine-match close season tour. The major absentees were the two half-backs who had recently hung up their boots, but replacements Gareth Davies and Brynmor Williams were thought to be more than satisfactory successors to Edwards and Bennett. But not only did Europe's reigning champions lose both Tests, they also went down in two matches against provinces.

The Wallabies had certainly been working out how to avoid defeat, but a vital weapon which worked in their favour in the Tests was the refereeing, which featured the obligatory 'homer' officials, notably Bob Burnett who had done duty in Queensland's victory over the tourists. Despite protests from tour manager Clive Rowlands he took charge of the first Test at Brisbane, where Australia's victory by 18 points to eight contained four penalty goals. Phil Crowe got their try, while Gerald Davies and Brynmor Williams replied for the Welsh. It may be that the visitors were a little jaded after an exhausting season back home, and their display at Sydney (17-19), when Cardiff's Terry Holmes made his debut at scrum-half, was not good enough to draw the series. Wales, recalls Dawes, were still relying too heavily upon inspired individuals, flair, opportunism and an injection of magic. As time marched on such ingredients needed to be under-pinned by better planning.

New Zealand had certainly done some planning before their visit to Cardiff that November, though not of the most respectable kind. A furious forward offensive by the Welsh had been rewarded with penalties by Davies and Fenwick, and with only minutes to go Graham Mourie's men trailed 10-12; Stu Wilson had scored a try, while replacement Brian McKechnie placed a couple of penalties. The perspiring All Blacks then

The end of international rugby for Dawes came with the defeat of New Zealand by the Barbarians in 1973, a match which has passed into rugby folklore. *Top*: Dawes prepares to pass inside in the move which ended in Gareth Edwards famous try. Derek Quinnell is in support. *(Colorsport)* *Bottom*: The victorious captain is chaired off to retirement. *(Western Mail)*

Terry Cobner, in whom Dawes would put so much trust on the 1977 Lions tour, scores his debut try for Wales, against Scotland in 1974. Phil Bennett and Dai Morris are in attendance.

Graham Price, Bobby Windsor and Tony 'Charlie' Faulkner, the famous
Pontypool front row who also did duty for Wales under Dawes.
(Associated Sport Photography)

The legendary Gareth Edwards sets the Wales backs moving against Australia at the Arms Park in 1975. Cobner and Mervyn Davies watch on as Shaw fails in the tackle.

So often Edwards's partner at half back, 'King' Barry John, playmaker, try-scorer and controller of games. Here he attacks the Irish backs with Gerald Davies in support, in the 1969 international.

(*Colorsport*)

Captain of Wales, Phil Bennett kicks under pressure from Ireland's Mike Gibson and Fergus Slattery, at Cardiff 1977.

Another pressure kick. Here winger JJ Williams gets the ball away despite the attentions of England's John Spencer. David Richards is in support.

A classic centre pairing for Wales. On the left, Steve Fenwick – for the Lions on this occasion – relieves the pressure on the 1977 tour of New Zealand. To the right, Ray Gravell shows no signs of his pre-match nerves once on field and involved in the action. (*Colorsport*)

managed to find touch between Wales's ten-metre line and the 22. Here it was that lock forwards Frank Oliver and Andy Haden hatched a cunning plot. As the throw came in the two men each dived out of the line-out to lie prone on the turf, the aim being to persuade the referee that they had been barged. Roger Quittenton blew – but when his arm went up it was signalling a penalty to New Zealand.

The crowd, especially those in the adjacent south stand and enclosure, raged and hooted, but the unruffled McKechnie stepped up to thump his kick cleanly between the Welsh posts and New Zealand held on to win by the narrowest of margins. As the experts viewed and analysed the play on the BBC Wales Sunday highlights programme, the seasoned critic Clem Thomas exclaimed 'Hollywood!' In fairness to Mr Quittenton, photographs show Geoff Wheel's hand on Oliver's shoulder (though not gaining any leverage from his action), and that was why the referee gave the penalty. Regrettably for Wales, on the home team's side of the line-out he had not been well positioned for an over-view of the play.

Haden later admitted in his book *Boots 'n' All* that: "Our act, whilst pre-meditated, was born of desperation on the spur of the moment... It grew out of frustration at not being able to perform the job for which we were primarily selected". What he meant was that Wheel and Allan Martin had consistently out-jumped the two All Black locks throughout the game. Now, with hindsight, Dawes comments, "I just feel sad that an All Black team could resort to such a tactic, especially as we know that it was condoned by the captain, Graham Mourie."

At the time the coach said, "Our men made one of the best starts for a long time... perhaps a team with more experience would have put more points on the board" (it only included ten British Lions!). He was sad that some blame for the defeat fell on Geoff Wheel, of whom he was a great fan: "It was fun to see him in action with his club Swansea at St Helens. You would see a maul literally bouncing up and down until Geoff emerged with the ball. I often thought that he would prefer to win a maul than score a try."

The afterglow of the great days in Europe was to continue into the Five Nations tournament of 1979. Scotland went down to a now customary defeat in Edinburgh, but Ireland put up stiffer resistance at Cardiff, holding the Welsh to 24-21 prompting Dawes to observe, "One thing you always get from Ireland is fifteen tackling players. Welsh teams of the past have been able to overcome this, but my 1979 team did not have the same qualities. Those men who have replaced our top players are not world class yet." The verdict was borne out in Paris, where a French victory by 14-13 was sufficient to deny Welsh progress to a fourth Grand Slam of the decade.

But the game Dawes remembers most vividly, and gave him cause for rejoicing, was the 27-3 victory over England which brought an outstanding sixteenth Triple Crown. Geoff Wheel was injured, and an inspirational selection by the coach brought back Mike Roberts to the second row after a four year gap. The veteran London Welshman out-played England skipper Bill Beaumont, and scored a famous try with a sprint to the line from fully two metres range to clinch a notable result.

Now, the times were a-changing. Only Graham Price was left of the abrasive Pontypool front row. JPR (side-lined in the second half by a calf injury) went into semi-retirement. Gerald Davies had hung up his boots; Ray Gravell was in his dotage.

And the National Coach had fresh ambitions.

THIRTEEN

The masterly achievements of John Dawes in Europe during the second half of the seventies have been dealt with as a progression. Hence it is now necessary to back-track in order to deal with a short period in his life which was, at best, unsatisfactory and at worst mortifying. In 1977 a man who is judged by posterity to have been one of the rugby game's outstanding coaches was to experience a summer of great discontent. In New Zealand.

His achievements in Welsh colours and as his country's skipper, then as captain of the uniquely successful British Isles team of 1971, and latterly in charge of Wales's dominant Five Nations contenders of 1975, 1976 and 1977 (they met narrow defeats just twice in twelve outings) meant that he had no serious rival for the position of coach to the 1977 Lions. One of rugby football's most trenchant critics of the game's administrators, the maverick All Black lock Andy Haden, approved of his appointment: it was 'forward–thinking' of the Four Home Unions to send Dawes as coach to a country where he had captained the British Isles side to a series victory, a 'first' for the Lions, over the All Blacks. In other words, this man was something of an icon in the world game.

But in 1971 New Zealand's rugby public had successfully overcome deep disappointment at losing the series. Their team had been on top of the world for a decade when they played mistake-free, power rugby and beat most opposition. So now, when these cheeky Lions turned up and whacked the All Blacks – well, all good things come to an end; and the Lions, they weren't half good. The generous, sporting character of the Kiwi was dominant. And, of course, their team would be re-shaped.

However, in their recent publication *All Black Magic* Bob Howitt and Dianne Haworth recall how New Zealand's "eighth decade" (since her first Test, against Australia in 1903) "could scarcely have started worse". There was a draw in Dublin (the first time for an All Black side not to beat Ireland), defeat by France in Paris, and seven months later an "embarrassing" reverse against England at Eden Park. A partial recovery under J.J. Stewart against

195

Australia was followed by a mixture of "selection shortcomings and outrageous refereeing decisions" in South Africa which allowed the Springboks to win the series 3-1 and cost the coach his job in 1976. With time running out before the British Isles tour of 1977 New Zealand's selectors turned in desperation to Jack Gleeson. Doomed to lose his battle with cancer on the Grand Slam tour of Britain in 1978, the new coach buckled down to the challenge of the latest invasion force.

He knew that nothing but a victorious Test series against the visitors would silence fans who had become angry and disillusioned with the team as the seventies wore on. Fortunately for the All Blacks, if not for New Zealand's image and standing in world rugby, this unruly fringe vented its spleen upon the Lions as they spread alarm and despondency with eight victories out of eight in the tour's early stages. Players reported being spat upon near touchlines, having cans and beer bottles hurled at them from the terraces, and sworn at when they kicked goals or ran in tries. If a provoked Lion chose to swing a punch at his tormentor he was continuously booed until the final whistle.

This paranoid atmosphere, allied to a cold fear of defeat again at the dreaded hands of Dawes, penetrated elements of the media too. The periodical ironically called *Truth* lambasted the tourists after their defeat in the first Test, attributing it to womanizing, late nights and heavy alcohol consumption. The Lions management, John Dawes and George 'Dod' Burrell, decided to take no action against this and other publications lest a calculated blast from the British Isles camp should fan the flames of controversy and bump up the circulation figures of the yellow Press.

As if such hostile vibes were not enough ultimately to damage the tourists' mood, the stirrers found an ally in New Zealand's windiest, coldest and wettest winter for decades. From day one and their game against Wairarapa Bush at Masterton the Lions endured eight weeks of Antarctic weather including torrential rain and occasional falls of snow. In match play backs, especially wings, are naturally most vulnerable to such finger-freezing conditions; but whole squads can be demoralized by training sessions which end with wet hair, muddied limbs, soaked track suits and sodden boots. Day after wretched day of such conditions can affect the most sanguine of dispositions.

There was a notable name missing from the 1977 referee short-list offered to the Lions – that of John Pring, who had refereed all four Tests in 1971. "He has never been forgiven for that," a veteran All Black told John Dawes. However, the refereeing was, for once, 'adequate' (Dawes's comment) and cannot be cited as one of the factors contributing to the series result. There were, however, flaws in the Lions' approach to the tour which manifested themselves before the party left the British Isles in May. So said the critics after it was all over.

British forward play had been improving out of all recognition in the first half of the seventies. All Black power was absorbed and contained in 1971, while Willie John McBride and Co took once-mighty Springbok packs apart three years later. Thus although he was naturally delighted at his appointment to serve as tour manager George 'Dod' Burrell's right hand man, John Dawes did not allow himself to be carried away. He contemplated his role soberly: it appeared to be the next stage in a progression which British rugby was making. He wanted the Lions of 1977 to build on the decade's previous successes and to reach untrodden heights of excellence. His back division could be relied upon – couldn't it? – to deliver the goods. He would see that his forwards followed suit.

The men who picked the touring party were five in number and included Burrell through whom the coach's opinions could filter. Keith Rowlands was the Welsh representative, Malcolm Phillips the Englishman, while Scotland and Ireland were represented by Alec Harper and Syd Millar respectively. Not available for selection were several great Lions of the past including Gareth Edwards, Gerald Davies, J.P.R. Williams, Fergus Slattery and Peter Dixon.

Named as skipper, Phil Bennett was one of no fewer than sixteen Welshmen chosen by the selection panel. Alarm and despondency were just two of the UK-wide reactions to the names. The old canard about the Welsh being bad travellers speedily re-surfaced; and some critics had a pop at 'marginal' selections like David Burcher and Gareth Evans (both of Newport) and Aberavon's Clive Williams.

Had better players been rejected? Scotland was sad that Bill Gammell and Jim Renwick had been overlooked, while, although he let it be known that he would enjoy a third Lions tour, the prop Ian McLauchlan did not find favour either despite the wealth of experience that his inclusion would have guaranteed. Jeff Squire of Wales and Ireland's Moss Keane were the replacements when Geoffrey Wheel and Roger Uttley were advised at the last minute by doctors to give the tour a miss. The Englishman's withdrawal was a blow to Dawes; "Roger had run a close second to Phil in the captaincy stakes and was a senior citizen, a major player in our pre-planning. A big loss."

Dawes is at pains to make it clear that the ultimate numerical superiority enjoyed by the Welsh was not down to his influence. "To say that I got the team I wanted is strictly inaccurate," he insists. "I was at one remove from the selection clout, and there was no possibility of my getting my own way in an argument with four or five opponents. No, if there was a preponderance of my countrymen, it was because for two or three seasons Wales had been playing the most consistently successful rugby in the northern hemisphere. As it happened, I harboured doubts over the quality of one or two of the Welshmen in the party. But here I was guilty, I think, of playing the compatriotic card and not standing in the way of a man rated by the selectors. If four clued-up gentlemen thought one of my countrymen possessed the requisite qualities to be a Lion I was content to endorse their views!"

But so much would not mean that other nationalities would stand at the back of the queue for Test places. Now, more than a quarter of a century later Dawes still makes this point repeatedly in conversations about the Lions' early days in New Zealand. You get the feeling that back in 1977 his instinct would have been to name Terry Cobner as an official vice captain; something from which in practice he shrank for fear of its being branded as yet another flag on a Welsh band-wagon. Thus the early fixtures featured captaincy by Ian McGeechan and Fran Cotton as well as Cobner. The tactic appears to have worked; and it is the case that no anti-Welsh sentiment simmered or surfaced at any stage of the tour.

Incidentally, when Cobner assumed control of the British forwards shortly after the tourists' defeat in the First Test, the pack felt the full force of his personality and the dynamic which he had packed into Pontypool's game. The Lions responded. There was a transformation of their attitudes and application which carried through to the bitter end of the tour. John Dawes contends that, ultimately, the 1977 Lions contained sixteen forwards of supreme calibre, and could put together two eights either of which would be world-beaters. Certainly the All Blacks went under the cosh. But sadly the team coach will never know what would have happened had he abandoned ethnic scruples and given Cobner a loose rein in May to whip Lions' packs to the controlled frenzy seen in August. The other plus-point deriving from such a decision would have been that Dawes himself could have spent more time with his backs, working out why they were under-performing and prescribing remedies. A quarter of a century on, he admits making the incorrect assumption that men of experience like McGeechan and Gibson would readily accept responsibility for taking training sessions. He was at fault in not perceiving how badly the three-quarters needed his oversight.

Ethnic considerations – a repetitious theme – also dissuaded Dawes from following Carwyn James's example of 1971 when his ideal team for the First Test was pencilled in from the outset of the tour and its backbone could be discerned in each Saturday XV that took the field. The names, however, were disclosed only to Doug Smith and Dawes, so that each player in the tour's early games gave a hundred per cent, in the belief that he might win a Test place. In contrast Dawes's 1977 obsession with banishing the spectre of Welsh dominance meant that men needing to get to know each other's play were not selected together nearly as frequently as was desirable. For example, in the nine games leading up to the First Test the preferred centre pairing of Fenwick and McGeechan had taken the field only once. It was the same with the back row; the tour ended, some said, without the British Isles management declaring which was the best trio they could field.

Nevertheless, the faces of New Zealand fans were glum in May as the 1977 Lions tour gathered momentum, criss-crossing its way from venue to venue. There was a 41-13 victory in the opening game against Wairarapa Bush and soon King Country -Wanganui plunged to a 60-9 defeat which included five memorable tries by Scotland's Andy Irvine. Of course there were some narrow escapes, too, with Hawke's Bay going down by just 13-11 and Otago putting up the usual rugged resistance before suffering a 12-7 defeat. However, the overall picture looked rosy as, after eight games, the tourists had a hundred per cent record and had scored 210 points while conceding 83.

Hence at this crucial juncture, with the First Test a week away, John Dawes felt cautiously optimistic about the outcome of the Test series – which is what really matters to Lions on tour. "In 1971 we did better than I had dared to hope," he says. "It would not have been a good idea for me to have stated publicly that we might lose a Test or the series. That would have been crazy – admitting self-doubts, about myself and my players. On the other hand, I may as well admit it: of course I had private fears about what might happen. It did cross my mind that we could be beaten – don't forget, that was only five years after the 1966 whitewash. Captains and coaches are only human. They, too, toss and turn during the wee small hours.

"But in 1977 I truly believed that we would win. Where 1971 had been all about containment, the pack of 1977 was, in the end, a genuine strike force. I said to myself, and I told my players, 'This time we're really going to get stuck in to these Blacks.' The sole niggling doubt at the back of my mind in the preliminary games was that only one back, Irvine, was a 'flair' player; that is, a man who created tries with speed and elusive footwork and also appeared as a support runner who finished them off. My captain, Phil Bennett, would normally have belonged in this category, but he was finding it hard to hit top speed or to jink on the rain-soaked playing surfaces. He was also targeted by Kiwi back row men who didn't mind arriving on their victim a few seconds late, and suffered injuries that sapped his confidence.

"But all in all we were relishing the prospect of locking horns with the All Blacks. Before that there was the little matter of a Tuesday match against New Zealand Universities at Christchurch which the T & Ws could take care of."

Happily, big rugby falls short of being predictable, and there are glorious afternoons when underdogs tear out of their kennels to see off the rottweilers. On June 14 1977, four days before the Lions were to meet New Zealand in the First Test, a student XV were the heroes who snarled and snapped their illustrious opponents out of contention. Admittedly the Lions' selection for the game was high risk, with the fitness of several men in doubt; they included Elgan Rees, who had waited a month to make his debut after tearing a hamstring before the first game of the tour, and Scotsman Douglas Morgan who was recovering from ribs damaged a fortnight earlier.

But captained from first five-eighth by Doug Rollerson, soon to win a series of caps for New Zealand, the students proved to be no respecters of reputations. They targeted Morgan, slowing down his delivery and hence the forward movement of the visitors' three-quarters. Up front, they waded into a Lions pack which had yet to undergo the Cobner revolution and found themselves leading 9-3 at the break. All the points had come from penalty goals, but immediately on the re-start Derek Quinnell forced his way over for a try converted by Morgan. Soon arrived one of the fateful occurrences which would haunt the British Isles for the remainder of the tour and are remembered sourly by John Dawes.

"We were on terms," he recalls, "and Morgan decided that he could kick a penalty awarded to us just inside the opposition half. He hit it well, and the crowd clapped in the belief that the ball had cleared the crossbar. The students appeared to think so too, and one of them kicked the ball back towards the half way line as if accepting that the re-start would take place from there, with a kick by them. The touch judges were right under the bar, which is not the best position from which to observe the ball's flight-path. One of them signalled a goal, while the other kept his flag down. The referee agreed with the latter and the score was disallowed.

"We should have taken the lead, and would probably have held onto it until the end," Dawes recalls. "Instead we allowed the incident to upset our concentration and let the students in for a try (which, I have to say, contained one if not two knock-ons). It was converted, and a couple more penalties by Rollerson and full-back Heffernan killed us off. So the Lions lost an unbeaten provincial record which stretched back to 1968 and their defeat by Transvaal at Ellis Park."

The defeat prompted John Dawes, for the first time on tour, to reveal a patch of thin skin. When asked what the team would be doing that evening, he snapped: "I will tell you one thing: we are not having a party tonight." But instead of a civilized evening, tinged with regret, out and out mayhem held sway as the tourists, notably those who had been in the defeated XV that afternoon, vented their frustration upon their hotel and its occupants. Fire hoses were employed to flush well-behaved team-mates out of bed, while guests who had nothing to do with the rugby and were minding their own business were also drenched as they negotiated the hotel corridors. At breakfast-time the following morning a number of ashen-faced, hung-over Lions chewed their pencils as they composed suitable letters of apology to the management and other offended parties. Doubtless there was relief in Christchurch as the party left to catch the afternoon flight to Wellington and the Hotel St George.

Dawes was later to grimace, "New Zealand did not win this Test series. The British Isles lost it." What he meant were the critical mistakes on the part of certain individual men in his teams rather than any collective failures by them. One such error cost them victory, plus a flying start to the series, in the all-important First Test at Wellington's Athletic Park.

The All Blacks' line-up on a miserable afternoon was full of experienced men, with Colin Farrell at full-back as the only newcomer. Among the men winning Lions caps for the first time were locks Allan Martin and Moss Keane, whom the selectors had to pick because of injuries to Horton and Gordon Brown. Number nine was the uncapped Brynmor Williams, who was able, at last, to play his own spirited game, out of the shadow of the great Gareth Edwards. The fact is that Williams was understudy to Edwards at Cardiff RFC (in days before replacements trooped on to play the last twenty minutes) and, arguably, was short of eighty-minute experience at the highest level. Wrote John Hopkins in *Life With the Lions*: "He could be a match-winner... he had a tendency to make one bad error in each game."

Well: you have to hand it to Dawes. Not a Welshman, Scot, Irishman or Englishman could possibly have guessed the combination that eventually took the field for the Test. However, it did include nine players from Wales.

All the meaningful action took place in the first half. With a couple of minutes left before the break New Zealand were trailing 12-10 but had scored two tries, one converted, to a series of penalties kicked by Irvine and Bennett for the Lions. The tourists looked set to increase this narrow lead as half time approached and a break by Brynmor Williams took them to the All Blacks' ten yard line. Here Fenwick supported and put Trevor Evans into territory occupied by three team-mates but guarded only by Grant Batty. That was when Evans held onto the ball just one stride too far, and the pass he tried to give Bennett was deflected by a desperate Bruce Robertson in Batty's direction. The little wing jumped to secure possession and, though carrying a ligament operation that had not properly healed, generated a strong enough head of steam to go fifty yards for a vital 'twelve-point try', as a dismayed John Dawes would afterwards call it. Batty would have known that if he failed to get hold of the ball the Lions would surely score; so he gambled – successfully.

Although the elements favoured New Zealand in the second half the Lions matched them for the full forty minutes and neither side was able to add to the score-line. The series was off to a negative start for the tourists. However, they had three weeks to lick their wounds, during which they got through some heavy scoring against combined sides in South Island, scraped the narrowest of wins over Canterbury at Christchurch and beat Wellington in a low-scoring game. This run of success, culminating in victory back in Christchurch over the All Blacks, was judged by many to be the most impressive part of the tour. There were, however, disturbing undercurrents which rocked the boat – and again they could be put down to the weather. Dawes insists that its baleful influence lay behind much of the discontent experienced by his men: "The rain was so heavy and sustained that the social side of our tour just never took off.

"OK, whatever the weather, we had to train. But after that, there was little chance of sampling the delights of New Zealand's outback such as power-boating, fishing and mountain scenery, while even race meetings were being cancelled because of the sodden turf. It was all pretty demoralizing, and for some weeks the players left the hotels only when they had to. The rest of the time they formed card schools, watched television, or simply lay on their beds reading the newspapers. That was about it until the evening, when after dinner some of us might take in a cinema visit.

"Unfortunately this had a knock-on effect on the Press and

media coverage we were getting, which bordered on the scurrilous and made Dod Burrell and me very angry. Because of the Lions' stay-at-home routine, which included 'do not disturb' instructions given to hotel reception desks, the journalists were not able to obtain the sort of background material they would normally acquire. They thought the Lions were being awkward (though, in truth, because of our inactivity we had precious little to say to them). They set out to get their own back, in the most lurid way imaginable.

"A headline in the *New Zealand Truth* screamed 'Lions Are Louts', which carried on: 'There has been only one word to describe their behaviour since the team arrived here – disgusting... During their stay at Wellington after the First Test two Lions urinated down a stairwell and team-mates ripped seven hotel doors off their hinges....They threw glasses, overturned tables, uncoiled fire hoses and sprayed water.'

"A short time after this the Auckland *Sunday News* carried a story headlined, 'Lions are Lousy Lovers'. This was the verdict of a girl who said she had slept with four of the tourists, adding, 'I found them boring, self-centred, ruthless, always on the make and anything but exciting bedmates'.

"The Manager and I reached the conclusion that there was little point in contesting such malign reportage, which was sheer invention. However, it had broken the unwritten rules which accompany touring, and something had to be said if only because the stories were getting back to the homeland and drawing anxious telephone calls and letters from wives and sweethearts. I therefore told the media, 'Normally if stuff like this appeared we would not take any notice. It is all lies and invention. What troubles me is that it appears to be rooted in hostility towards my players. I do not understand this, and I have never known anything like it'."

The sniping from the sidelines abated slightly, only to resume after the Second Test. Dawes decided to hit back, once telling a Press conference, "If there was a DC10 leaving here for London tomorrow the whole of my team would choose to be on it."

The team he was referring to for the Second Test showed five changes from that which lost in Wellington. Peter Squires was omitted, J.J. Williams moving into his place on the right wing and Gareth Evans chosen at left wing. Only Graham Price survived in the front five, from which Windsor, Orr, Keane and Martin made way for Wheeler, Cotton, Gordon Brown and the recently arrived replacement for Nigel Horton, Bill Beaumont (who impressed the management from his first outing in the training arena). Now Dawes did what he could, and maybe should, have done at the beginning of the tour, inviting Cobner to choose and take control of the forwards.

Pontypool's Ray Prosser had been a prop with the 1959 Lions in New Zealand, from where he had imported valuable lessons in forward play. His club's heavyweights moved around the field as a black, white and red clone of All Black packs, grinding opponents into the ground and rarely trusting the backs. If the ball went further than number ten, that was a 'move'. And Prosser did not encourage 'moves', where control of possession might be lost by his packs. Flanker Terry Cobner was his acolyte, appointed captain of Pontypool in 1969-70, the first of nine consecutive seasons in charge. In *A Century of Welsh Rugby Players* (1980) Wayne Thomas wrote of the skills and commitment which won him a place on the 1977 tour:

> Cobner led by example, with fiery assertiveness, tackling everything that moved with a pounding certainty. A brilliant mauler, he was expert at turning men in a tackle to make the ball available for his own team. He was fast, and never stopped moving around the field, showing an unflagging determination at all times.

John Dawes adds, 'Terry suffered from homesickness, so that the responsibility for the forwards which we now placed upon him was a kind of therapy. In one respect he resembled Carwyn James – that is, not being interested in second rate ability. Also, his tunnel-vision of preparing for battle was focused upon the pack. He was truly uninterested in what the backs did, and half-backs were only allowed near his scrummaging practice to put the ball in. However, the fact is that his input lifted the Lions' forward play to a level at which it could dominate the All Blacks' Test XV and all subsequent opponents. A major adjustment by him was the choice of Derek Quinnell, whose line-out presence matched that of Ian Kirkpatrick.

From the start the difference showed, especially at the line-outs where the Lions' re-vamped pack completely closed down a hitherto reliable launch-pad for All Black attacks. Soon Bennett kicked a penalty given against Going, after which the visitors registered the sole try of the game: "It was an admirable score," recalls the coach. "The early running was made by Bennett, Brown, Quinnell and McGeechan, who fed J.J. Williams. He thought of passing to Andy Irvine before, realizing that the fullback was marked, selling a dummy and slipping in for a classy try, his ninth on tour. It was the difference between the two sides, Bennett kicking two more penalties while Brian Williams kicked three for New Zealand." The Lions survived fierce assaults by New Zealand through the second half before leaving the muddied arena having squared the series with their 13-9 victory.

To all and sundry it seemed that the tour was back on the rails. Two of the four provincial fixtures that preceded the next Test brought outstanding rugby from the tourists, notably a defeat of the Maoris who were leading at one stage by nineteen points to six before succumbing to a hurricane finish which yielded four tries (two by Squires and one each for Gibson and Orr) that brought the British Isles back from the dead. Waikato and New Zealand Juniors were dealt with, and finally an Auckland side whose coach had been bad-mouthing the British Isles was crushed 34-15. A group of Lions from bygone eras including Clem Thomas, Barry John and Mervyn Davies had arrived by now to report the closing stages of the tour for various newspapers in the UK, and were pleasantly surprised at what they saw.

New Zealand's selectors certainly took fright at the Lions' run of ten successive victories which had followed the First Test, making six changes for the crucial meeting in Dunedin – after which the side that won could not lose the rubber. Lyn Davies was brought in at scrum-half, a choice which ended the Test career of the great Sid Going, while at full-back the twenty-one-year-old Bevan Wilson from Otago would win a first cap. Robertson returned to the centre after injury, Brian Ford was chosen on the wing, while Mourie and McEldowney had jobs to do in the pack.

The Lions spent a few days before the Test relaxing in North Island's scenic Bay of Islands – where even to gossip about rugby football was forbidden. They swam in their hotel's heated pool, but more importantly enjoyed some sunshine for the first time in many weeks, getting out on the golf course and going fishing. John Dawes knew only too well how demoralizing was the wretched weather which his men had experienced from the outset of the tour, and this brief change of climate raised their spirits. He recalls that confidence was high as the party flew south to Dunedin. But here it was still raining.

The centre David Burcher was the sole newcomer named for the Third Test by the Lions, ousting McGeechan (who would replace an injured J.J.Williams in the second half). But the high-risk selection was that of Brynmor Williams, who had severely pulled a hamstring at Waikato a fortnight earlier and on the eve of the match was unable to pass a full-scale fitness test monitoring his recovery. As it was he lasted for only fifty minutes before having to be replaced by Doug Morgan. Was Williams wholly candid about the gravity of the original injury? If he concealed it, he had done the Lions a bad turn by delaying a call to the UK for a replacement.

But Williams was only one of a back division that performed lamentably on 30 July at Carisbrook. In particular, Phil Bennett was completely out of sorts. In *Everywhere for Wales* he wrote:

> I kicked and passed like a novice... and ended up apologizing to the forwards and Terry Cobner... I felt a failure as captain and would willingly have given the responsibility to someone else at that stage.

That was a brave admission – and told the truth. The captain's catalogue of errors which contributed to the defeat of his team included: a failure to convert Duggan's try, a missed clearance giving possession to the All Blacks, a drop-out 22 behind chasing forwards, an easy penalty missed, several kicks charged down, and loss of the ball in a tackle. The skids were under his confidence; he went from bad to worse.

John Dawes recalls: "Comparisons are odious. But, inevitably, that winter New Zealanders were comparing the Lions' stand-off half with his predecessor Barry John. The management was not asked questions about their relative merit, but I think a comment is fair enough in 2005 bearing in mind that we are talking about two supremely gifted men. My summation is that, when Barry moved the ball to the midfield he was telling us – 'It's good ball - use it'. In contrast, when Phil passed, he was saying to the centres, 'I can't go any further – I'm unloading.' All Black flankers had worked out how easily he could be forced to crab across the midfield – where Fenwick could not always straighten the three-quarter line.

"The other failing in Benny's game was a strange one, especially bearing in mind his early days on soccer pitches – the inability to kick with the left foot. The dodging and weaving capers to which he would resort to make room for his right boot left onlookers gasping with admiration – but the spectacular side-steps would have been unnecessary had he possessed the ability to use both feet. Barry John was so 'two-footed' that I could not honestly tell you which came more naturally to him."

Most people who saw the test or reported it were in agreement that up front the Lions gave Tane Norton's pack a real beating (though, oddly, the two All Black tries were touched down by forwards Kirkpatrick and Haden). Old stager Bruce Robertson dropped a goal and new boy Bev Wilson placed two penalties, while the only responses by the Lions were Duggan's try and a penalty by Irvine. But in Dunedin's bars and bistros that night the consensus was that if the British Isles' backs could stitch their game together they could still win the last Test.

The three former Lions who saw the Dunedin defeat had to grasp the nettle and print a few home truths in their Sunday newspaper columns back home. The story of the day at Carisbrook was big enough to stand on its own two feet; but by the time it had been sexed up by Fleet Street sub-editors and teleprinted to New Zealand for consumption by the Lions' management it was a major ingredient in the disgruntlement of Dawes. The media's small arms fire, first heard early in the tour and muted after Christchurch, had never quite gone away. Now, on the Sunday morning, salvoes were again being fired with 'Limping Lions' the major theme. Then, as if defeat was not a big enough blow, as if the criticisms in the Kiwi Press were not hurtful, as if Dawes's hopes for a series victory had not been blown away – on the wires came forthright comments by one-time team-mates. The coach could take the criticism, but he found the fact that it had been generated by friends unpalatable.

The period between the final two Tests clearly strained the coach's nerve almost to breaking point. He felt desperate disappointment of the worst kind – having been so sure at the outset that his Lions would win. So his judgement was imperfect. In the final Test at Eden Park, Auckland, the tourists could only secure a drawn series, which would be less than earth-shattering. Such considerations equated, in his view, to a mission unaccomplished; perfectionists are their own severest critics, to whom failure and consequent feelings of frustration are a potent cocktail. Thus the media, Clem Thomas later wrote, were made to feel wholly unwanted by the siege mentality which developed. He felt the lash of Dawes's tongue (and later graciously accepted an apology); Barry John was scolded; even Carwyn James's rugby credentials were mocked late one evening by the coach of 1977.

Dod Burrell took an even fiercer line on the visitors from the past. When Mervyn Davies was invited into the team room for a chat by Allan Martin the Manager instructed him to leave and gave Martin a dressing down. While talking with the former Lions number eight at a post-match function Derek Quinnell and Bill Beaumont were told to break off. Davies remembers being ordered by the Manager to leave the official NZRU function at the end of the tour. "Mr Burrell, I'm here as a guest of the New Zealand Rugby Union," was his response. "But don't be upset; I was just leaving anyway." Dawes often found himself an ill-at-ease messenger boy for the Manager's menacing instructions.

In such an atmosphere the last thing the Lions wanted as they cleared the final provincial hurdles and looked forward to the climactic Test was selection problems. Alas for their hopes; Brynmor Williams's tour had ended at Dunedin and now, in the tour's final week Cobner, Quinnell and J.J. Williams joined him as walking wounded. Given the unavailability of these key members of the Test side the Lions' performance in Auckland was unbelievably brave, once again forward-led with newcomers Tony Neary and Jeff Squire fitting perfectly into the eight-man machine. Doug Morgan was at scrum-half, with recent arrival Alun Lewis (London Welsh) covering for him on the bench.

Bevan Wilson opened the All Blacks' account with a penalty goal to which Morgan replied twenty five minutes into the game. Then came a fine try by the Lions to leave New Zealand a memento of the tour's highlights. Cotton, Duggan, Beaumont and Price handled in turn before the backs joined in, Fenwick setting up a maul from which Morgan raced on to touch down. The scrum-half converted for 9-3, which was how the score stayed until ten minutes from time when Wilson kicked his second penalty. In the light of the treatment the Lions' pack was handing out to the All Blacks (who frequently settled for three-man scrummaging to minimize damage) it seemed that the tourists could hold their lead, now down to three points, until the end.

It was not to be, and again the villain of the piece would be the captain. With five minutes left of the Test, and the series, Bennett fielded a loose ball deep in Lions' territory and, under pressure from Brian Williams, failed to put a clearance safely away into touch. The ball fell to Osborne, who pumped it straight and high to the Lions' 22 where Graham Mourie hit Wheeler with a tackle that knocked the ball from the hooker's arms into the grasp of Laurie Knight. The All Black number eight went like an express train for a decisive try which, though unconverted, was enough to deny the tourists their hoped-for consolation prize. Eden Park erupted with joy as the beaten Lions trudged away to their changing room, some close to tears. They had been denied a result that their forwards had surely earned by a single mistake from a man whose screw-kicks could hit the Stradey Park touchlines unerringly week in, week out. Thus the last-gasp victory by New Zealand was symbolic of a tour on which the visitors' backs were less than adequate. For this, the coach carried the can.

Nearly three decades on John Dawes no longer feels, or at least manifests, the hurt of major defeat. The rugby world looks back at him as one of the game's philosophers, for whom 'it is only a game.' His coolness in action is well remembered, and although he was undoubtedly a stern, even ruthless leader and driver people remember that he rarely lost his temper. If a team captained or coached by him played badly he preferred to argue through its failings coolly and reasonably rather than bawling men out; always searching for answers which he preferred to be voiced by the players themselves. However, when he looks back to the summer of '77 I judge him to be bitter – if not angry – that a side with such high hopes and so much promise failed its acid test. In this chapter blind spots which he never cured have been highlighted, in particular leaving his backs to sort themselves out. So much he admits, taking the blame rather than naming fall guys. "We lost in Fiji on the way home," he smiles. "Maybe that was my fault, too."

The immediate reactions in the UK were less than kind, and critics lamented the 'decline' of the Lions after the great accomplishments of 1971 and 1974. Books came out with titles like *The Long Lost Tour* and *Lions Down Under*. In his *History of the British Lions* Clem Thomas wrote, "After the two great tours in the early 1970s, 1977 was a case of 'after the Lord Mayor's Show' and turned out to be a huge disappointment". Dawes's Lions finished a sad second best that year.

But when the statistics are examined the tour can only be described as a failure in the context of the Tests, two of which were lost through one-off, unique eventualities featuring individuals not combined play, and a third was won by the Lions. Twenty-one games were won against robust provincial opposition and there was only one defeat (by the NZ Universities). The 1977 side's predecessors, 1971 excepted, would not have turned their noses up at such a record. The 1904 British Isles side scrambled one draw and lost the other three Tests. The 1930 Lions won one Test and lost three. The post-War team of 1950 got a draw and lost three, while 1959 yielded three defeats and a narrow victory in Auckland. The 1966 whitewash is better forgotten, and lastly the 1971 side were, well, something else.

In short, the 1977 Lions' record compares favourably with that of the majority of their predecessors. They were beaten, but not disgraced.

FOURTEEN

O ther great captains of Wales in the twentieth century left their mark and a legacy. Gwyn Nicholls's inspirational leadership had brought a first Golden Era at its start while John Gwilliam's successes after World War II were golden too (as was the contribution of Bleddyn Williams, albeit that his reign at the helm was a brief one). Arguably, however, the 1970s, with John Dawes always influential in the van of international achievement, must go down in history as the outstanding era in the Welsh game: indubitably a Third Golden Era. There was an element of style under-writing its uniqueness. Gareth Edwards, Barry John, Mervyn Davies, JPR, Gerald Davies and their peers were a constellation that twinkled in the rugby heaven, sometimes in the context of tours by the British Lions. The Welsh enjoyed huge success in Europe: besides three Grand Slams Dawes, as captain and then coach, delivered five Triple Crowns, four of them in succession from 1976 to 1979. Well might the unassuming man from Newbridge now say to himself, "Been there, done that." This consideration now prompted him to ponder a next career step.

The direction he should take was to a great degree determined by events going on around him. July 1980 would see the launch of the Welsh Rugby Union's Centenary season, and a year earlier Ray Williams had quit his role as Coaching Organiser to become Centenary Officer with a huge range of celebratory events and major fixtures to devise and schedule. He remembers John Dawes dropping in at his office one afternoon saying, "I'm interested in the post you're leaving. Tell me all about it." Williams's reaction was one of delight: Dawes "had the rugby world at his feet" and he was willing to put vast experience, plus a high profile worldwide, at his country's disposal. The conversation was positive, and in Williams's opinion there appeared to be no man better qualified for the job.

Dawes says, "After five years as National Team Coach I felt that it was time to look to my future. As an amateur, my role had been a powerful one, but the demands it made on my time and my private life was becoming well nigh unbearable. I felt that becoming Coaching Organiser – that is, a professional member of the WRU's staff – was a logical next step. Available to succeed me as National Team Coach was a former Wales captain and success-ful coach at Bridgend in the shape of John Lloyd. Hence I felt able to accept the WRU's invitation when it came and John stepped into my shoes in December 1979. I was pleased that Malcolm Lewis, who had been Ray's right hand man, overcame his disappointment at not being promoted and agreed to serve under me. The future looked good."

That is more than can be said for the National XV. The ninety-ninth season of international rugby football in Wales was far from being the most successful in WRU history, with two defeats out of four, at Twickenham and in Dublin, which saw them finish the Five Nations tournament with four points and second place behind England's joyful Grand Slam. But if the Welsh lacked their normal aggression it may well be that France's supremo Albert Ferrasse began to undermine it with remarks at the dinner which followed France's defeat at Cardiff in January 1980. The French President suggested that their hosts were "over-vigorous" – a clear case of the pot calling the kettle black. He had been abetted by his captain, whose scalp was gashed in a collision during the match: Jean-Pierre Rives made sure that his jersey was lurid with the blood he smeared all over it.

Many held the view that such insinuations inhibited the Welsh for the remainder of the campaign and even in the seasons that followed. It is possible, however, that they had shot themselves in the foot. Just over a year before Ferrasse's accusation Coaching Organiser Ray Williams had gone into print with a stern warning about foul play in Welsh rugby:

> There is currently an unacceptable level of violence [in our game] which should not be tolerated... Selection committees must have enough courage to reject those whose behaviour falls short of accepted standards. Coaches must be very careful how they motivate their men, especially before a match. It is possible with certain players to induce an arousal state where logic and skill go out through the window – and this is where trouble begins.

Such strong language from a top-ranking WRU official would have been, in effect, a prompt for those anxious to put a cork in the Welsh bottle. By now watching from the sidelines, Dawes remembers the then President of the RFU attending the 1980 match between England and France at Parc des Princes where he fanned these controversial embers. After the visitors' 17-13 victory Bill Ramsay looked forward to his country's next game, against Wales at Twickenham, saying pointedly, "Our game in Paris was a really good clean contest. I am hoping very much that we shall see a similar display. at Twickenham in a fortnight's time."

Referees acquaint themselves with many aspects of a big game which they are down to control, and the referee for Wales's visit to 'HQ', Ireland's David Burnett, would have been well aware of the powerful undercurrent of criticism focused upon hard-as-nails Welsh abandon. Thus, after a fractious ten-minute opening to the match full of off-the-ball scuffles he took aside the two captains, Bill Beaumont and Jeff Squire, delivering a warning – to be relayed to their teams – that the next man to commit an act of foul play would be dismissed from the field.

That player turned out to be Paul Ringer (formerly of Ebbw Vale but by now playing with Llanelli). At fifteen minutes, the aggressive flanker went late into John Horton and the referee sent him off. Although the England stand-off half was disconcerted rather than injured, given the warning and the climate of opinion Burnett's decision was inevitable; the tackle was high and reckless. In his book *Thanks to Rugby* Bill Beaumont wrote:

> I would defend Ringer in so far as his tackle was not, by a long way, the dirtiest one I have seen on a Rugby pitch; but knowing the attitude of the referee, which had been clearly and forcibly relayed by the two captains to all the players, his act was one of the utmost, unbelievable folly... the height of stupidity and the action of a fool.

Beaumont adds later, "Had Ringer not been sent off Wales would probably have won." As it was the fourteen visitors played wonderfully well for sixty-four more minutes: Squire and Elgan Rees got tries, but the place-kickers failed to add vital points. In contrast Dusty Hare was on target with match-winning penalties for England, the third of which came in the eightieth minute – a masterly shot aimed from the right-hand touchline which gave England only their second victory over Wales in sixteen seasons. The crowd was exultant.

"It is incredible what an atmosphere of tension and even hatred had built up before the game," John Dawes remembers, "and we were on the back foot from the start. The Welsh XV was booed onto the field at Twickenham, something hitherto unheard of. John Scott and Terry Holmes clashed in the opening minutes, stoking things up. But even after giving his warning Burnett should have been able to distinguish genuine foul play from exuberance. Ringer's tackle merited a penalty, but not the ultimate sentence of a sending off. I believe the incident affected our game for several seasons. The Welsh started to feel that they did not dare throw a punch – something forwards have to do now and then in order to assert themselves.

"It's also true, however, that the conveyor belt of talent based on our domestic game was not now yielding players of the maturity shown by their immediate predecessors. A teachers' strike at that time ended with the withdrawal from tutoring and coaching of the schoolmasters who had traditionally moulded first XVs at our secondary schools. They now showed their discontent by declining to put in extra-curricula effort such as staying on after school to run a First XV practice or travelling with boys to away games. Further, there was strife and demoralization in the declining Welsh heavy industries like coal and steel which had provided the tough cores of our packs. Hence there was a big challenge for John Lloyd and the National XV to recover and maintain Welsh momentum – while I had to look hard and constructively at the grass roots and the smaller clubs who traditionally fed the higher echelons of the game."

Dawes, then, well understood his mission. However, as a salaried operator within the WRU he was no longer a bird of passage who could fly in and out of southern Wales for lightning visits to watch rugby and attend meetings. His base could no longer be London; it had to be Cardiff. His wife's priorities, however, still lay in the metropolis, where her teaching career could prosper and semi-pro engagements could advance her reputation. There were bullets to be bitten on.

"I needed to accept at this point," Dawes admits, "that Janette had been no more than mildly interested in my work routines and ambitions – which, it has to be conceded, took up a big slice of my time. The fact was that she had become totally disenchanted by the situation, and there was no hope that she would make the move back to Wales with our children, whose up-bringing she had shouldered brilliantly. She was adamant that London was where her opportunities existed and that the Welsh musical scene held no openings for her. Thus my acceptance of the Coaching Organiser job at Cardiff Arms Park was, for her, the last straw; as for me, I knew that there was no going back and I had no other option. At that stage, then, we accepted the situation to see if it would work and whether we would continue to have a relationship.

"That proved not to be the case. It has gradually but terminally waned. For a while we used to meet up and spend Christmas with our offspring, but now that is over and for both of us it is simply the maintaining of contact with them and the grandchildren that keeps us in touch. Michael is in the West Midlands with three children Rhodri, Emily and Iwan, while Catherine, her husband, and daughter Lily are at Telford. All very tough and complicated; but people who have been through such an experience will understand."

His move to Cardiff brought a light-hearted interlude when John Dawes dropped anchor with Carwyn James in the Cardiff suburb of Penylan. He recalls: "Carwyn shared a flat, which could accommodate me as a new asylum seeker, with the legendary and volatile 'Doc' Jones, who worked for an international drugs company. This native of Penygroes had such a persuasive manner that he allegedly commanded the biggest expenses allowance of any such rep in Britain. His role was that of head cook and hoover-master; and he also fed the cat, whose name was Angharad Trenchard-Jones and spent most of her time romancing out on the tiles. James, too, was by this time a creature of the night who returned to Penylan in the small hours, enjoyed a stiff gin and tonic with me, before leaving for BBC Radio Wales at six am to present the morning sports summary. The rest of the day he spent resting in a large room where scattered on the carpet were invitations to speak at dinners from Land's End to John O'Groats – not to mention contracts and cheques from the Beeb."

But James's ear and Doc's were ready ones when the Coaching Organiser wanted to chew over the challenges encountered in his new job. Dawes was grateful for the company and support rendered to him by both men (and grieved deeply at Carwyn's premature death in 1983), but he felt the need for a place of his own and before long took an apartment in Penarth. In due course his circle of friends, in and out of rugby football, grew and widened, and in recent years he has lived in a pleasant house not far from the shops and agreeable pubs and bistros of Llandaff.

The first major change in life-style was encountered in Dawes's early months on the staff of the Union. He realised that there was now a professional accountability which he had not encountered in his amateur days. The vibes he was getting told him, "You are our servant. You have to do as you are told." This attitude was heavily present within the Cardiff Arms Park headquarters of the WRU, but it was also encountered during the visits the Coaching Organiser began paying to clubs on the circuit.

On the whole his reputation and ability brought him a warm welcome from the squads and coaches that he dealt with in practical sessions out on the pitch; but committee-men and officials whom he met after a shower were less than cordial. Dawes knew that his first priority lay with the coaches; but the nominated men with whom he was working were not always the right raw material. All too often they would be recently-retired players who wanted to keep in touch with their clubs and thought that becoming coach was suitable recognition after many seasons of loyal service out on the pitch. It did not follow, however, that just because of seniority such people had the professional qualities required. A coaching diploma is almost a post-graduate qualification and the clubs he dealt with had not properly realised this. All too often the men they put up were bossy sergeant-major types who found it difficult to interact with players wanting carrots as well as constant stick. Dawes had to go right back to basics and educate committees about the virtues needed by a good coach.

As Centenary Officer Ray Williams had a lot on his hands and Dawes felt unable to make demands on his time. He sought advice and good practice from the Government-funded National Coaching Foundation which was not specific to rugby but laid down valuable principles which were relevant to his needs.

As a conscientious employee Dawes was never a clock-watcher. But it is clear that the new work-load he had taken on stretched him to the utmost. He and Malcolm Lewis had divided their responsibilities so that his assistant liaised with the schools and youth stream while he dealt with the clubs. He soon found himself coping with an eight-hour day and five-day week at his Cardiff base, as well as the evening and weekend stints when most of the rugby-playing population was enjoying itself at leisure. He thus found it difficult to create time for himself in which to relax, for if he was not at his desk during office hours there were colleagues who thought he must be skiving.

Throughout its history the WRU has usually been a reactionary body. Early on the Coaching Committee, chaired at this time by the former Swansea coach Ieuan Evans, did agree with Dawes to the appointment of 'development officers' to whom routine coaching matters out and about could be delegated. But instead of embracing the concept in its entirety and placing one such officer in each of the Union's nine Districts the Committee took on just four men, or five less than the number required.

"This was a compromise," Dawes recalls, "by a Committee that was the opposite of dynamic. Malcolm and I still found ourselves travelling many miles to spend evenings with the clubs, while our presence was also demanded whenever the Committee met. Other promising but short-lived initiatives included the introduction of international athletes Lynn Davies (1964 Olympic Gold Medal winner in the long jump) and sprinter J.J.Williams to advise on fitness levels. After a publicity photograph was published featuring Terry Holmes on a treadmill in an oxygen mask this constructive innovation was abandoned. When I suggested creating a running track around the touchlines of the new stadium, our masters of the half measure agreed but stipulated that it would have sharp bends at the corners and only two lanes.

"Yes, the Union was full of die-hards in those days. The old gentlemen who, for the most part, ran it had great, glorious memories and were determined that their reputations should not be threatened or eclipsed. Then you had pressure from lower down; our international players of the 'eighties did not wish to be reminded of the great deeds of the previous decade. No-one seemed able or ready to analyse the direction in which big rugby was moving – towards professionalism. The boot manufacturer Adidas penetrated the camp giving boots bearing their logo to some of our top men (plus, I guess, some pocket money). While protesting its horror that rugby's amateur status should be flouted in this way, the Union fell short of holding an enquiry to discover if any of its personnel or players had broken rules. Then there came a complacent consensus that Welsh rugby could not be all that bad when Wales finished third in rugby union's first-ever World Cup (though conceding an unprecedented fifty points to New Zealand in the process). Leagues came in, but there was strife about which clubs should play in the premier division – as if there was not already a select group whose pre-eminence in the game dated back to the nineteenth century. To me the WRU seemed incapable of contemplating radical change.

"Also, it will be remembered that at this time the re-built National Ground was nearing completion, and it sometimes struck Malcolm and me that this was what WRU personnel were really excited about – to the detriment of nurturing our grass roots. All in all these were trying times for its members of staff, especially as the Secretary, Bill Clement, was marking time as he prepared for retirement."

Dawes's disenchantment was evident to the personnel closest to him. Ray Williams thinks that changes to what had been his cheerful disposition date back to the 1977 Lions tour – its failure in the Tests and a less than cordial relationship with critics in and outside the media; but this may be simplistic in the light of the two great seasons over which he presided following his return home, when his confidence was fully restored. I think it is more likely that the break-up of his marriage and the professional frustrations which he was experiencing, lay at the root of his discontent. Whatever the reason, critics noted an occasional lack of punctuality at important meetings (even when Dawes himself had set them up). His mood might be negative or destructive when he arrived in Committee. Some of all this was doubtless down to an absence of approval and enthusiasm on the part of its members for the policies he was shaping. Even Coaching Organisers need the occasional pat on the back.

Now, he is inclined to agree that the trauma of a marital severance proved greater than he expected. His drinking habits

219

underwent changes. He never took alcohol on routine trips (since his job depended on mobility and he did not dare to be 'over the limit' when driving home). However, he felt that, as a player and then as National Coach his contact with Welsh clubs in general had been minimal. Now there was a need to get to know their personnel, in all age groups, and sit down with them to talk about the game, thus revealing himself as an ordinary guy who was on their side. So, if he were staying the night at a distant destination like Pembrokeshire or Clwyd he would enjoy a pint or two after a coaching master class in order to build and cement a relationship with the locals – something he would never have done in the past. Clubhouse hospitality was nothing if not warm and generous.

Although he never, or at least very seldom, drank alcohol at home he grew to welcome a pint or two, or some wine, at rugby occasions and get-togethers. He knows that he often became 'boisterous', a mood whose effect was to mirror the frustration and impatience he felt as he sought to bring about change in Welsh rugby's outlook and methods and effect a streamlining of the ruling body. He became quick to pick arguments and, instead of presenting a case reasonably, to rubbish opposition. Old friends were hurt and bruised. He concedes, "I guess I simply didn't control the habit, and became over-aggressive when there was no need. Social beverages loosened my tongue and made me a bit bolder, perhaps. However, I have to say that at no period in my life have I felt a *need* for, or a dependency on, alcohol."

Ray Williams says, "I think John was gradually realizing that he had taken a wrong turning. There was a lot more administration to the job than he had expected, whereas he chiefly wanted to identify coaching talent and talk with men who just needed the right encouragement to reach the top of the coaching ladder. In other words, he was a track suit man not particularly interested in the endless behind-the-scenes politicking."

Dawes agrees: "That's right. I had made a mistake. Meekly turning up at an office to fix timetables and schedules on the telephone was not my forte. What I best enjoyed was talking and analyzing rugby with men who were coaching or playing it. People also seemed to think there was an elitist streak in my make-up. If that is true it was because I had reached the summit of the game and could match the experience of anyone in my peer group.

"But having said all that, I believe I can claim that my contribution was constructive. For a start, one aspect of the job was playing a supportive role arranging the National XV's movements and activities for coaches who followed me like John Lloyd and John Bevan. I was, in effect, a team manager who timetabled the week-to-week routine of the players, provided practice facilities, organised training sessions, hired team buses, arranged flights and booked our personnel into hotels. This meant that I could regularly watch Wales in action, something which pleased me. Of course I was careful to keep a low profile and not interfere with my successors' routines, but if someone needed a shoulder to groan on I would be ready. Furthermore, just as Ray Williams had always been at hand with counsel during my stint as National Team Coach, so I was always ready and willing to talk with my successors if invited to do so. What I had lost, however, was any direct influence upon selection."

Dawes was conscientious about his relationship with the clubs and ran lively conferences for their coaches. For a while these took place on the playing fields and lecture rooms at Aberystwyth, where years before he had obediently attended one of Ray Williams's courses to support his application to become National Coach. But it became clear that the cost of continuing to use this far-flung facility was prohibitive to both the WRU and the clubs. The Dawes solution, therefore, was to to take courses to personnel – in their own Districts. He remembers a successful launch of this system, which grew until, in his final period in office, he visited 115 venues in twelve months.

Something that gave him comfort during what had turned out to be a formidable challenge was the retention of his links with London Welsh, who were ever mindful of the transformation which he had effected at Old Deer Park. For his part he says that he remained a true London Welshman (something that still rankled with certain elements in the homeland), and was delighted to be honoured with life-membership of the club in 1979 when he left London for Cardiff Arms Park. In 1998, although by now firmly settled in Cardiff suburbia, he accepted the position of President and is grateful to the modest, affable Jack Lowis, his immediate predecessor in office, for taking the title Deputy President and being willing to represent the club at more routine functions in Middlesex and Surrey, thus saving him spending more time on the M4. Dawes has always sought to be at Old Deer Park once or twice a month when he looks forward to entertaining guests of the club in the Room which bears his name – with the concomitant OBE awarded to him in 1971 'for services to British rugby'.

A number of Dawes's one-time playing contemporaries are always delighted to see their skipper of old when he calls in for a chat or maybe to watch Welsh Academicals in London. The 'Accies' are mainly field teams comprising university men and the occasional large schoolboy, appearing at London Welsh's HQ each year to play a fixture in memory of Denis Horgan, a stalwart at UCW Aberystwyth in John Dawes's time and a coach to London Welsh in the halcyon days. The character of the club-house is perhaps less fervently Welsh than of yore; yet those who enter it are made well aware that they are not 'in England'. Certainly the President approves of this atmosphere.

He knows, too, of disappointment at some of the Exiles' hopes which have been dashed since the WRU established leagues in 1990. The club has continued to see itself as a Welsh presence in English rugby, but has harboured ambitions to compete in a Welsh league system. Entry to what was initially called the Heineken National League was on offer at the outset, but to their chagrin London Welsh would have been expected to start off by competing in a humbler division and working their way up to Premiership ranking. This was unacceptable both on principle – that is, it was an insult – and practically, since members accustomed to watching high profile opposition like Cardiff, Llanelli, Wasps or Harlequins could hardly be expected to show the same levels of enthusiasm and support for fixtures against second and third echelon clubs from the homeland. Dawes thinks that old-established anti-London Welsh attitudes prevailed in the general committee of the WRU, with veteran members like the hard-liner Jack Young insisting that the Exiles should be treated "like any other club". Evidently "other clubs" did not include the likes of Cardiff, Llanelli, Newport, Swansea and old-established high-fliers.

The net result has been that London Welsh have dutifully played within the RFU's league system. In 2005 the club still hankers after a place in the Welsh competitive structure, but to Old

Deer Park this is a less attractive proposition now that the cream of Wales's players appear in regional sides or the Celtic League. "You could almost say that the RFU have been kinder to us than our own countrymen," John Dawes reflects. "They bounced us around during the early seasons, when clubs were often demoted to fit their leagues without actually being relegated – before being promptly re-instated. This could mean London Welsh travelling to all sorts of previously unknown venues in, say, East Anglia, where 'crowds' comprised a few men and their dogs. But the financial assistance from Twickenham has been invaluable and the Exiles have never felt discriminated against.

"In recent seasons we have coasted along near the top of Division One just below England's Premiership. This has been acceptable so far on these grounds: if we were to win promotion into the elite division, the rules state that our ground capacity would need to be increased to a minimum of 10,000 (from around four thousand). This in turn would require fund-raising which would stretch our resources to the utmost – and there would be no guarantee that we could hold our place in the top echelon and continue to draw big crowds to Old Deer Park. So the club is a victim of Catch-22, with ambition needing to be tempered by reality.

"In this context the Exiles are fortunate in having a resourceful Board of Directors who are both generous and prudent whose names I would like to record here. David Hammond, a financier, is its Chairman with Bill Carey-Evans as his deputy. The industrialist Kelvin Bryon, whose generosity knows no bounds, has been a tower of strength, along with John Taylor, Sir Alan Thomas, Dr Ceri James and Tudor Roberts. Also on the Board is a former Cambridge captain in Adrian Davies, a highly-effective Director of rugby who, I think, is the stuff that National Team Coaches are made of and keeps our semi-professional players fine-tuned. I ought also to pay tribute to our membership whose support, through a difficult period in our history, has never waned."

After Ray Williams had resigned from the Secretaryship of the Welsh Rugby Union in the autumn of 1988, "for personal reasons," David East, Chief Constable of the South Wales Police, did a short stint in office which lasted until December 1989 and was marred by feuding about what should be the WRU's policy towards South Africa, where apartheid still ruled. The Union was guilty of misplaced secrecy relating to its input to the Republic's Centenary celebrations: "a thoroughly distasteful episode," said the Welsh Brewers *Rugby Annual for Wales* and one which resulted in a special general meeting at which the clubs voted overwhelmingly to break off relations with South Africa, reversing a decision of 1984. Into East's shoes in January 1990 stepped Denis Evans, brought up in the Gwent hamlet of Trefil and the holder of one Welsh cap. The newcomer brought to his role nearly two decades of high-powered business activity in Hong Kong.

Evans spent his first months in office examining and assessing the state of the game in the homeland before publishing an in-depth report called *The Quest for Excellence* – a Plan to take the Welsh game into the twenty first century. "We cannot afford to fail," it said, "and we will not fail". It went down well, and empowered the Secretary to wield a new broom who turned out to be the former Wales hooker Jeff Young, now Technical Director.

Among those now swept away was the Coaching Organiser of the last decade, John Dawes, along with his assistant Malcolm Lewis. Says Dawes, "To say I was shocked when the Coaching Committee asked for my resignation would be an understatement. All Denis Evans could say was that the two of us had become surplus to requirements. Sadly, I cleared my desk, pondering where I seemed to have gone wrong.

"There may have been two factors behind the WRU's decision to fire me. Firstly, I had boxed my corner vigorously and could claim to have put in place a workable system which was faithful to, while up-dating, the guidelines laid down by Ray Williams. So the track record stood up to scrutiny. However, I have indicated that I showed my impatience and frustration at the slow-moving WRU machine and may have lost supporters in this way.

"Secondly, Ray Williams had always held that the performance of the National XV was a 'shop window' for Welsh rugby which now, as time went on, was desperately short of quality goods for display. Our last Grand Slam lay a dozen years earlier and we had played over a decade without a Triple Crown. The only Championship title had come in 1988 and was shared with the French. New Zealand had put together a sequence of twelve victories in a row over us (a run which has extended to the present day). Romania had beaten us twice in the eighties. There was, in short, precious little of which the game in Wales could be proud. So it is more than likely that the WRU were looking for fall-guys, and Malcolm and I were available. In a decade, our critics com-plained, the National Coaching Organiser and his staff had failed to deliver the goods. Despite our input, new Welsh heroes in the game were not coming through. Ieuan Evans, Hadley, Norster and Jonathan Davies promised much, but there were not enough men at their level of excellence."

John Dawes reflected that the train had hit the buffers. Fifty is not a good age at which to be cast upon the labour market. His long seasons at London Welsh meant that his circle of genuine friends and allies lay outside Wales, and the powerbase which he had considered strong had been knocked from under his feet. What hurt was that after a decade's loyal and constructive service there was scarcely a word of thanks from the Welsh Rugby Union.

At this point in time he returned to London and the family home at Sunbury, turning again for consolation and involvement to his old friends, the Exiles. He does not seem to have rediscovered an ambition to teach professionally, but was still ready to don a track suit and coach players. Bill Calcraft, an Australian, was the club's semi-professional coach and readily agreed to an offer of assistance. "I suppose I made myself useful," Dawes recalls. "But after a while my enthusiasm waned as I realised that there wasn't really a job for me with the First XV and that the club were doing me a favour by inviting my contribution. The workload in the evenings and on Saturdays was considerable, but during week-days time hung heavily on my hands."

In 1998 Dawes moved back again to Cardiff – becoming grateful to old, Welsh-based friends for their companionship – and decided that he would settle for a comfortable retirement. "Besides the Crawshays visits to Old Deer Park I pay occasional visits to the Millennium Stadium and the Old Internationals' attractive lounge. But otherwise my contact with rugby is via the television screen. I don't think that, in over a decade, any interest has overtaken the game in my list of priorities. But if I am not enjoying a match I switch off; and similarly if the occasional visit to Cardiff Arms Park disappoints my expectations I have sometimes left the grandstand at half time.

"There are my grandchildren to keep in touch with and support, at least one of them (Rhodri) a very promising sportsman, so there are regular visits to the Marches and the Midlands where they are with their parents. Of course, I cannot cut links with rugby entirely, and in the morning Press I take care to keep up with trends and happenings in the world of sport – and usually turn to the back pages first. Certainly in the latter part of 2004 the manoeuvrings of Clive Woodward, the Lions' coach elect, have been something to keep up with. As for tackling novels and non-fiction I have been an avid Dick Francis fan, though there are one or two of his books still on my shelves waiting to be read – for agreeable escapism. When in the past I have had time on my hands, in the car, for instance, or at a hotel, it was usually spent thinking about the job in hand and the consultancy work awaiting me with the clubs. I never really got the reading habit.

"But I walk. Several times in a year Jill and I (with the dog) set off to familiarize ourselves with a new part of Britain. We may drive a couple of hundred miles to an area which we don't know before launching out into the unknown. We choose a period like Easter, Whitsun or late September when good weather is likely, and try to go somewhere different each time. Despite all my rugby travels I had never been along the coastline between Tenby and Milford Haven, for instance, which revealed itself to us as beautiful and full of grandeur. When this manuscript goes off to the publisher we intend to tackle the north Somerset coastline between Weston-super-Mare and Minehead for the first time. These are our route marches of discovery, with vigorous exercise thrown in.

"And peace of mind. Now I have time to reflect – on moments of triumph in rugby and times when fate seemed to turn her back on me. Certainly my story has elements of the roller-coaster about it, but life has never been dull and to have enjoyed a career heavily involved with a sporting society that I love has gone far beyond the dreams of my youth. I have written of it briefly before, and am grateful to Professors Gareth Williams and David Smith for allowing me to print here the paragraph I supplied which brought down the curtain on their masterly work *Fields of Praise* which celebrated the Centenary of the Welsh Rugby Union – and the greatness of the Game:

There is so much enjoyment you can get... if you are prepared to work at it in training and in organization and coaching that there's no price you can put on it. You can't buy it. The enjoyment from its eighty minutes is, in sport, the most I've ever had, and the magnificences of the game were something to be envied. We played it, and engendered so much enjoyment for ourselves and the spectators that they used to come... to enjoy it too.

JOHN DAWES: AN EPILOGUE

Since David Parry-Jones and I embarked on this life-and-times memoir we have been overtaken agreeably by events, and decisions happening in both Europe and New Zealand. Not the least of these by a long, long way is the Grand Slam brought off by Wales in the 2005 Six Nations Championship. It should guarantee the presence of a goodly number of Welshmen in the British Isles tour party due to visit New Zealand in the middle months of 2005. And, happily, the Kiwis have looked very hard and searchingly at the structure of the tour.

From the outset, visits by the Lions have always been tremendously popular, and New Zealand took note of the successful Test series of 2001 in Australia. With 20,000 supporters likely to follow the tourists, the NZRU can expect a financial bonanza. To their credit, its administrators listened to public opinion and reached the conclusion that it would be impractical, and even insulting, to offer their guests a mere handful of games. The fans were demanding a return to the 'old fashioned' multi-venue style of tour which their country has not hosted since South Africa's visit in 1994.

For some time, though they were not unsympathetic to this pressure, the NZRU's hands have been tied by their SANZAR commitments which leave room for a maximum of three International fixtures outside the Tri-nations series. But a window has now been identified between the Super Twelve tournament (whose 2004 Final was on 22 May) and the Tri-nations which will probably kick off a week later on 23 July. Into the gap thus created the Lions tour of 2005 should fit snugly.

As well as the host country's Test venues, therefore, it will be possible for a good spread of fans who live, geographically speaking, along the perimeter to watch the Europeans locally. Auckland, Wellington, Christchurch and Dunedin are used to being in the big time, but other venues too will now entertain Sir Clive Woodward's men in non-Test encounters. At the time of writing these are Rotorua, New Plymouth, Hamilton, Invercargill and Palmerston North. Such a spread of locations will give pleasure not only to New Zealanders but also to the British Isles players; having travelled twelve thousand miles it would be a pity if the 2005 tourists did not see as much as possible of what is a very beautiful, unspoiled part of the world. And the British will hope that some time before the end of this decade a tour in the UK and Ireland by the All Blacks will include some of the old traditional fixtures.

How the Lions will adapt to the new demands remains to be seen. Sir Clive's pre-planning proposals have been revolutionary, and have not pleased all supporters in the British Isles. In August 2004, in prolonged talks with the RFU, he appeared to be arguing that he could preside over the build-up to the 2005 Lions tour and at the same time master-mind England's Six Nations campaign, with the donkey-work being done by his right hand man Andy Robinson. In retrospect no self-respecting governing body could have agreed to such an arrangement, and I am glad that ultimately Woodward freed himself from the England responsibility to bring his first-class organizational skills to bear on selecting and grooming the Lions.

At the time of writing he hopes to take two full squads (44 players and 26 support staff) to New Zealand, though he must expect the Four Home Unions Tours Committee to consider, and maybe prune his ambitions. Veteran tourists like Dr Jack Matthews are scornful of the concept of two Lions XVs, an 'A' team for the Tests and a 'B' squad to mop up provincial fixtures: bad for 'bonding' and possibly a second-rate deal for provincial opponents and spectators.

For representing the British Isles should remain the summit of British players' careers, and personnel should regard going on tour as a pinnacle. Men are picked for their countries, and can now hope to play in a World Cup tournament. But becoming a Lion remains something special, involving the *crème de la crème*. Certainly that is the view of all Lions of bygone years, and they deplore developments that threaten it.

I have indicated that my contact with the game of rugby is now minimal compared to the time when it was in my mind, and on my mind, for seven days a week. My London Welsh visits continue to be something I look forward to, but the absence of a high profile, high intensity input to playing rugby, or its administration, has left in me what might be called a void. Then I remind myself that when the game turned professional (or 'went open' as the change was called) it closed the door to the highest levels of the game upon teachers, electricians, doctors, plumbers and others from a wide spectrum of backgrounds who played rugby for fun, sharing the pain, the pleasure the socializing and the friendships it offered.

I fear that professionalism has eliminated all that, at the highest level, in one fell swoop. I regret such a sea change, and am doubtful whether the game's new character would have included a role for such servants as myself. The ambitions and experience of the young men who now populate rugby's higher echelons are narrower, with coaches demanding professional commitment and the 'body beautiful', as I call it, from their employees: that is, muscularity and the ability to just keep on running – sometimes like headless chickens. Unlike soccer players, for example, who train most mornings but have the rest of the day off, today's rugby men must carry out their demanding team routines each morning before doing weight training on their own in the afternoon (boring but necessary). I ask myself how much time Welsh players can devote to thinking and talking about the opportunities to acquire and demonstrate the skills which the game offers.

From the start of the 1980s, when I became Coaching Organiser, the three major southern hemisphere nations began placing special emphasis on fitness levels, with attention given to body-building and diet. Through my travels and contact with our clubs, and despite modest reforms that I could put in place here and there, it was clear to me that Wales was not taking full note of these new trends. Individual players were not getting fit; club training remained perfunctory. Towards the end of the decade we won third place in the first-ever World Cup tournament, a feat that the nation applauded – conveniently forgetting the semi-final reverse at New Zealand's hands by an horrendous 49 points to 6. Complacency took over, and was not dispelled by the All Blacks' two victories the following year by 52-3 and 54-9. The Welsh preferred to dwell in the past and expect our traditional flair to reassert itself and restore pride. But our physiques and mental conditioning were far from ready. Even during the nineties anyone watching a Welsh squad train could not fail to note undesirable bulges around the participants' tummies. The net result of such shortcomings is an unprecedented run of failure; in the Five (and Six) Nations series we have won only a single title outright in the last quarter of a century. This is woeful and demoralising.

For many years Wales boasted an admirable system headed by four senior clubs, (in diplomatic alphabetical order) Cardiff, Llanelli, Newport and Swansea. They had grounds which attracted the biggest crowds; they supplied most of Wales's International players; they enjoyed sustained success in cup and league competition; they played matches against major touring sides; and our best up-and-coming players gravitated in their direction. There was a perceived second rank containing clubs like London Welsh, Pontypool, Bridgend and Neath who could, on their day, beat one of the Big Four. A third group contained, for example, Maesteg, Newbridge, Cross Keys and Glamorgan Wanderers, who once in a decade were capable of killing a giant. It was all very gentlemanly, and the top echelon clubs behaved graciously to the lesser brethren who retained fixtures with the mighty. In their sporadic visits to Wales, many New Zealand luminaries admired its framework (while continuing to beat us).

What had been happening, however, was that our top men would play against their peers, and be extended, only once or twice a month. In other matches they could cruise to victory. Thus when they played in the Six Nations, or the Heineken Cup, or even the Celtic League against Scottish, and especially Irish, opposition it was difficult to adjust upwards to the pace and intensity of games. That accounts for the drastic surgery which needed to be carried out by the new Chief Executive of the WRU, David Moffett, before the start of the 2003-4 season. It hurt; many old-stagers were mortified by the cavalier treatment he meted out to venerable member clubs. But by September 2004 the fans knew what to expect and were rallying to support the Blues, the Scarlets, the Dragons and the Ospreys. They now carry the flag for Welsh rugby. I have no doubt at all that the changes were necessary and can deliver success.

Next question: coaching. Why were the Welsh so spectacularly unsuccessful in the seasons around the turn of the twentieth century? I think that WRU policy was probably to blame. They never allowed the coaches they appointed to play themselves in.

This had an effect on the players who formed squads to compete at International level, in that they found it hard to adjust to new systems and game plans.

After a series of sad Welshmen who held the post of National Coach before their services were dispensed with, the Kiwi Graham Henry spent a busy period in control at the height of which South Africa were defeated for the first time. However, he left little else in the record books, departing before his contract with the WRU was up. Although many think it was the promise of coaching New Zealand's team which prompted him to go (after Wales lost 54-10 in Dublin) he made his feelings clear in a book published after the Lions 2001 tour of Australia, which he coached. He is quoted as saying "I did not want to be associated any longer with the incestuous, mediocre rugby culture fostered by the WRU."

His successor, another Kiwi, Steve Hansen, failed to live up to his promise and has not been missed. He was in charge of Wales when they gave, first, New Zealand and then England terrific battles in the 2003 World Cup – but no-one seems to know whether he can claim the credit for that or whether his players decided to ignore him and do their own thing. Mike Ruddock stepped in to fill the vacancy.

I am writing all this as a kind of 'Stop Press' on the day after Wales beat Ireland to complete a magnificent Grand Slam – 19 March 2005. All that is needed henceforth from the National Coach is 'more of the same'. There is only one concrete suggestion I will offer. Mike should abandon the practice of players leaving the field at half time. They return to the changing rooms simply to take revised instructions from the coach – possibly about the next seventeen or eighteen phases that they have to execute (pardon me while I yawn). I think the coach should confine his interventions on a match day to suggesting options before kick-off, leaving his captain to lead on the pitch, delivering the half-time pep-talk out in the fresh air and re-sharpening his players' will to win. The skipper is involved in their struggle. He shares their battle. He knows how it feels, and what is needed in the second forty minutes.

The key thing that a coach can and must continue to do is release Welsh talent, as demonstrated for example by Shane

Williams. There is a certain bravado possessed by Welsh backs and half-backs which can make crowds – and often opponents – gasp with admiration and amazement. The coach can make sure the ball is moved regularly and speedily to men like Shane and the lethal finisher Tom Shanklin. High-risk tactics leading to tries are what spectators pay to see. Our players must be willing to live dangerously in order to score them; they must be able to say to themselves, 'OK, if that may mean that the opposition gets three tries against us we will score four'. This appeared to be the Welsh attitude in the 2003 World Cup, and although it did not carry them to the semi-finals it won the unstinted admiration of hard-nosed Australian onlookers. Our players had shown that they were not duffers. Since then younger men like Dwayne Peel and Gavin Henson have come of age and the National XV has looked mature and well-constructed in the glorious spring of 2005.

It helps that we play home games in one of the world's finest arenas. There is a core of opinion in Wales which still believes that its predecessor ought to have been up-graded rather than knocked down; but that is hindsight, and the Millennium Stadium is a marvellous creation with a more-than-adequate crowd capacity and a terrific atmosphere. It also has flaws, such as the inability, from all seats, to see the big TV screen and the score-boards. And, for the rugby public, it is no longer a shrine known as Cardiff Arms Park but an all-purpose sports ground where, as well as major rugby fixtures, soccer, speedway and even day-night cricket are attractions.

Sadly, given the importance of finance in today's sporting world, the Millennium Stadium has not been marketed in the last five years with the vigour that was needed. On the contrary it has landed the WRU with the very problems it was built to solve, and at some events the crowd appears to be out-numbered by stewards. One thing is for sure, though: if Wales puts attack on a pedestal our supporters will still pour along Westgate Street and into its great grandstands to watch International Rugby.

And so I lay down my pen. Soon I shall be packing my bags and, in my capacity as London Welsh's President, setting off with the club's Male Choir to follow the Lions around New Zealand and entertain our Kiwi hosts in the post-match evenings. Their country's face has changed radically since my early trips there and the big cities are prosperous and glossy – but what counts are the people. It will be great to link up again with friends and opponents from 1969 and 1971 and more recent years.

All Blacks are hard as nails and near-impossible to beat on a rugby field in their own country – even by tourists who include a number of the players who delivered a Grand Slam in Europe. How the Lions will get on against them is anyone's guess. But I feel sure that there will be one triumphant combination in the New Zealand winter of 2005: the London Welsh RFC Male Choir cannot fail to win the Kiwis over!

Index

Index of International Games

ACKNOWLEDGEMENTS

I am enormously grateful to John Billot, the *Western Mail* and Associated Sport Photography for the photographs in the plate sections.

Also by David Parry-Jones

PRINCE GWYN
Gwyn Nicholls and the First Golden Era
of Welsh Rugby

The period between 1900 and 1911 has come to be known as Welsh Rugby's First Golden Era, thanks to six Triple Crowns and victories over New Zealand, Australia and new entrants into the European Championship, France. Much of this success derived from a particular style that was both eye-catching and devastatingly effective. Its development owed everything to the influence of Gwyn Nicholls.

Born in Gloucestershire, Nicholls came to Wales as a toddler when the family moved to Cardiff and "in all but birth was a Welshman" as the obituaries would put it. A centre three-quarter, he represented Cardiff 242 times, captaining the club during four seasons. He was skipper in ten of his twenty-four games for Wales, of which the most memorable was the (sole) defeat of New Zealand's first All Blacks. Team-mates, and the Press, nick-named him 'Prince'.

The dominant stature of Nicholls in Rugby Football bears comparison with that of W.G. Grace in the world of cricket at the start of the twentieth century. His skills were unsurpassed; the tactics he devised were innovative and definitive; he was a great leader of men. Yet this book shows how the squeaky-clean Nicholls of legend was also subject to vacillations and procrastinations which involved him in embarrassing controversies.

Prince Gwyn's canvas portrays what is today the world-wide game of Rugby Union Football at a fascinating and volatile early stage in its history.

www.seren-books.com

THE GWILLIAM SEASONS
John Gwilliam and the Second Golden Era of Welsh Rugby

In the late forties and early fifties the Welsh rugby team was at its highest highest peak since Gwyn Nicholls' day. Indeed, the 1953 side remains the last to beat New Zealand. Lining up for Wales at that time were some of the all-time greats: Cliff Morgan, Bleddyn Williams, Lewis Jones, Ken Jones. If the backs were outstanding, they were aided by a pack of rigour and technique which provided quality ball and was destructive in defence.

The team was lead by the No. 8 John Gwilliam, a name perhaps overshadowed by those glamorous three-quarters, but a captain whose stamp the side bore indelibly. Gwilliam remains something of an enigma: he left Wales to serve in the army in the Second World War and took teaching posts in Scotland and England during his working life. Consequently he seldom played in Wales and was not part of the close rugby scene of inter-club rivalry and politicking. His army and teaching background helped to maintain a certain distance as captain. As a player he was an athletic and technically gifted forward, but also a deep thinker about the game, who liked to produce the unexpected. His was an early contribution to the idea of fifteen man rugby.

With his customary attention to the period, David Parry-Jones has produced an enthralling biography of the man and an overview of one of the great periods in Welsh rugby.

DEREK BEVAN (with Owen Jenkins)
The Man in the Middle

A referee can't make a bad game good, but he can make a good game bad. Based on this assumption, Derek Bevan became one of the world's best – and best known – rugby union referees. He retired at the end of the 1999-2000 season, aged fifty, after quarter of a century as the man in the middle. During that long career he refereed in all four World Cups, including the 1991 World Cup Final; almost 50 internationals, four Welsh Cup Finals, World Cup Sevens, Hong Kong Sevens, Dubai Sevens and the Students' World Cup Final.

Forced to stop playing by an industrial accident – he'd been sent off three times as 'an aggressive flanker' – his love for rugby turned Bevan to refereeing and brought a prominence that he would never have achieved as a player. He saw huge changes in the game: player professionalism in terms of money and on-field attitude; world cups; the growing importance of the smaller nations; television money; the development of the IRB and national Unions; rule changes to make the game more popular: in short, a new rugby culture.

In his autobiography Bevan explores the changing game, the great matches, the great players, modern refereeing and the future for referees. He also owns up to a few mistakes and deals honestly with the Louis Luyt affair in an engaging book which charts rugby at international and club level over the last thirty years.